RISE AND GRIND

RISE AND GRIND

Outperform, Outwork, and Outhustle Your Way to a More Successful and Rewarding Life

DAYMOND JOHN

WITH DANIEL PAISNER

CURRENCY
NEW YORK

CURRENCY and its colophon are trademarks of Penguin Random House LLC.

Currency books are available at special discounts for bulk purchases for sales promotions or corporate use. Special editions, including personalized covers, excerpts of existing books, or books with corporate logos, can be created in large quantities for special needs. For more information, contact Premium Sales at (212) 572-2232 or e-mail specialmarkets@ penguinrandomhouse.com.

Library of Congress Cataloging-in-Publication Data
Names: John, Daymond, 1969—author. | Paisner, Daniel, author.
Title: Rise and grind : how to outperform, outwork, and outhustle the competition / by Daymond John with Daniel Paisner.
Description: New York : Currency, [2017] | Includes index.
Identifiers: LCCN 2017029856 | ISBN 9780804189958
Subjects: LCSH: Success in business. | Strategic planning. | Entrepreneurship.
Classification: LCC HF5386 .J597 2017 | DDC 650.1—dc23 LC record available at https://lccn.loc.gov/2017029856

ISBN 978-0-8041-8995-8
Ebook ISBN 978-0-8041-8996-5

PRINTED IN THE UNITED STATES OF AMERICA

Jacket photograph by Peter Hapak

10 9 8 7 6 5 4 3 2 1

First Edition

Guess you could say I'm a creature of habit. Or, that I've got my priorities straight, because in the past I've used this space to dedicate my books to the powerful women in my life. Back then, there were just four of 'em—my mother, Shark Momma John; my ex-wife, Maria; and my daughters, Destiny and Yasmeen. Now I've got the love of my life, Heather, and our beautiful baby girl, Minka, to add to the mix. I am blessed to be surrounded by these six extraordinary souls. They're the reason I rise and grind. Everything I do, I do for them.

Man surprised me most about humanity. Because he sacrifices his health in order to make money. Then he sacrifices money to recuperate his health. And then is so anxious about the future that he does not enjoy the present, the result being that he does not live in the present or the future. He lives as if he is never going to die, and then dies having never really lived.

—Dalai Lama

CONTENTS

RISE AND INSPIRE

OKAY, SO YOU'RE checking out this book, thinking about spending your money on it. Even more important, you're thinking of spending your time on it—and time . . . well, that's the only thing we can't get back in this world. Once you spend it, it's gone, so you've got to make sure you're spending it wisely.

Let's face it, the one thing they're not making any more of in this world is attention, but now that I've got yours I want to honor it, make it worth your while.

I get that your time and your attention are valuable. **So this is a book about spending it productively, meaningfully, purposefully.** After all, we all get the same twenty-four hours a day, whether we have a million dollars in the bank or a hundred. This book is about how to put those hours to work for you, how to use them to outperform, outwork, and outhustle your way to the top.

Hey, I've seen some things, met all kinds of interesting, ridiculously successful people. I've hung around with world leaders and game-changers. I'm constantly learning from these people, and one of the things I've learned is that there is no secret formula for success. However, there are certain essential ingredients that are always in the mix. Truth is, there is one common trait I notice in all the people I meet who are thriving and striving: every single one of them has got a killer work ethic. Seriously, they are up and at it each and every day, and they are at it hard. You could call it drive. You could call it determination. You could call it oomph, grit, or hustle.

I call it rising and grinding. And I'm out to shine a light on it here.

Maybe you're thinking you've already read one or two of my books and you're wondering what there is left to say. I've written about the power of broke, telling readers that you don't need a big budget to be successful as an entrepreneur. I've written about how we all stand as our personal brands. I've written about my own rise from the streets of Hollis, Queens, to the very top of an urban fashion industry I helped to create. But now it's time to do a deep dive. It's time I took you behind the scenes and let you in on how I power through my days. I'm going to tell you all about what gets me *rising* and *grinding* every morning—how things were for me when I was just starting out, and how they are for me now. I'll show you how I've changed my approach, as I learned to rise and grind and hit all these new targets that were set out in front of me.

I'll share a bunch of my day-to-day habits and routines to show how I make the best use of my 24/7, and I'll break down the rituals of some of the world's most successful people, from all walks of life—people who inspire me, who amaze me, who push me to be the very best I can be.

The idea is that by pulling back the curtain and showing how these folks live and work, I can highlight some takeaways for readers looking to change things up. Maybe you'll get a whole mess of ideas. Or maybe you'll take just one primary strategy and find a way to attach it to what you're doing in a way that transforms your life forever. That's how it happened for me, the third or fourth time I read Napoleon Hill's great book *Think and Grow Rich*. It lit something in me, turned me on to a very specific practice that I started using myself, one that set me on a path to success. I'll tell you more about that a little bit later on, but the point here is that we can all learn something from the people around us, from the people we admire.

Think about the people you look up to in your life—the folks in your field or in your community who seem to have it going on. It's great to be *inspired* by the successes of others, but one thing I want you to think about as you read this book is how important it is not to be *intimidated* by the successes of others. Those who are ten times, twenty times, a hundred times more accomplished than those around them are almost always driven in a more focused, more determined way than their peers. What's the differentiator, between being okay and being great? Between poverty and prosperity? Well, one of the keys is having the right attitude—that was the message I shared with readers in *The Power of Broke*. But another important key is knowing how to make the best use of your time, how to maximize every moment, and that's going to be our focus in the pages ahead.

I happen to believe that a small percentage of our lives are determined by acts of God—say, two percent or so. Tsunamis, earthquakes, winning the lottery, chance meetings with people or opportunities that can ignite meaningful prospects . . . good or bad, these are the things that happen *to* us and are out of our control. But if we accept this notion, then we must also accept that the other ninety-eight percent of what happens in our lives has to do with the decisions we make or don't, the actions we take or don't, the strategies we put in place or don't.

It has to do with how we *rise* and *grind*.

Here's the deal: I'm hoping the people you meet in this book will inspire, amaze, and push you, the same way they do me, and that you'll pick up on some of what they're doing and apply it to whatever it is you've got going on. Even if you look through the table of contents and see the name of someone who might stand on a different side of an issue that's important to you, I hope you'll take the time to see what they're about. Hey, I can't say I see eye to eye with every one of these people on every single issue either. But I'm sharing their stories because I've learned something important from each of them—something I had to share with you as well. Even if you can't relate to them directly, I hope you'll stay with them, learn from them, be inspired by them.

Maybe you're not a mother trying to raise three kids with learning difficulties. But trust me on this, you can learn from that mother's struggle—and you'll meet one such mother here.

Yeah, chances are you were born with all of your arms and legs. But you'd better believe you can pick up a couple of things from the guy who wasn't—and you'll meet him, too.

Look, **I wrote this book for two types of people. The first is someone who is already rising and grinding.** That person is out there getting things done, every single day, and they're looking to sharpen their routines, get more bang for their buck, and stay motivated. Maybe that someone is you. Maybe you've got something to learn from Nely Galán, the former head of the Telemundo network, or Carlos Santana, the legendary guitarist, or Catherine Zeta-Jones, the Academy Award–winning actress, about what it took to rise and grind their way to the very top of their fields.

I sat with all of these people, and a dozen more besides, and asked them questions they told me they'd never been asked before. I asked them what they do as soon as they get up in the morning, where they turn for inspiration, how they organize their days. I asked them some tougher questions, too—questions

I'm asked almost every day by aspiring entrepreneurs who want to make something of themselves, and by corporate leaders who bring me in to motivate their employees and get them to start thinking outside the box.

Obviously, each of these interviews grew in an organic way, so even though I came with a set list of questions, our conversations were open-ended and free-flowing. Each of them might have started in the same place—me wanting to know what their days were like when they were just starting out, what their days are like now, and so on.

I've taken the answers that came back to me and created a kind of blueprint you can follow as you do your own thing—whatever that thing happens to be. Honestly, it doesn't matter who you are or what you do—whether you're trying to move up in the corporate world, make it as an artist or creative, strike it big as an entrepreneur, or even just be happier and more fulfilled in your life. If you want to succeed, you have to put in the work. Remember, these ultra-successful people get the same 1,440 minutes in every day as you do, and there's plenty you can learn from how they use them. Who knows . . . you might come across one simple tip or habit in these pages that will change your life forever, if you can find a way to make it your own.

Point is, I've learned a ton from all these people about what it takes to be successful—and now, through this book, so can you.

I also wrote this book for readers who are already in a kind of leadership position, and who want to inspire others to rise and grind. Maybe you're an entrepreneur or an intrapreneur. Maybe you're in charge of a team of a hundred or a thousand people, or maybe you've got just one or two people looking to you for guidance. Maybe you're a parent looking to model powerful behavior for your children. Doesn't matter—you're still looking for ways to teach, to lead, to set a positive example. You know as well as anyone how it sometimes takes a while for a lesson to register. We don't always absorb things the first time around. It might take three or four or ten or twelve times for a message to sink in. That's why I've collected so many different stories here, because you never know when something will click, or when something will speak to you in such a way that you can't help but pass it on.

I saw a cool stat as I was writing this opening passage and putting the finishing touches to this book, and it struck me as a great metaphor for what I'm after here. **Did you know that Walt Disney World is the second-largest purchaser of explosives in the United States? The first is the US Defense Department.** The military part makes sense, but the Disney part surprised me, although when I kicked it around I started to think of what it means to be explosive. **We tend to think of blowing things up in a negative way, maybe as a line of defense, but all those fireworks they use at Disney World have more to do with offense than defense. At Disney, they're a symbol of joy and celebration. In our military, they're a display of power, a weapon to keep us safe and sure and strong.**

It all comes down to perspective, right? The same goes for the tactics and habits you're about to see from the people you'll meet here in this book. Some of these approaches will resonate with you, and some of them won't. Some of them are meant as a way of playing defense, putting out the fires that tend to come up as we go about our business, our daily lives, and some of them are meant as a way of playing offense, igniting a new strategy that might take that business, that life, in a whole new direction.

Some of them are used to create moments of joy and celebration, and some are put in place to guard against the forces in our lives that line up against us.

I'll leave it to you to grab at the lessons that speak to you and set aside the ones that don't. Along the way, I'll tell you the story of how my grind just about saved my life, when my determination to keep fit and healthy so that I'd be able to take care of my family and my business for a long, long time led directly to the discovery (and removal!) of a stage II thyroid cancer that would have gone undetected—and untreated—if it weren't for the rise-and-grind mentality that guides me.

Bottom line: I rise every morning ready to get to work, and I make sure that when my head hits the pillow each night I'm dead tired, from running this way and that. I make sure that I don't quit until I've got nothing left to give to my cause, my mission, my purpose. I give everything I have. And while I'm at it, I make sure that when I open my eyes each morning, I'm up and I'm at it. That I'm challenging myself, stretching myself, driven by the belief that anything is possible. That everything is possible.

This right here is my *grind*.

ONE

ALL RISE

MY THING IS to push, to reach, to *grind*. I get up—before the sun, some mornings—and start grinding at my goals, hard. I go to sleep—stupid-late, most nights—still grinding. Because when I hear people say there isn't time enough in the day to do everything they need to do, it gets me hot, and not in a good way. *Time enough?* Yeah, I get that it sometimes feels like there aren't enough hours in the day, but the feeling only hits me when I'm not using those hours wisely. When I'm not efficient, organized, *on it*. But if I'm on top of my game, in tireless pursuit, there's always time. And if it starts looking like the clock is about to run out on me, I'll work even harder.

I'm burning the midnight oil.

The early bird catches the worm.

Early to bed and early to rise makes a man healthy, wealthy, and wise.

You've heard all the expressions—probably got a few of your own to get you *up and at 'em* in the morning. Here's one that inspired me, when I was just getting started: **It's time to make the donuts.** Do you remember that Dunkin' Donuts ad campaign? That was like a rallying cry to me and my boys! If you ask me, they should still be using those ads, but now we're supposed to be "runnin' on Dunkin'," so those days are gone. Still, I've done some work with the company over the years, which seems fitting because it reaches all the way back to what got *me* up and runnin' when I was a kid.

(Hey, bet you didn't know—those spots were named one of the five best commercial campaigns of the 1980s by the Television Bureau of Advertising, so obviously they made an impression on lots of people, not just on *me*.)

I'll tell you, when those *It's time to make the donuts* ads first hit, they got me thinking. I'd see that guy with the mustache, Fred the Baker, getting up at some ridiculously early hour and shuffling off to the donut shop to start his day, and I got the message that hard work was hard work. That when a thing needs doing you've got no choice but to get your butt out of bed and do it. It might seem obvious, but you have to realize, outside of my mother, there weren't too many positive examples of folks in my neighborhood *rising and grinding* in this way—getting up and getting things done when everyone else you know is dead asleep. (That said, looking back, I realize it's not that no one in my neighborhood was *rising and grinding*—it's just that they were up early and off to do their thing, so I never saw them).

Point is, these days, when I stumble out of bed to catch a predawn flight to who knows where, and shuffle to the bathroom to brush my teeth and splash some water on my face, I've still got that phrase bouncing around in my head . . . *It's time to make the donuts.*

Maybe there's some other phrase that gets you going, like this great line: *The dream is free. The hustle is sold separately.*

Or this quote I once heard from Jerry Rice, the legendary

football player: *Today I will do what others won't, so tomorrow I can accomplish what others can't.*

Then there are these oldies but goodies:

A little hard work never killed anybody.

Hard work is the yeast that raises the dough.

No one ever drowned in sweat.

We've given ourselves these little bumper-sticker expressions, and we've repeated them into the ground. And that's exactly where the trouble starts. See, these phrases have become clichés, and the thing about clichés is that we tend to race over them. We hear the words but not the truth they have to tell us. They become like background music. We forget why they caught on in the first place.

But it's not about the words, for me. The words, they'll only get you so far. It's about the action. It's about the goals you set for yourself and how you go after them. It's about the structure you lay out and your ability to stick to it. It's about whether you actually get up and make the donuts, or you just think about it. **Doesn't matter what you say you'll do . . . doesn't matter what you *mean* to do . . . doesn't matter what you *hope* to do . . . None of that matters until you *rise* and *grind* and get to it.**

THINK BIG

There's no cap on what you can accomplish.

If you can picture it, you can make it so.

Be the change you want in your life.

We hear these kinds of mantras from motivational gurus all the time. But they often leave out the most important part: *if you're willing to put in the work.*

I know this because I've lived this. I know this because I

grew up watching my mother find a way to work two or three jobs and still keep a close watch on me to make sure I didn't get into any trouble. Once I caught the reading bug a little later on in life, I was all over books like *Who Moved My Cheese?* and *The One Minute Manager,* but my mother's good influence found me in a more organic way. She was a daily inspiration to me, just by the way she carried herself. Her *grind* was the background music to my growing up. It was in the air and all around. I talk all the time about the ways she set the bar high for me—like when she hung up a giant can opener on the wall in our house, with a sign saying THINK BIG, to give me something to shoot for, to reach for each and every day. Those words were such a meaningful reminder to me I put up a THINK BIG sign of my own in the reception area at Blueprint + Co, the coworking space I opened up in midtown Manhattan for executives and entrepreneurs, so the change agents who shared our space would get a daily jolt of my mother's homespun advice.

Think big! There's no other way to think, if you ask me. Anything less than big, what's the point?

But my mother didn't *just* teach me to think big. She also taught me to reach big, to go big. One of the things she used to get on me about was whenever I'd say I didn't want to take the time to put into this or that. I'd throw up my hands and say something like, "It'll take too much time." And she'd just shake her head and say something like, "Daymond, the time will pass anyway. Might as well use it productively."

Out of that, I came up with a line of my own: **"The time will never be perfect, so you can only make perfect use of your time."**

(I'm still using that one!)

You know, one of the positive habits I've developed in this area has more to do with what I *don't* do than with what I *do* do, and it goes to making sure I have "time enough" for the big stuff. And what I *don't* do is watch a lot of television. That was never really my thing, although these days, with all these great, great shows like *The Walking Dead* and *Game of Thrones* that everyone seems to be binge-watching left and right, it gets tougher and tougher to resist that temptation. I'm made to feel like I'm missing out, and I guess I am, but I've got things to do, man. Nothing against all you folks who make the time to binge-watch these shows, but it doesn't feel to me like I have all that time to sit in front of the television. Oh, I'll watch a nature show every once in a while, or a documentary. I'll keep up on the news and anything educational or business-related. And, of course, I'll be sure to tune in to every new *Shark Tank* episode. But I try to avoid all these great story-driven shows like *Homeland* or *Empire*. Why? Because they're just *stories*. Because you get caught up in them. Because they're addictive. Because there's a lot I have to get done, and as good as these shows are, they're not worth what I'd have to give up.

So my thing is, I don't binge-watch. I'll take the time to see a movie, but I can't get caught up in six or seven seasons of a show, and every time I'm tempted to check out *House of Cards* or *Orange Is the New Black* or whatever, I think back to how things were with my mother, when it was just the two of us. When we just had our few local channels. I just can't imagine ever seeing my mother getting so hooked on some show that she would spend an entire weekend catching up on old episodes—would never have happened.

Her good example became mine: **get up early, work hard, do what you have to do, don't complain, and do it all again the next day.** The thing of it is, when I was a kid, my time wasn't totally my own. My grind had to happen outside of school. Those eight hours a day we were in class, they were off the table. I'd get to school, go through the motions, and wait for the bell at the end of the day to tell me I could go off and do my thing. Later on, in high school, I started working in a co-op program with First Boston in Manhattan, so I was able to get a jump on what the real world might look like for me, so *that* became a part of my grind. *That* became my hustle—and soon as I set my mind to making money and chasing my own dreams, I started working my sidelines like they were a full-time deal. Like my life depended on it.

And, in a way, it did—but not just yet. The dreams, the hustle . . . they could only set me up for what was still to come.

Let's forget for the moment the extra *grind* that came my way because school was so hard for me. For those who don't know, I was dyslexic—I've written about it, talked about it, worked to call attention to it as one of the biggest obstacles to success for way too many kids. (For some of us full-grown kids, too!) In order for me to get by in school, I had to put in all this extra time just to keep up. Homework that took most kids an hour or two to complete took me four or five, so that just piled on *even more* time I had to slog my way past. But as a kid, all the way through high school, what choice did I have? I mean, it's not like there was some pill I could take, the way there might be these days, say, to help a kid deal with his or her ADD or ADHD. And because it was something you couldn't medicate, there wasn't a whole lot of information, not a whole lot of helpful resources, because there was no way for the medical establishment to make any kind of money off of it. I wasn't out there looking for a cure, wasn't looking to hide behind the fact that I had some trouble reading, studying. Wasn't looking for an escape. I was just looking for help. But you know what? If I could go back in time and take a magic pill, I wouldn't. Because to fix my dyslexia, to overcome it, I had to work twice as hard, and maybe that's another way I found my grind.

> **POWER FACT:** Dyslexic entrepreneurs are more likely to launch multiple businesses, and to grow those businesses faster than nondyslexic entrepreneurs.... *If you find yourself struggling with learning issues, know that you're in good company: Richard Branson, Charles Schwab, Henry Ford, David Boies, Ted Turner, Tommy Hilfiger, and yours truly are just a few successful CEOs who've been diagnosed with dyslexia.*

I wrote in my previous books about some of the tiny hustles I had going on back in the day. Fixing up old bicycles. Selling mirrors or pencils or whatever else to the other kids at school. Recycling broken toys. Shoveling snow. I had all these ways to make myself a little money so I could maybe go to the movies, buy myself a slice of pizza and a Coke . . . whatever. I don't want to suggest we were dead broke, me and my mother. Wasn't like that. We had a decent house, lived in a decent neighborhood— that is, until crack came along. Still, if I wanted a little extra walking-around money, maybe buy myself a new pair of kicks . . . that was on *me*.

I came to realize very early on that each one of my enterprises would live or die by the time I put into it. And so, when I was in the bike business, for example, that meant getting out the door early on Saturday morning before the garbage pickup and harvesting parts from the beat-up bicycles folks would leave for trash on the curb. It meant figuring out the best times to go dumpster-diving out behind the mirror factory for those little handheld mirrors, then finding time to hit up the Ideal toy store, where they used to throw away all the busted-up stuff the people would return. The bottom line was I needed to get a jump-start, stake out my territory, and do my thing in a hurry to make sure nobody else could beat me out of a deal.

Time is money—that's another cliché you hear all the time in business. You hear it from young wannabe entrepreneurs, all the way up to the titans of industry, in the upper reaches of the one-percent class. First time I heard it, I owned it. Figured it out for myself, really. Came to me on one of my very first gigs, shoveling snow. **In my neighborhood, you had to get out the door pretty damn early to make some paper shoveling snow.** If you slept in, or dug out your own driveway first, or stopped to eat a good breakfast, your day was over before it ever started—because, let's face it, the kiss of death in the snow removal industry, when everyone with a shovel and a strong back is working the same route, chasing the same business, is a late start.

And keep in mind, it wasn't *just* about the cash. The same *rise and grind* mindset even found its way into the schoolyard, into how I got on with my friends. One big reason for this was that I was on the small side as a kid—a decent athlete, but no giant—which meant that if I wasn't the first one out there, or the one to bring the ball, I might not get picked when they got to choosing up sides. If I was there first, I could run the game, especially if it was *my* football, *my* basketball, so I'd always try to be the one to get things going and make sure I could play. Baseball, I was cool—that was never a problem for me. But football and basketball, being one of the smallest kids in the neighborhood, it was easy to get overlooked, so I hustled to make double sure I got to play.

Here again, **there was nobody to figure out all this stuff for me**—nobody saying, "Daymond, you've got to do this here." No, this was on me. I was an only child. My mother didn't have the time to help me navigate through all these growing pains, and I didn't want to bother her with my nonsense anyway. She had enough to worry about. And what I learned out of all that was that I had to find a way to work my own *grind*. Wasn't any kind of magic formula I could bend and borrow and make my own. There was just my mother's fine example of that killer work ethic, and I could rise to meet it or not.

The choice was mine.

G-R-I-N-D

In *The Power of Broke*, I shared what I hoped would be an easy-to-remember acronym to bring across some of the essential themes of the book—five empowering calls to action I'd made a part of my life and career that I thought readers might grab at in their own way. **I called them my SHARK Points,** because of the similarities I saw between the characteristics of the shark species (aggressive, resourceful, hungry) and the traits we all need to succeed as entrepreneurs.

I'd been using a version of that acronym for years as a public speaker, ever since I landed a spot on the *Shark Tank* panel, because I thought it was a great way to enhance and promote the exciting new brand I was now honored to be a part of, and to tie in the takeaway elements of my talks to the popularity of the show. But it wasn't meant as a gimmick. Readers seemed to really respond to those lessons, just as keynote audiences had for years, so I'll revisit them here—and then I'll offer up a whole new set of points more in keeping with the themes we're looking to highlight in these pages.

My **SHARK** Points:

Set a goal.

Homework, do yours.

Adore what you do.

Remember, you are the brand.

Keep swimming.

S-H-A-R-K . . . Like I said, people really dug the lesson of these letters—they turned out to be a great teaching device. But, in truth, the reason so many people connected to it was that *I* connected to it. Because I'd internalized these **SHARK** Points to where they were a part of me. It was genuine. I'd lifted my game on the back of 'em, and so it was easier to motivate others to lift their games on the back of 'em as well.

This time out, I thought I'd lean away from those majestic creatures of the ocean—and the fierce creatures who sit with me in the *Tank*—and focus on the core message of this book . . . on the *grind*. At this point you might be wondering, what does he mean by *grind*, exactly? **Look up *grind* in the dictionary and you'll see a ton of different meanings: to crush something into a powder . . . to rub together . . . to sharpen or smooth a knife or an edge . . . to operate a mill or a machine by turning a handle, like grinding coffee.** And there are a couple of definitions that aren't exactly appropriate for a family audience. (You can go ahead and look up those for yourselves.)

But what I'm talking about here are street or slang definitions of the word—the ones that have seeped into our culture to express, and in some cases celebrate, the idea of good old-fashioned hard work: to roll up your sleeves and get into it, to push yourself to new heights, to tackle the tasks before you in a relentless and spirited way. And whether your *grind* is about making money, or killing it at work or at school, or whether it's about being the best damn parent you can be, the grind isn't just a concept, it's a way of life. Just like the "power of broke," it's a mindset—and if you learn to live by it, like I've tried to do, you put yourself in position to succeed each and every day.

And so, I offer my **GRIND** Points:

Get on it. Look, anybody can talk a good game. Anybody can dream big, or resolve to make a change. Go ahead and hang up that giant THINK BIG sign where you'll see it every day, but know that the words alone won't take you where you want to go. **You can't start moving toward your goals until and unless you take that all-important first step.** But here's the thing: **That first step doesn't have to be a big one. It simply has to move you forward, even just a little bit.** That's the great thing about incremental change: it sneaks up on you; it adds up; it amounts to something, eventually. So write down your goals, if that's your thing. Come up with a strategy, if you need a kind of road map to follow. But whatever you do, get moving. Now. **Whatever tough road you're facing, it's not about to get any easier tomorrow, so start hitting it today.**

Repeat. This is the essence of what it means to *grind,* because if you want to see those incremental gains, you've got to have at it in a systematic way. Act . . . learn . . . *repeat* . . . it's a basic formula for success, whether you're talking about meditating at the same time each day, working out, reading, praying, or leaning on some other habit or routine that helps to give your days structure or meaning. **Do something once and achieve a successful outcome, and it might just be dumb luck. Do something again and again and achieve that same successful outcome, and you just might be on to something.** So go ahead and build a meaningful routine . . . and then stick to it. Each and every day. Develop good habits . . . and then refuse to break them. Each and every day. If you're like me, the word *repeat* calls to mind those old shampoo commercials, the ones that told you to "lather, rinse, and repeat." Remember? The phrase became so common, we started seeing it as part of the directions on the shampoo bottle. As a marketing tactic, it's pretty interesting, don't you think? That advertising executives can condition us into believing their product is so essential to our health and well-being that we must not only use it but use it *twice*. . . . For me, the phrase serves as a useful reminder for this second **GRIND** Point: we humans are indeed creatures of habit, and the idea here is to carry this reminder into the ways we structure our days.

(Let's be clear: good habits are hard to break, but you've got to *make* them first . . . so *get on it,* not just once, but again and again. And more to the point, *stay* on it. Today. Tomorrow. Here on in.)

Insist. On your very best. On the very best efforts of your team. On the conditions you'll need to put in place in order for you to hit all the right notes in what you do. **If you demand excellence in what you put out, it might just find you in what you get back.** So go ahead and insist on it—because **life isn't what you accept, it's what you negotiate**.

Navigate. This is the *grind* version of keep swimming—same deal, different environment. What we're going for here is the relentless spirit we're so quick to celebrate in others, even though we sometimes have difficulty tapping into our own version. One interesting fact about sharks—some species, anyway—is that they can swim while they're sleeping. In fact, they must, because in order to breathe they need to keep water flowing over their gills. Which means that they have the amazing ability to navigate their way through the water—even as they sleep! Up here on dry land, it's not enough just to find your way from point A to point B—any GPS system can help you with that. No, the key is navigating those larger journeys in life and moving with speed and precision, like a killer shark in the water. Did you know that when they're feeding or attacking, most sharks can swim at up to two and a half times their normal speed? The mako shark, one of the fastest swimmers in the ocean, can move at bursts of more than thirty miles per hour! So the message to us mere humans is to keep our eyes on where we want to get to in life—our goals, our passions, our dreams—and keep moving in that direction with fury and purpose when necessary.

Something to think about: we see the best, most literal examples of this *keep moving* mentality in our elite athletes, who take their grind to superhuman levels—in their training, in their mental preparation, in competition. They grind because they have to. If they don't, they'll get stepped on, or fall behind. But that's true in business, too, don't you think? The most successful entrepreneurs I know are athlete-warriors in their own right. They refuse to give up on a dream until they can hold it. And that generally applies to their workout routines as well, because almost every successful, hard-charging person I know makes sure to get off the couch and get moving, in some way or another, almost every day. It's just like with our friend the shark: their thing is to keep moving, all the time. They're not always moving in for the kill, but they *are* always moving. That's more of what I have in mind when I talk about not quitting. Press on, ever forward. Don't be discouraged by setbacks along the way. **Know that disappointments will find you, from time to time. And know that the only way to make sure a project or endeavor fails is to quit on it.**

Desire, **d**rive, **d**etermination. One *d* just won't cut it here. A lot of aspiring entrepreneurs feel like they're counted out before they're counted in—meaning, it's like there are two strikes against them before they even step to the plate. I know this firsthand, because when we started out with FUBU, a lot of people thought we were plain crazy. Even when we came back from our first trade show in Vegas with hundreds of thousands of dollars in orders, we couldn't get a loan to get the money we needed to fill them. So when people tell me how nobody believed in them, or in their vision or product or whatever, and then tell me how they still managed to power past these low expectations and succeed in a big-time way . . . well, I get how that can be the sweetest vindication of all.

So my message to you is this: don't ignore all those *naysayers* in your path, as you make your way to the top; instead put that negativity to work *for* you. Let it *drive* you, even if it's just to prove everyone else wrong. **Be *determined* to blow past those expectations, clear whatever low bar has been set before you, and make sure you do it with room to spare.**

This right here is my deepest *desire*—you should think about making it *yours,* too.

G-R-I-N-D . . . it might not have that ready hook of my trusty SHARK Points, but it gets the job done. **G**et on it, **R**epeat, **I**nsist, **N**avigate, **D**esire/**D**rive/**D**etermination . . . In the end, that's what it's all about. So take these points as your marching orders, and while you're at it, keep in mind that all those SHARK Points still apply. Just be sure to add these new ones to your game as well.

WHO YOU GONNA CALL?

The folks you'll meet in the pages of this book, they find a way to **G**et on it. To **R**epeat whatever ritual or formula they put in place to help them get to the starting line. To **I**nsist on the very best from themselves, and from the people around them. To **N**avigate their careers and their days with the precision and instincts of a shark in the deep. And to tap the **D**esire, **D**rive, and **D**etermination they need to accomplish the outcomes they set out in front of them.

So let me tell you a little more about them. Some of them, you already know—entrepreneurs, entertainers, athletes, business moguls, and thought leaders whose approach to their own daily *grind* has taken them to the top of their fields. Some of them, you'll meet here for the first time—advocates, artists, small business owners, up-and-coming movers and shakers—successful individuals who've tapped their *own grind* to power past a difficulty and find a meaningful path.

I'm hoping the stories and strategies of the people profiled here will inspire you to move the needle in your own lives and careers. Each of them was chosen because there was *something* about them that inspires me—and I'm betting there will be something about them that inspires you, too.

....

For more information on my GRIND Points and how
to apply them in your own life, check out
www.DaymondJohn.com/Grind

BE PRECOCIOUS

FIND YOUR FIRE AND STEP INTO THE LIGHT

CATHERINE ZETA-JONES
Actress, Designer, Mom

MOST OF US know her face from the movies and the Broadway stage and the pages of *People* magazine, but I'm betting few people know the *real* Catherine Zeta-Jones. Oh, yeah, she's just as gorgeous in person as she is on the big screen, but what's really beautiful about Catherine is the way she's not content to sit still and coast on her many accomplishments.

Catherine might be an A-list movie star, married to Hollywood royalty in Michael Douglas, but deep down she still sees herself as a small-town girl growing up on the coast of Wales, in a little town called Swansea. She's still the same kid who was drawn to the London stage and would have stopped at nothing to get there, the same kid who kept on grinding after that, moving to Los Angeles to try to make things happen in Hollywood. What's interesting to me about Catherine's story is that her dream was all her own. Her parents weren't theater people. Far from it. Her father ran a candy factory—or a sweet factory, as they call it over there. Her mother was a seamstress, as they call it over there. I guess you could say Catherine got her entrepreneurial streak from both of her parents. But the theater piece? Catherine's not sure where that came from, although she did start taking dance lessons and appearing in local plays when she was just four years old.

"I grew up with a strong work ethic," she remembers. "We weren't extremely well-off, but we certainly had everything that we needed. And I was taught to dream big. To this day, I dream big. You can always pull it back. I knew my dreams and ambitions were going to take me further than Swansea, South Wales."

Even though Catherine and her two brothers were encouraged to pursue their dreams, I don't think her parents ever imagined that hers would lead her to the stage. Even though they supported her talents with dance classes and acting lessons, Catherine believes that her parents fully expected her interests to fall into line as she grew up. She was expected to finish high school, to maybe go on to college. The dancing and the acting was meant to be a little-kid activity, a creative outlet, but they came to mean something a whole lot more to young Catherine. It got to where the bright lights of London were all she could see, and when she finally told her parents she wanted to quit school and become a full-time, card-carrying actress, it was like she'd up and told them she was running off to the circus. She was just fifteen years old, and she was determined to chase a life in the theater, whether they liked it or not.

To their credit, Catherine's parents found it in their hearts to let it happen. They weren't crazy about it, but they went along. Before signing off on the idea, though, they went to talk it over with the headmaster at her school, and he put it to them straight. He basically said he'd seen Catherine in all the shows she'd done since she started at that school, and he'd spotted her passion, her drive . . . her talent. She had a little something extra, he said. A little something special. He also said that as smart as she was—and she *is* whip-smart—she was never going to be happy as a banker or a surgeon.

"You have to realize," she says, speaking like the child of a sweet factory owner, "that me wanting to leave school and get my equity card was like finding that golden ticket in *Charlie and the Chocolate Factory*. But I'd been performing professionally since I was nine years old, when I'd gotten a part as one of the little orphan girls in a West End production of *Annie*. So when we sat with my teacher, my father was like, 'aw, shucks,' but he heard him. He listened. My parents knew I wasn't a typical teenager. I was never wild or a problem child. I was always a little more grown up and focused than my peers. As they've said themselves, I never gave them a moment's worry. And so with that my parents allowed me to sign out of school, and I went off with a touring traveling company of *The Pajama Game*."

STAY FOCUSED

To hear Catherine tell it, **it really did feel to her like she'd won some sort of lottery, being able to pursue her dreams in this full-on way.** However it came about, she was making it work, making a name for herself, although she admits there were a couple of hiccups here and there. Once, one of the "adults" in the company saw that Catherine was crying over some slight Catherine no longer remembers. That person looked over at her and tsked and said, "Oh, stop it, you precocious child."

Catherine had no idea what the word meant, but she thought it sounded horrible. She went home and looked it up in the *Oxford English Dictionary,* and learned it wasn't so horrible after all.

It just meant that she was a little wiser than other kids her age, a little advanced. That she was maybe a little more mature.

"I thought to myself, That's not bad, actually," she now says. "But up until then, if I heard the word at all, I heard it as a negative. I heard it and I was like, 'Oh, no, don't be that.' But now I say to my kids all the time, 'Please, be precocious.' Because as grown-ups you might lose a little bit of that. Really, it's so easy to lose your drive. You know, **when things start to get good, we all have a tendency to get a little complacent. We lose whatever it was that pushed us to act in the first place, that feeling that we can do anything.** That's what drives us, when we're first starting out. That precociousness. And then, just like that, it can slip away. It's like when they asked me to sing at the Oscars. That's something I didn't want to do at first, to sing and dance at the Oscars. But then I thought about it and I asked myself why I didn't want to do it. What was I afraid of? You see, as we get older, that fear starts to come in and it knocks us down. And you start to tell yourself, No, no, no. I can't, I can't, I can't. So I will go back to my petulant little self, that childhood precociousness, and tell myself, Yes, yes, yes. I can, I can, I can. I will tell myself all over again that I can do anything I set my mind to."

Yes, she can. Yes, yes, yes, she can. I know, because I've been working with Catherine on an interior design and home furnishings company she's launching, Casa Zeta-Jones, and I can see that precocious child she's talking about. I can see it in her passion, and her tireless approach to the work. (Plus, she's got an incredible eye and a signature sense of style—just check out her Instagram posts at #StyleByZeta to get a sense of her vision.)

You know how when you meet someone for the first time, you have these preconceived notions about them? We form these first impressions in our mind, and sometimes they're difficult to get past—especially when we meet someone we know from movies or television. In Catherine's case, I didn't know her at all, but she reached out to me because she and her family are big *Shark Tank* fans. They watch it all the time, could probably quote from it if you asked them to. Matter of fact, when she first tried to get in touch with me, I thought one of my friends was playing a practical joke. I mean, why would the amazingly talented Catherine Zeta-Jones want to talk to me about an interior design and home furnishing line? I was known for designing some stylish baggy jeans, not necessarily for my decorating style.

But it turned out the call was legit, and the two of us hit it off right away. (Hey, we were both taught to sew as kids!) One of the things I most admired about Catherine was that she was fully invested in this idea of starting her own company and making it her own brand. I actually tried to talk her out of it, first time we met. I said, "Catherine, you can probably go out there and get an endorsement deal with a home furnishing company for more money than you'll make off this business in five years."

She wasn't interested, so I went at it again.

I told her that she was getting herself into some seriously hard work and that in order to ramp this thing up she'd have to fly all over the world, visit all these different factories, learn about all these different types of fabric.

And she just looked at me and said, "I can't wait."

Really, with Catherine it was the thrill of the grind that got her excited—not the paycheck that may or may not come her way.

Soon, her excitement became mine, and she started sending me a flurry of emails with drawings and photos of all kinds of designs. She'd see a certain silk out of India, or a certain pattern from Brazil, and she'd send me pictures. I'd look at the time stamps on her emails and see that she was up at two and three o'clock in the morning, her time.

> **POWER FACT:** Successful people are always in pursuit of a new challenge. . . . *Whoopi Goldberg, for example, has gone into the medical marijuana business, after making a name for herself in entertainment. Shaun White went on to dominate the world of skateboarding, after he made a name for himself as the world's best snowboarder.*

"It all comes down to passion," she says, when I ask her what drives her. "And this is something I'm passionate about. It's in my gene pool. My mother used to sew, so of course I sew. **I've been wanting to do something like this for a long time, but the timing was never right. I had my career. I had my family. But I also felt like I needed the right partner,** and then something hit me. Something told me that I had to meet this guy on *Shark Tank*. That there had to be a reason we watch it all the time in our house, right? It was one of those things. And I told myself I could just sit there and do nothing, or I could pick up the phone and do something about it."

That's kind of the way Catherine has lived her life. She sees something, sets her mind to it, and goes after it. Like when she went off to London at fifteen years old, to pursue her theater dreams. It isn't about fame or fortune—it wasn't then, when she first left home, or even now, as she's lighting out on this new path. Back then, she just wanted to act. On the stage, she felt truly alive, more like herself than she felt in her day-to-day life, and she just wanted to keep that going, to feel that way all the time.

"When people used to ask me what I wanted to be when I grew up, it was never to be famous," she says. "That word was never even a part of my vocabulary. I just wanted to be on the stage. It wasn't even television or movies. For me, it was the stage. It was the art and the craft of the theater. That's what I wanted to do."

Trouble was, she was so good onstage that television came calling, and soon she was becoming pretty famous in and around London, despite herself. She was being offered bigger and better roles, but at the same time she felt this pull to keep doing what she was meant to be doing—basically, to honor the calling that drew her to the theater in the first place.

Out of that, she decided to move to Los Angeles, to see what opportunities lay in wait. She was in her mid-twenties, and it felt to her like the time was right to try something new. Here again, she summoned that precocious child. And that child wanted to rediscover the pure joy of acting she had known when she was just starting out, when nobody knew who she was. So she traded the life of a working British actress for the life of a Hollywood hopeful just waiting to be discovered, although in Catherine's case it might be more accurate to say she was waiting to be *rediscovered*.

She fell into a routine. She'd get up every morning at seven and head straight to the gym, and here I think we have to acknowledge that she was motivated at least in part by the desire of every aspiring actress to look her best, although I now know her to be the kind of grounded soul who also drew strength and confidence and structure from her routine. **She was almost fanatical about it, and determined to chase her dream with a clean mind and a clean body.** "I didn't want to go to LA and become a statistic," she explains. "You hear all these stories about drug and alcohol abuse in this business, so I was determined to take care of myself, and to make good decisions."

After the gym, she'd come back to her apartment and get on the phone with her agent in London.

"It was the end of the day there, so he'd have a full day to report on," she says. "For some reason, that would motivate me for the rest of my day in Los Angeles. He'd have me reading lots of scripts, and I'd be going out on auditions, and learning to drive on the right side of the road, and basically just getting familiar with this new life of mine."

At the end of each day, Catherine would catch up on the world news. She tells me now that it was one way she could kind of make up for the fact that she never finished high school, never went to college, so she vowed to keep connected to what was going on outside her building in Los Angeles and back home as well. She read a bunch of newspapers, watched the news on television—not the celebrity-driven infotainment shows that the people she was going up against in auditions tended to watch, but hard-hitting news and analysis. It was a way to keep sharp, and focused. One could say that she started her days as a young actress in Hollywood by exercising her body and she closed them out by exercising her mind.

Another way she kept herself focused and centered during this time was an extension of a habit she'd developed when she first lived on her own in London—a habit she continues to this day. When we first met, she told me it felt to her like the life of an actress was like the life of a gypsy, so when she started traveling in all these different touring productions she started doing what she could to make herself comfortable in whatever room she was renting on the road.

"I started taking candles with me wherever I went," she said. "I'd take my sari, too, and every morning I'd put it on and light a candle. I'd blow them out when I left my room or my apartment where I was staying, and light them again when returned. I had a whole little ritual, these little prayers I used to say."

Like I said, Catherine's still lighting candles, every day. They're all over her house. They're in her dressing room when she's shooting a movie. They're with her when she travels. She lights her candles and makes the space her own, wherever she happens to be. And I've come to appreciate how the practice grounds her. It goes beyond the calming or soothing effect of the ritual itself. It's about more than the mood she creates when she sets the lights down low and fills the room with candlelight, although I guess that's a part of it. No, it's mostly about *owning* the space she's in. It's about being able to feel at home, wherever she is.

....

POWER FACT: Studies show that workers are 38 percent more likely to perform at above-average levels when they are in a positive, engaging physical work environment.... *Go ahead and light those candles, crank the Muzak, whistle while you work, and make yourself comfortable as you go about your day.*

....

The strength and spirit Catherine draws from all these candles is the fire behind her design work as well. She's out to help people feel at home in their own spaces, to let you know that wherever you are, however you got there, you're exactly where you're meant to be.

Catherine's Grind Checklist

✓ create an atmosphere in the workplace and at home that helps you to feel relaxed and connected to the values you want to express, and the emotions you want to share with friends and family . . .

✓ seek news and information that broaden your worldview instead of confirming whatever it is you already *think* you know . . .

✓ make the time to exercise your body *and* your mind . . .

✓ don't be shy about reaching out to potential partners, even if you don't know them or have any contacts in common— sometimes, you see a spark in someone's eye, or get a good feeling in your gut that tells you there's a connection to be made, and you need to follow your instincts . . .

✓ when you come across a word and you're not quite sure of its meaning, look it up—in other words, if it applies to you, make sure you understand the meaning of everything you see, hear, and read . . .

✓ go ahead and follow your dreams, but win consensus among the people in your life who care about you the most—they're the ones you'll need to call on if things don't go your way . . .

....

For more information on Catherine and how she uses the Rise and Grind mindset, check out
www.DaymondJohn.com/Rise/Catherine

BE DETERMINED

DON'T MAKE EXCUSES

KYLE MAYNARD
Athlete, Speaker, Author, Dynamo

MAYBE YOU KNOW Kyle Maynard as a headline-making, head-turning, expectation-shattering mixed martial artist. Or maybe you've heard one of his empowering talks, or seen him give an inspiring interview on television. You might *think* you know what motivates this guy to make the giant obstacles in his path seem small—but like anything else, there's always more to the story than we can see from the outside looking in.

Here's one thing I didn't know until I visited with Kyle to talk about the themes of this book: **the best way to climb a mountain is to look back at the base instead of ahead to the summit.**

Let me explain: Kyle was born with a rare condition called congenital amputation, which means he came into this world with no arms or legs. A lot of folks, facing that kind of challenge, they might just fold. Actually, I should restate that: I've got no idea how you move forward from that . . . it's just completely beyond me. But Kyle and his parents chose to look on his situation as a gift. That brave attitude was his parents' choice at first, but Kyle picked up on it soon enough—he had no other options, really. Kyle's dad was military, so even though he and his wife were floored at first by their son's apparent disabilities, they adjusted to the family's new reality with a kind of military precision. They decided to focus on what was right about Kyle instead of what was wrong—and, naturally, that positive outlook helped to shape Kyle's dogged personality.

Right off the bat, Kyle's mother made sure he was treated like every other kid in the neighborhood, although she knew the other kids might have a hard time including Kyle in their activities. They were kids, right? So she made their house into the go-to hangout! She bought Kyle a Super Nintendo, at a time when that was a big-ticket purchase the family couldn't really afford, so the other kids would want to come to his house to play. Incredibly, Kyle was into sports, big-time. So she organized street hockey games, making sure Kyle was on one of the teams.

What struck me when I got to talking with Kyle was that he didn't see himself as different when he was growing up. He was just Kyle. That started with what he took in from his parents, but Kyle grabbed at it and made it his own. He looked in the mirror and saw a kid who could do or accomplish whatever he wanted—a kid with friends and hopes and dreams.

"It was almost like my parents pulled the ultimate Jedi mind trick," he says now. "They just put it out there that I was not disabled. And so, I'm not disabled. I was eighteen years old before I knew the name of my condition. I still don't know the technical name, because that was never the central focus. It didn't matter. So many times, we get wrapped up in our identity. We think we're this one thing, and that can become a limiting factor."

This dude doesn't know limiting factors. In fact, you'd be hard-pressed to find something that you and I could do that he couldn't. Like use a keyboard—he taught himself to type using his elbows, on a normal keyboard. (He can crank out fifty to sixty words per minute!) But he didn't teach himself to type so he could do well at school, or communicate by email. No, he was big into video games, and he needed to work a keyboard if he wanted to beat the game and beat his friends. So he figured it out. That's how it goes, a lot of times. **When there's something you want more than anything and it requires a bit of reaching, you find a way to reach.**

Same with football—he'd suit up, and the kids on the other team, on the other side of the field, they had no idea what he was capable of. Kyle, too, had no idea at first—but because of the "can-do" mindset instilled in him by his parents, because of his instinct to "reach" for what might have been beyond his grasp, it never occurred to him that he couldn't figure this one out, too. It never occurred to him that he was *incapable* of anything. He played nose guard, and it turned out that nobody could block him. He'd dive under their legs, squirm this way or that, whatever it took. And then, if one of his opponents tried to just belly-flop on him, or knock him out of the play, Kyle would make him pay—he'd just start smashing his helmet against the kid's leg. It was a tough assignment, going up against Kyle.

"I had something to prove," he reflects. "Even as a kid, that was a part of me. Everything inside of me was determined to prove I wasn't helpless. A lot of what I would go on to do in my life, I'd go back and look at them and connect the dots and see that so many of my strengths were really about wanting to bury that fear of being seen as helpless. That's what drove me."

BE TRUE TO YOURSELF

Kyle looks on one specific incident, all the way back in kindergarten, as a defining moment. It happened during show-and-tell, and the way it worked at his school was that the parents were invited to each child's first presentation, so his mother was in the classroom. You remember show-and-tell, right? It was like a TED Talk for your little classmates—a chance to share something with the other kids that was important to you, maybe something you knew a lot about. On this day Kyle had brought in a special toy he wanted to show the class, and he accidentally dropped it. No big thing, except in those days Kyle wore prosthetics out in public, which, ironically, is where the problem started.

Here, let him tell it:

"I had these prosthetic arms on with hooks on the end of them, and prosthetic legs with a buckle to collapse the knee, and I just couldn't jump to the floor and grab the toy the way I would at home. Without the prosthetics, there'd be no problem, I could just pick it right up, but with them I was effectively disabled. I was immobile. And I was so embarrassed. The teacher had to get the toy and hand it back to me. So I went home that night and told my parents I didn't want to wear the prosthetics anymore. I called them my 'big arms' and 'big legs' and I hated them, just then. My mother spoke to the teacher before school the next day and they worked out a way to tell the class about it, because when you're five years old, it's a big thing to get your head around, explaining why Kyle had these arms and legs one day and the next day he comes to school without them."

That was the last time Kyle wore his prosthetics, and you can just imagine the commotion he made when he showed up at school the next day. I mean, when he had pants on and a long-sleeve shirt over the prosthetics, the other kids couldn't necessarily see what was going on with him, and now here he was, without any arms or legs. But the teacher, she was on it, and she helped the class understand. By the end of that next day Kyle was mixing it up on the playground, same as all the other kids. In fact, a lot of them went and told the teacher they liked Kyle so much better this way—said he was so much more fun.

That's the kind of respect that comes from staying true to who you are.

....

POWER FACT: More than 1 billion people live with some type of disability. . . . *That's about 15 percent of the world's population, and that number is going up, up, up. Of course, Kyle's disability is extremely rare, and you're not likely to find too many people facing his kind of struggle, but everyone's got a little extra something to deal with, right? The key to success comes in recognizing your own little extra something and finding a way for it to lift you instead of bring you down.*

....

SHUT UP AND WRESTLE

Kyle may have been a force to be reckoned with on the football field, but his true athletic ability didn't show itself right away as a kid. In fact, he struggled with it at first. In sixth grade, he convinced his parents to let him sign up for the wrestling team, but then when things didn't go well right out of the gate, he wanted to bail. He remembers that even after he lost his first thirty-five matches, his parents still wouldn't let him quit. "My friends were saying it was borderline child abuse, that they were making me [keep wrestling]," he says. "But their thing was I had to tough it out and finish the season."

You can't quit in the middle of something. That's another great lesson Kyle took in from his parents—only, it wasn't meant as a lesson, I don't think. It was more of a direct order: *this is not up for discussion . . . now, shut up and wrestle.*

The next year, Kyle's father tricked him into wrestling a second season, telling Kyle that he himself didn't win a match his first year, either, and reminding him that he had gone on to a great wrestling career. "Years later when I was doing research for my book, I found out that was a complete lie," Kyle told me. "My father started winning matches right away, but at least it got me back out there, and after that I started to win a lot."

Kyle didn't just win a lot—he won *a ton,* and by high school he was wrestling for one of the top teams in the country. At one point, when his team was ranked twelfth in the nation in Kyle's weight class, some of the opposing coaches and parents and wrestlers were saying that Kyle had an unfair advantage because without that extra leg weight and arm weight he was wrestling in a class that didn't match his body type. Can you believe it? The kid had no arms and no legs, and people were crying foul. **It just goes to show you that people will always find a reason to point at you and say you've had some sort of advantage.**

It was in high school that Kyle was able to take the *don't quit* mindset instilled in him by his parents and work it, but looking back he doesn't think the message had fully registered . . . not just yet. Yeah, he was having success as an athlete. Yeah, he was doing well enough in school. Yeah, you'd look on and see Kyle do his thing with a measure of independence and good cheer you couldn't help but admire. But to hear him tell it, there was no *rise and grind* to the way he went about it. He was doing what he needed to do to get by, but he wasn't pushing himself to any kind of next level.

That didn't happen for him until a couple of years later, until he started working on that book I mentioned earlier. Really, it was that book that kicked Kyle's grind into gear. He got the idea to write it after he'd been interviewed on a bunch of national media outlets, by people like Larry King and Bryant Gumbel, started working on it when he was still in high school, and got it published when he was just a year or so into college. The book was called *No Excuses* and it became a national bestseller. It even got Kyle a spot on Oprah Winfrey's show, which if you remember was like a sun-kiss from the publishing gods back then. The book made so much noise, it got him thinking that maybe college wasn't for him. He understood that he had something to say—something that people wanted to hear—and he was determined to get out there and let them hear it.

"When you get an opportunity to launch a book on *Oprah,* it kind of sets your life in a different direction," he says. "Looking back, I think my education really started the moment that I left school."

It was at this point, finally, that Kyle's days began to take on a new focus. He talks about his new life as a kind of process, something he had to get good at, like picking up a spoon or putting on his own socks. "I was terrible when I first started speaking in public," he admits, "and it really was like learning to put on my socks. The way that happened was I used a paper clip and reshaped it to form a fishing hook. It used to take me forty-five minutes, and now it takes like ten seconds, and I think that's really the thread that runs through my entire life. There's a front-loaded period of a lot of failure and struggle that has to occur, a learning curve. It's like an experience curve, really. And then at a certain point I know it's going to tip and I'll be in a totally different spot. So eventually, this public speaking thing, I started to get more comfortable with it."

The more you do a thing, the more you *own* that thing—that's the truth behind Malcolm Gladwell's theory that you need ten thousand hours of practice before you can truly master your talent. Kyle picked up a version of that theory from one of his heroes—Bruce Lee, probably the greatest martial artist of all time. "It was Bruce Lee who said, 'I don't fear the guy who knows a thousand kicks,'" Kyle shares. "He said, **'I fear the guy who's practiced one kick a thousand times.'** Because when you do something over and over, a thousand times, you're just beginning. You realize how much you don't know at that point, and there's an infinite amount to discover after that."

LIVE THE LIFE YOU'RE PUTTING OUT THERE

Kyle was out there practicing his one kick a thousand times, logging his ten thousand hours on the speaking circuit, sometimes sharing the stage with heavy hitters like Michael Phelps, Colin Powell, and then-senator Barack Obama. During that time he'd often catch himself thinking, *What am I doing here?* But then he'd catch himself again and remind himself, I have something to say that can help to make a difference in people's lives. He was twenty years old at the time, and his days had yet to take on a meaningful shape. He'd get up early when he needed to because he was traveling. He stuck to a relentless schedule so that he could make it to wherever he was scheduled to appear. But it still felt to him like he was being pulled along by the momentum of the moment. He wasn't *driving* his days so much as he was *being driven* by them. He wasn't eating right, wasn't sleeping right, and wasn't filling his mind with the right influences. Even though he was achieving some success and notoriety and helping to move the needle in the lives of others, he says his own life was like a train wreck for a time there—that's what I mean when I say that from the outside looking in you can't really appreciate what someone's going through. On the outside, he had it going on. He was getting it done, making good things happen. But on the inside, he was still finding his way.

It wasn't until he rediscovered his love of athletics and started training with Forrest Griffin, the former UFC light heavyweight champion, that Kyle began to develop the sense of discipline and purpose that would come to define him. "There's a purity to a combat sport that doesn't let you think about anything else," he says. "You can't think about whatever stresses you've got going on, or the trips you've got coming up, the appearances you have to make. I realized I wasn't living the life I was talking about. I was out there talking about achievement, living a bigger life, going outside your comfort zone. The message of the book was *no excuses,* but at the same time I was kind of stuck. It felt to me like I was in this massive stream and I didn't have any way to guide the boat."

It took this new physical outlet to shake Kyle free from all that. He turned his focus from theory to practice. He started working as a trainer. He started a supplement company. He opened a gym. Not all of his efforts succeeded, but at least he was *doing* something instead of just *talking* about doing something. And out of that shift in focus, Kyle started setting big, tangible goals for himself. One of the first—and definitely the *biggest*—was climbing Mount Kilimanjaro, the highest peak in Africa. Every year, about twenty thousand people try to reach the summit, and Kyle guesses about half of them make it. "At nineteen thousand feet, stuff gets weird," he explains. "And it's not just the altitude. There's weather, ice, all kinds of conditions people just aren't prepared for."

....

POWER FACT: *55 runners completed the first New York Marathon in 1970.... More than 51,000 crossed the finish line in 2016....* This is just one example of the power we seem to draw from pushing ourselves to the max. People are testing the limits of what they think is possible like never before. What's on *your* bucket list of impossible dreams? What are *you* doing to make those dreams a reality?

....

Of course, Kyle had other conditions to think about besides just the altitude. Once he got the idea to climb Kilimanjaro, it took him about a year and a half to prepare. He had a custom shoe designed, but basically he would have to make his ascent on his elbows and knees—a thirty-mile bear crawl.

What in the world makes someone want to take on a goal like *that*?

"I was just realizing that I needed to listen to the message that I was putting out there," he says. "I had wanted to climb Kilimanjaro since I was a kid, and I was spending so much time talking to other people about their goals and their dreams, and not focusing on my own. And finally I was doing a CrossFit competition and had to climb this tiny mountain, Stone Mountain. It's only nine hundred feet, and I tore a lot of the skin off the ends of my arms doing it. I had these leather welding sleeves going over my arms, but they didn't help, and when I came home that night I told a friend of mine I wanted to climb Kilimanjaro and she looked at me like I was crazy. She said, 'You just tore up your arms doing Stone Mountain, how are you going to do Kilimanjaro?' And I just looked at her and said, 'I don't know.'"

Those three words—*I don't know*—turned out to be the most powerful, most impactful words of Kyle's life,

because in those words there was the certainty that he would figure it out. Same way he figured out how to put on his socks, or type, or dive beneath the legs of a blocker in a youth football game. He would *rise and grind* his way to the top of that mountain—and that's exactly what he did.

After Kilimanjaro, Kyle went on to climb Aconcagua, the highest peak in South America. And one of the most surprising things he learned from those experiences was the power of looking *back* at what he's accomplished, instead of looking only ahead. Perspective is all, he says.

"We get so focused on the summit, we get discouraged," he explains—meaning that the goals we put out in front of us can seem pretty big, pretty intimidating. "But it was when I looked back down the mountain and could see how far we'd come, that was the most empowering moment I had on that climb. . . . When we were about two thousand feet from the summit, sitting on an ice field, and as the sun came up we could look down and see the rain forest where we'd started like ten days before, when it was like eighty-five or ninety degrees. Really, we'd come so far.

"And it's not just about climbing Kilimanjaro, of course, because I've definitely had periods of feeling lost and wondering what my life is about, where I didn't have that sense of direction I found on that climb. At twenty, I just had no idea. I was so consumed with my book, and with my speaking career, but I never really took the time to look back and appreciate that I was standing on the stage with these people who'd done phenomenal things. Sometimes you just have to look back to appreciate how far you've come. That's something I get from one of my favorite writers of all time, Joseph Campbell. To 'return with elixir,' that's his term for it. When we're out on our hero's journey, and we achieve the reward we believe we've been seeking, that's when we turn and see what it is we've accomplished, how far we've come. That's when we think to turn and share that reward, to become a mentor to others. **That's the greatest gift you can make of your own life, to help someone else find the ability to create their own fortune.** That's what I want my life to be about now."

My kind of grind, people.

Kyle's Grind Checklist

✓ be authentic—when Kyle talks about how he started out as a motivational speaker and felt like a fraud because he wasn't exactly practicing what he was preaching, that really resonated with me . . .

✓ look at how far you've come instead of how far you still need to go . . .

✓ keep a picture of yourself in your mind and like what you see, because if you're not good with you the world probably won't be either . . .

✓ make the necessary adjustments—the human body can adapt to just about anything, but only if we embrace the concept of change and keep open to new approaches . . .

✓ don't conform to the expectations of others (unless of course the expectations of others make a whole lot of sense, in which case, might as well change things up) . . .

✓ be the guy who practiced that one kick a thousand times—I love this thought because it reminds me that we don't have to do *everything* well as long as we're able to do one thing really, really well . . .

....

For more information on Kyle and how he uses the
Rise and Grind mindset, check out
www.DaymondJohn.com/Rise/Kyle

TWO

EMBRACE THE GRIND

KIDS THESE DAYS . . .

Hey, I'm almost fifty—got a right to say things like "Kids these days . . ." Although, got to admit, a line like that, it makes me feel like some crotchety old man, sitting on his front porch, shaking his cane at the teenagers goofing off on his street. Still, there's no denying that millennials are wired a little differently than us Gen Xers, same way the boomers were different than the greatest-generation folks who came before *them*. And since I plan to keep *grinding* until I actually need that cane someday, I've had to adapt to some of the millennials' ways. So here I want to spend a little time looking at how the world has changed, how *my* world has changed, how it's changing still.

In *my* day (another expression that makes me want to take out my teeth!), we got to work early, grinded hard, left the office at six, seven, eight o'clock at night, but once we were out of the office we were mostly out of touch. Our time was our own. **These days, young people are at it 24/7.** They're always on the clock—no such thing as being out of touch, because if you miss out, you miss out. Young people today know they need to jump on every prospect as it appears, or someone else will beat them to it, so they'll answer that email at three o'clock in the morning—and send out another few of their own while they're at it. I'll do that, too, from time to time, but that's a *learned* habit for me, and the reason I had to learn it was these damn kids. They grew up like that, didn't know any different. Feels a little bit like they're built without a Pause button. And so, to keep pace, to keep relevant, I've had to bend to this new idea of a never-ending workday, even though I try to remind myself I can always hit Pause.

This constant contact with our colleagues and our customers has become part of our cultural core. And that's both a good thing and a not-so-good thing. It's a good thing because we all get to work on a bigger canvas. It's as if a whole new world of opportunity has been spread out before us. There's no end to it. We're no longer bound by a traditional workday, or even by a traditional office setting. We work on the fly: walking down the street, at home in our underwear, sometimes in the middle of a meeting on another project entirely. **When inspiration hits—whenever and wherever—we've got the tools at our fingertips to act on it.** So what could be bad about that? Well, if we don't power down, we'll run out of gas. We can't stay in full-force grind mode all the time. If we don't take the time to recharge and refresh, we'll end up just going through the motions. Whatever energy we might have had going in to some new project, some new deal, we'll have a whole lot less of it after a while. At that point we'll have to double down and work even harder. At least, that's what we tell ourselves, so what happens is there's this constant tug-and-pull, between keeping to a routine we know is smart and healthy and keeps us productive, and hustling to make sure we don't get beat by the guy who grinded just a little harder. It's the same kind of thinking that got me out of the house first thing on a snow day, making sure all those other shovels didn't get the gig that was meant for me. Thank God it didn't snow every single winter day in New York, because if I had had to keep to that schedule for a couple of months straight it would have worn me out.

Don't know about you, but I *need* to hit that Pause button every now and then. I *need* to catch my breath, reflect, consider. But it sometimes feels like there's no time to just chill.

So what do we do? We figure it out, strike a balance, and come up with our own style that works for body and soul *and* bottom line. That's what this book is all about, really. **It's about the ways we answer the call when our time is our own.** If you're working for someone else, you've got no choice but to follow their lead—same way my mother had to do when she was juggling all those jobs. Your hours are your hours. But once you start to be your own boss, or once you get something going on the side away from your nine-to-five, that's when it's time to develop your own grind.

Look, I like to party as much as anyone. Line up all the pictures I've posted on Snapchat and Instagram the past couple of years, and you might think I'm partying all the time. But **I've found a way to make my grind my joy,** so what *looks* like a big ol' time is really me finding a way to network, to hustle in a social setting. There are no walls to my office, so what might look like me just chillin' with someone could just as easily be a conversation about a deal we're trying to do, or a project we're about to kick off. I might love the beach, but I'm not unwinding for a full week with my toes in the water and an umbrella drink in my hand. I might love to snowboard, but I'm not hitting the slopes first thing in the morning and grabbing that last lift up the mountain at the end of the day. Instead, I'll slot in little points of pause in my day-to-day: moments where I can step back, catch my breath, maybe ease off the gas a little bit before getting back to work. My idea of time off ties in to the way I was raised. Like my mom said, the time is going to pass anyway, so might as well use it productively. This applies not just to work, but also to how I spend my free time.

What that means, in practice, is that if I'm traveling to California, I'll try to stay at a hotel on the beach. If I'm hitting up a trade show in Denver, I'll carve out time for a side trip to a nearby ski resort. If I'm in Miami, I'll take a couple of calls by the pool. If I'm in some landlocked city, at sea level, with nothing to distract me, I'll find some local adventure or a great nearby restaurant and lose myself in what the region has to offer . . . even if it's just for a while.

....

POWER FACT: *Forbes reports that 45 percent of vacation property managers have seen a spike in the number of millennial renters in recent years. . . . That's a sure sign that our younger entrepreneurs are recognizing the importance of maintaining a healthy work-life balance as they build their careers.*

....

Everything is relative, right? Even the grind. **One man's heavy burden is another man's feather.** The key to success, really, is learning to carry the load you've been given, without getting crushed by it. . . . To make it seem like it isn't a burden, but a blessing. To make it your joy. And the way I've learned to do *that,* over the years, is to build these little bits of downtime into my schedule. To stitch each day together in such a way that there's time for me, time for what I've set out to do, time to keep focused on the road ahead, and time to fill up the tank when I'm running out of gas.

We all carry our load in life differently. There's no magic

formula telling us how. But like anything else in life, there's a lot we can learn from the people who seem to have it all figured out.

Something to keep in mind as you read—I don't expect you to see yourself in each and every one of these individuals. Be inspired by them, sure. Be impressed by what they've accomplished, absolutely. Be connected to them through your connection to *me,* hell yeah. But like I said up top, I'm hoping you'll pick and choose from their strategies and approaches as you figure out what works for you.

....

POWER FACT: "Pareto's principle" says 80 percent of your results flow from just 20 percent of your resources. . . . *You might know it as the 80/20 rule, and most of the people I interviewed for this book have embraced the concept. Think how the formula applies in your case— and, if you must, adjust accordingly.*

....

In talking to all these good people, I've been struck by the common ground they all seem to walk. Never forget, we're all cut in different ways, but at the same time it helps to note that the folks you're about to meet share a lot of similarities, too. I'm generalizing here, but let me just highlight a few of the traits most of these folks tend to carry:

- *they work out on a regular basis*—and most hit the gym first thing in the morning, before the day takes shape and time starts running on them . . .
- *they spend a portion of each day networking*—only not in the most obvious ways . . . they keep connected, plugged in, but they've each developed a signature style, a way of keeping on top of their contacts that

doesn't feel forced—in other words, they've found a
way to keep it genuine . . .

- *they take some time to expand their base of knowledge,*
  to research their market, their customer base, their
  competitors . . . to stay on top of their business . . .
- *they set goals for themselves or for their business—*
  writing them down, in a lot of cases, visualizing or
  internalizing them . . .
- *they meditate*—got to say, I'm endlessly (and, happily)
  surprised at the number of successful people who find
  a way to mute the noise of the world, and calm the
  chaos all around, just to reconnect with their core and
  their sense of purpose . . . even if it's only for a few
  blessed minutes . . .
- *they delegate*—that is, they have come to depend
  on trusted people around them to help grow their
  games and scale their businesses, while also allowing
  them an extra measure of freedom to pursue other
  opportunities and occasionally step off that moving
  treadmill they rode to the top in the first place . . .
  successful people know which tasks to tackle
  themselves, and which ones to assign to folks who'll
  see them through . . .
- *they have trained themselves to think like an attorney
  chasing his or her billable hours.* What do I mean by that?
  They manage their time like someone else is paying
  them for it—which, I guess, they are—but the way
  that works out is they're looking to fill their time in
  meaningful ways. Every chunk of time is accounted
  for, even if it's set aside as downtime. Every phone
  call, every meeting, every strategy session . . . it's all
  programmed into their calendars in such a way that
  they can stay on top of whatever it is they're doing,

whatever it is they're about to do. I saw the most extreme example of this when I visited with President Obama, back when I was serving as an ambassador for his Global Entrepreneurship program: his schedule seemed to be microprogrammed into three- and four-minute chunks of time. That's how you get things done! Or put another way . . .

- *they tend to focus on moments instead of hours and days*—after all, there are only twenty-four hour-long chunks of time on your daily calendar, but there are 1,440 minutes you can fill in a meaningful way . . . spend them wisely . . .

- *they learn to "fail fast"*—meaning, they stumble right out of the gate a time or two, and then find a way to honor and learn from those early missteps as they move forward . . .

- *they have managed to downshift from the 24/7 grind that stamped their early careers*—allowing them to discover the work-life balance they need to survive and thrive . . .

- *they keep a primary goal in mind*—it might feel to you like you've got a million things going on at once (okay, maybe that's an exaggeration—maybe it's more like a thousand things) . . . but successful people keep their eyes on *one* big prize at a time . . .

- *they get home in time for dinner*—obviously, there are business trips and business dinners that can make it difficult for us to spend evenings at home with our families, but successful people make the effort . . .

- *they follow the "one-touch" rule*—this basically says that you should act on every bill, every email, every phone message the very first time it crosses your desk . . . just think how much time you waste *rereading* all

this stuff when you eventually get around to it . . .
successful people see it, process it, and act on it—
immediately . . .

Now, I don't want it to seem like I'm giving away the store
before you even have a chance to see what I've got on the shelves,
but I believe it helps if you're on the lookout for these things
as you read. It'll drive the lesson home. Or maybe it'll get you
thinking about some of the habits you've developed in your own
life and career—the good ones *and* the not-so-good ones—and
push you to try a new approach.

Another thing I want you to look out for as you read are those
moments when someone defied expectations and looked doubt
in the face. I don't want to swear in these pages, so let's just call
these To Hell with You Moments. (You can just imagine what I'd
really like to call 'em!) You've probably heard of that famous study
at UCLA that reported that the average one-year-old toddler
hears the word *no* more than four hundred times a day. That's a
whole lot of negativity, right? And yet somehow that child is able
to get to yes . . . maybe not right away, but eventually. Same goes
for every successful person I know—they started out hearing no
and they didn't stop until they heard yes . . . maybe not right
away, but eventually. You'll find examples of this throughout this
book. I'm thinking here of the warrior you just met, Kyle Maynard, who became an award-winning athlete, bestselling author,
and one of the most unstoppable individuals on the planet, despite people telling him he'd never amount to anything, and that
he had to just suck it up and deal with being disabled. I'm thinking too of Nely Galán, the warrior you're about to meet—one of
the top producers of reality television shows, who wouldn't have
even gotten to the starting gate if she didn't stand up to one of
the nuns in her Catholic high school who accused her of plagiarism. And entrepreneur extraordinaire Brian Lee, the cofounder

of LegalZoom and Shoedazzle and The Honest Company, who stood up to his father's low expectations when he announced that he wanted to quit school to become a rapper. And Wendy Williams, the one-of-a-kind shock jock turned television talk-show host, who changed the structure of syndicated television because she saw a better way—a better way to use her time, make more money, and capture a bigger share of viewers.

And on and on . . .

I want to emphasize that every one of these successful individuals has followed his or her own path. **There is no *one* *way* to grind,** just as there is no *one way* to make it to the top, to accomplish your goals and dreams, or even to simply make it through your day with a smile on your face and a whole bunch of checkmarks on your to-do list.

But these folks do have one thing in common. They rise . . . and they **G-R-I-N-D**.

BE RESILIENT
STAND FOR SOMETHING

NELY GALÁN
Television Executive, Reality Show Producer, Empowerment Broker, Force for Good

YOU MIGHT NOT know Nely Galán by name, but you probably know her work. Chances are that, even if you don't speak any Spanish, you've stopped to watch something on Telemundo, where Nely served as president of entertainment for a stretch, and where she created and produced some of its top shows.

When I run into people who've never heard of Nely, I tell them she's like the Tyler Perry of Latino programming, and then they get it. Really, it's incredible what this woman has accomplished, the programming she's helped to put out into the world, and when you think about how she started out . . . well, then it's downright astonishing, too.

Nely and I crossed paths around the time I was promoting *The Power of Broke* and she was promoting her *New York Times* bestselling book, *Self Made: Becoming Empowered, Self-Reliant, and Rich in Every Way*. In a nutshell, her book was all about how to think like an immigrant—which, when you break it down, has a whole lot in common with the message I was putting out. **We were both trying to get our readers to flip a switch and start thinking of the disadvantages they were facing as advantages in disguise.**

"That's totally true," she says, when I make the comparison. "We didn't know each other, but we were on the same page."

Nely's backstory is unique. She was born in Cuba and came to the United States when she was five years old. When she tells me her family history, I can't stop thinking how different the immigrant experience was in the 1960s. "It was nothing like today," she says, "when immigrants are talked about so negatively. Back then, different churches were sponsoring all these different refugee families, and taking them in."

That's kind of what happened to Nely and her family. They lived for a time in southern New Jersey, in the home of a woman whose two sons had both died tragically—one in Vietnam and the other in a swimming pool accident. Nely remembers that the woman's minister had counseled her to live a life of service to help get over her grief. Specifically, he suggested she adopt a Cuban family, which is how Nely's family got a place to stay for a year or so while her parents found work and got settled. Eventually, her father took a job painting cars on the assembly line at Ford, while her mom went to work in a local factory.

"That left me as the family translator, the therapist, the shrink, the everything," Nely recalls. "That's how I grew up in America, like so many kids of immigrants."

Let's face it, we're all immigrants, at bottom. That's who we are, how we got here, and I believe we can all learn from the people we know who came to this country with nothing and found a way to turn it into something.

What Nely learned from the example of her parents' tireless, selfless work ethic was that good things come to those who wait. From an early age, she started thinking of herself as a turtle— knowing that wherever she was going, she would get there eventually. Might not be on the same timetable as everyone else, but she'd keep powering ahead, same way her parents kept grinding and eventually found a way to build a life for their young family by punching a clock at their factory jobs.

Nely tells me a heartbreaking (and, ultimately, heart-*lifting*) story of how the other kids used to pick on her when she was in first and second grade—which is unfortunately the story of growing up in America for too many kids of immigrants.

"The kids would call me names," she says. "They would say, 'You're a spic.' I wouldn't even know what that meant, but I'd come home and tell my mother the kids were saying all these things about me. And she goes, 'You come from this incredible island. You come from an African background. You come from a Spanish background. You speak multiple languages. How could anyone think more is less? They're ignorant. Whenever those kids call you names, you just remember that two languages, three cultures, two countries is more.'"

Such an empowering message, don't you think? And in Nely's case, for her and her younger brother, it took. From those humble beginnings she found a way to become a leading voice for women in television—specifically, for Latina women in television, and I have to think it all flowed in some way from this right here. Nely grew up believing her heritage was a blessing, an advantage instead of a disadvantage, and out of that she got it in her head that she could do anything, become anything. Along the way, she also learned to stand her ground—that was really the key to a lot of the turning point–type moments that found her along the way.

One of the stories she tells from her childhood, for example, is about how her family struggled to afford to send her to an all-girls Catholic school. Her parents didn't have the money for tuition, but at the same time they didn't think they could afford *not* to send their kids to the best possible school. Nely wanted to help out in whatever little-kid ways she could. Eventually she was encouraged by a neighbor to start selling Avon products and doing so she made enough money to cover what her family owed that year. She arranged a clever little charade with the nuns at school and had them send a letter home saying the money came from a scholarship, so her proud parents would be okay with it.

Forget for a moment what those nuns were thinking, helping a little girl lie to her parents. There was a greater good at play here, as far as Nely's development was concerned. Even as a child of twelve, she was building the kind of negotiating skills that would serve her well throughout her career. Nely points to the story as example of how her family worked together as a team. In a lot of ways, learning to work within the family unit, to do her part to make sure everyone had what they needed while also making sure that everyone's feelings and personalities were taken into consideration, was great preparation for running a big company, she says now, but at age twelve Nely couldn't know that just yet. She still had some growing up to do.

....

POWER FACT: Women of color make up about 33 percent of the female workforce, and they're twice as likely as white females to be employed in low-wage jobs. . . . *Not exactly an inspiring statistic, but I set it out to inspire readers to go against the norm. If you hope to stand out, you need to know where you stand!*

....

DON'T LET THEM PUSH YOU AROUND, EVEN WHEN THEY'RE PUSHING YOU OUT THE DOOR

Nely's career really began to take shape around a misunderstanding that found her in high school. Actually, to call it a *misunderstanding* is probably generous, because it was really more like a false accusation that Nely was smart enough to play to her advantage. What happened was, in her sophomore year, Nely wrote a story for an assignment in English class that was so well written, the teacher accused Nely of plagiarism—a charge that was probably a little racist, and probably a little ignorant, but Nely didn't see it like that. To her, it was just a problem to get past, so she did.

She says, "They suspended me for three days, so of course I went home and told my parents, and my mother said, 'You go ask the nun for forgiveness.' That was the immigrant perspective. My parents were always afraid. They would never speak up. My mother was always taking the side of authority, even if authority was wrong. So I go, 'But I didn't do anything wrong.' It didn't make any difference. I was home for three days, and I wrote an article about it for *Seventeen*. That was the magazine I read as a teenager. It was called 'Why You Should Never Send Your Daughter to an All-Girl Catholic School.' I sent it in. Then I went back to school and the nun called me in and apologized. She goes, 'I'm so sorry. Your story was just so well written.' She compared it to *The Old Man and the Sea*. I got an A, and everything kind of blew over."

Only, things didn't blow *all the way* over. Three months later, Nely got a check in the mail for one hundred dollars from *Seventeen*. She was as surprised as anyone. She didn't know anyone at *Seventeen*. She was just a reader, on the outside looking in, but what she wrote struck some kind of chord. The magazine wanted to publish her article, and when it came out, she got called into the principal's office at school. One of the nuns said, "We don't like your kind in our school." (*Your kind* . . . can you imagine a teacher or administrator speaking to a child like that in today's environment?) Nely burst into tears and ran home to tell her parents she'd been expelled. Once again, her mother told her to apologize. She said, "Go back to them on your hands and knees."

Well, Nely wasn't about to do *that*. Matter of fact, she did just the opposite. She called the New Jersey Board of Education to complain. Pretty feisty for a fifteen-year-old, huh? But that's Nely Galán for you. She's not the type to roll over—never was, never will be—and soon she was taking her case to the local newspapers. When the story came out, Nely's mother once again took the opportunity to scold her daughter for stepping out of line. A lot of parents, they might have cheered if their kid took such a proactive approach to an injustice, but Nely's folks were embarrassed, and worried that their daughter's activism might come back to bite them in some way.

You know, I hear stories like this one from Nely and I'm reminded of the importance of teachers, only most of the stories we hear are about the good teachers who pushed us, inspired us, and introduced us to big new ideas. You never really hear how a bad teacher can also make an impact, and here you see Nely's experiences as a great example. To hear her tell it, this teacher was narrow-minded and prejudiced and lazy, and yet out of all that, Nely found a way to stand against these charges against her and learn from them, grow from them.

Good for her. Good for *all* of our proud, determined young people who are able to rise above the failings of the teachers who are meant to guide them and find a way to guide themselves.

Back to Nely's story. This time around, the whole family was called in to see the nuns, and Nely's mom was all set to apologize, but by the time they got there the school administrators had flipped. The nuns must have realized they were up against a force of nature (or, at least, a public relations nightmare), because all of a sudden they were falling all over themselves to praise Nely for her outspoken stance. They claimed they'd never expelled Nely, just told her that they didn't approve of her behavior. They said it was all just a big misunderstanding. (It's *always* a misunderstanding when you're on the side of right!) It was such a misunderstanding, in fact, that the nuns were prepared to allow Nely to graduate a year and a half ahead of her classmates.

"They really wanted to get rid of me," Nely says, laughing about it now, but it's clear as she shares the story that she still hurts from the experience. It might have toughened her up and taught her to go against authority, but it was a lot for a fifteen-year-old kid to process. And it pushed her to think about life after high school way before she was ready.

That's how it goes for a lot of us, a lot of the time. Life comes at us at its own pace, and it's on us to rise to meet it. Or, not.

Happily, the editors at *Seventeen* checked back in. It turned out the school's loss was the magazine's gain, because the publisher offered Nely a guest-editor position. Nely jumped at the chance, and her career just kind of took off from there. The position at the magazine didn't pay anything—it was more like an internship—and Nely was commuting on the bus from New Jersey to Manhattan, so it was actually costing her a little money. She ended up taking a job at the Limited, as a salesperson, evenings and weekends. And a babysitting job, too—that's three jobs in all, at fifteen years old!

Nely guesses this was when her *grind* really kicked in, because to get all this done she started waking up at five o'clock every morning—a habit she continues to this day. By now, her body clock is hardwired to get up before everyone else and allow her to get a jump-start on her morning. For her, getting an early start is essential. It gives her a couple of extra hours to prepare for the day ahead and gives her a head start on everybody else chasing the same goals.

MAKE IT WORK

Her first assignment at *Seventeen* was to arrange a fashion shoot with five models. Nely had no idea where or how to begin, so she asked her boss. Her boss just looked at her and said, "If you need me to show you, I'll have to fire you. Figure it out."

So Nely figured it out—that's what entrepreneurs do, and that's what visionaries do. And it's the kind of perseverance Nely showed throughout her career. But here it had its roots in desperation. She knew she had to find a way to make it work.

She kept up this ruthless work schedule for two years, when another opportunity came her way—this one from a television production company in Texas. A producer had been reading Nely's articles in *Seventeen* and thought of her to join a slate of on-air reporters for a newsmagazine show in development and targeted to teenagers and twenty-something viewers—think a youthful version of *60 Minutes*. They wanted Nely to fill the La-tina slot, and Nely was ready to jump at the chance. Her parents? Not so into it. In fact, her mother refused to let her go at first, but once again Nely stood her ground. She said, "If you don't let me go, I'm going to escape."

It was a turning point in her life, Nely says—and it turned on her resolve, her belief that good things come to those who put themselves in position to take advantage of them. Much like the story I shared about Catherine Zeta-Jones, Nely's parents' disapproval taught Nely to be willing to set aside the expectations of others as she set off in pursuit of her dreams.

··

POWER FACT: According to WalletHub, working moms find the best opportunities for employment in Vermont, Minnesota, Delaware, New Jersey, and Connecticut.... *These states rate highest in terms of work-life balance and child care, so sometimes you might have to move away from home to give yourself and your family the best chance to succeed. Because, let's face it, working moms are the ultimate entrepreneurs, and entrepreneurs go where the opportunities are.*

··

In the end, Nely drove herself to Austin in an orange Chevette she'd managed to buy—against her parents' wishes, at first.

"When I go around the country and talk to women of color, this is significant," she says, "because young women don't leave home. Family is just so strong, especially among Latinas, and women from Asia and India. Culturally, it's not cool to leave home. My mother was crying when I left. She said, 'I will never forgive you until the day I die.' Now, of course, she says, 'Where would we all be if you had not left that day?' But at the time, it was a big, big deal."

Once in Texas, Nely stuck to the same disciplined routine she'd developed in high school and as a young staffer at *Seventeen*. She still rose every morning at five o'clock, and even though her job required her to be at the studio by nine, Nely was usually there by seven, going over her notes, immersing herself in the stories she'd been assigned to cover. Success is what you do before and after you do everything you're *supposed* to do—this was

Nely, living the truth of that line. And it's a habit she's kept up over the years, making sure each day that she gets to work with plenty of time to spare—and plenty of time to make sure she's ready for the day before it gets under way.

Getting up at five every morning wasn't always easy, of course, but she picked up a great tip from one of Tony Robbins's books that helped her rise and grind on those mornings when she was feeling dog-tired. His thing was to buy an alarm clock that smells or sounds like something you love. "The idea," she explains, "is to reboot your brain, so that when you get up, you're happy to get up. Your brain is something you can rewire."

Personally, I *love* this idea—I'm thinking of getting a custom alarm clock that smells like the Baby Back Rib Burger at Carl's Jr. and Hardee's, made with the Bubba's-Q Boneless Ribs from my *Shark Tank* partners Al and Brittani Baker, of course. *Mmmmm* . . . now *that's* a smell I wouldn't mind waking up to each morning! (I couldn't resist . . . *sorry!*)

Even with her early wake-up time, Nely still managed to continue the good habit she'd developed back in high school of getting eight hours of sleep each night. Wasn't such a big deal when she was a kid, living at home, but now that she was out on her own, and scrambling to keep up at work, it was tough to find the time to justify all that shut-eye. But she also knew she relied on a good night's sleep to keep her grind going—maybe because her mind was always racing a million miles a minute.

How did she fit all that sleep into her crazy schedule? Easy. "I had no personal life," she says of her time in Texas. "I was this young kid, living in Austin. My whole thing was to succeed in that job. When young people say to me, 'Oh my God, I'm dying, trying to hold down three jobs,' I don't feel sorry for them. When you're young, there is no balance, and there shouldn't be balance. There's plenty of time later in life for balance."

DREAM SMALL

That hard-driving work ethic sure explains how Nely got herself from that newsmagazine in Austin to Channel 47 in New York, which she helped turn into the top Spanish-language independent station in the country and eventually grow into Telemundo—all before she was twenty-five years old. And just in case I haven't made myself clear, Nely kept climbing to the very top. After a successful stint as Telemundo's president, she went on to produce more than seven hundred episodes of television in English and Spanish, through her company Galán Entertainment, including the hit reality show *The Swan* for Fox. And then, after all *that,* she went back to school to pursue her master's and doctorate in clinical and cultural psychology. At each rung on the ladder she was climbing, she took the time to learn the lay of the land, do her homework, and get comfortable. Sometimes she'd even hire a tutor or consultant to guide her through the ins and outs of some new aspect of the business, just because she didn't want to let her bosses or her colleagues know she wasn't up to speed.

So what I'm about to say might surprise you, especially coming from me: Nely is all about setting her goals small. Now, I don't want to contradict that "Think big!" message I put out earlier—the one I got from my mother when I was a kid. The thing of it is, when I slap a header on this section like "Dream small," I don't mean to go against my mom, but only to add a little wrinkle to her advice—maybe even to make a different point entirely. But just as there is no one right way to grind, there is no one right way to set goals. What's the point of rising and grinding to meet your goals if they aren't your own, right? In order to meet hers, Nely learned early on to make good and careful use of her time, and she credits her own self-styled goal-setting technique with keeping her focused. Her method couldn't be simpler. At the beginning of each year, she comes up with three things she hopes to accomplish.

"I keep it to three big things," she tells. "Not twenty things. Not one hundred things. Three. And every Sunday I sit down and see where I'm at, and what I need to do that week. I break it down."

If one of Nely's goals is to lose weight, say, she'll give herself a big target. Then she'll give herself lots of little targets. For example, to lose thirty pounds in a year, she'll have to lose about half a pound each week, so she'll weigh herself every Sunday to see where she's at. She'll put a diet and exercise plan in place to help her hit that mark and then she'll work toward it each day.

"If you set out to do big things every week, you do nothing," she explains. "If you set out to do small baby steps to get to the big things eventually, you feel good about yourself, because you're able to succeed."

There's a lot to like about Nely's approach. I like how it sets things up so she can feel good about herself every night. I like how it's all streamlined, and simple—hey, it's a lot easier to track three things than six or eight or ten.

Another good habit she's been practicing for most of her life is meditation—specifically, she took the time to study Transcendental Meditation, so she's got a mantra and everything. "My mantra keeps me focused," she says. "If I drift away from it, I can come back to it."

End of the day, Nely's routine keeps her grounded, helps her keep a realistic hold on the busy life and career she's managed to build out of her immigrant experience.

"A lot of kids in America, we get told, 'Follow your bliss and the money will come.' I think that's a BS, first-world, entitled way of thinking. If you live in Afghanistan and you want to be a singer, but your mom's starving, are you going to be a singer?

Maybe not. Maybe you've got to work in a factory. To me, it's about mission and money. You have to always cultivate what you love, but alongside of that you have to make money. You have to keep the lights on. Always, take care of your family. And always, take care of business.

"Look," she says, "you have to take time to figure some things out. You're not going to fix all the parts of your life at once. People get very upset and they go, 'My life is screwed up.' Well, maybe it is. But I feel like if I look at my life, with the way I monitor everything, with the way I'm so introspective, I might see that only twenty percent of my life, at the worst, is screwed up. And when you look at it like that you start to think, Oh, that's not so bad. It's okay. And now you know it. Now you have an awareness about it. You will get to the parts that aren't working, but you might not get to it right away.

"You're like a turtle," she says. "Slow and steady baby steps."

Nely's Grind Checklist

✓ keep your goals big, but keep the steps to get there within reach . . . don't *just* shoot for the moon—grab at all the clouds you can on the way there . . .

✓ speak up . . . like a lot of first-generation immigrants, Nely's parents were handcuffed by a kind of second-class-citizen mentality . . . don't be afraid to get what's yours . . . and remember that when one path appears blocked to you, there is almost always a way around . . .

✓ seize the opportunities that come your way, even if you didn't go looking for them in the first place . . .

✓ be true to yourself . . . Nely's opportunities came about because she was self-assured enough to honor her voice . . .

✓ figure it out . . . when life hands you an opportunity, it doesn't always come with an instruction booklet . . .

✓ take chances . . . see what works, and if you're wide of the mark the first time out, change things up and try a new approach . . .

✓ it's okay to be the turtle . . . slow and steady wins the race, people . . .

....

For more information on Nely and how she uses the
Rise and Grind mindset, check out

www.DaymondJohn.com/Rise/Nely

THREE

MAKING TIME

THOSE THREE LITTLE words, man. Rise. And. Grind.

They've become my rallying cry, my mantra, my purpose. And notice I didn't just count those two action words—*rise, grind*—because I need that little conjunction in there—*and*—to put them to work.

Now, before you start thinking I've gone soft, using a big ol' word like *conjunction,* let me come clean: I looked it up. Sorry, but I was never much of a student back in middle school and high school when you learn all that stuff. I was dyslexic—still am!—which means I was also never much of a reader. But through will, effort, and stubborn insistence, I've made myself into a student over the years. I've also made myself into a reader. (And, last I checked, I've even made myself into a writer!) I just go about my reading and writing in my own way, at my own pace. **And these days what drives me is learning as much as I can, as *efficiently* as I can . . . no matter what obstacles are in my way.**

And so I *rise and grind*. There's no quit in me, no letup. I don't pump my brakes. And it doesn't end with the way I taught myself to read. It doesn't end with the way I run my businesses, or how I take in all these bits and bytes of information in my own unusual ways. No, the rise and grind runs all through my days, at all times. It's how I live, work, and play. It's who I am, and if you follow me on social media you'll know it's how I try to motivate those around me.

How did I get this way? Where will it take me? As you read on, I hope, those answers will come clear, but this is not a book about me. **It's a book about you.** It's a book about what it takes to power through, what it takes to get what you want. Whether it's making it to the top in your career, building a killer start-up, or making a major breakthrough in your goals, your interests, your relationship status, this book is about how to push through whatever it is that stands before you as some kind of obstacle. Because there is no mountain you can't climb, as long as you set about it—even if you've got to climb it on your damn belly, like my friend Kyle Maynard!

We'll talk a lot about goals in the pages ahead—setting them, keeping them, redefining them—but the most important goal I want you to think about as we take this journey together is this: get started. That's it. Doesn't sound like much, does it? In fact, it reminds me of that silly little "Put One Foot in Front of the Other" song from that "Santa Claus Is Coming to Town" special we all used to watch as kids. But sometimes that's all it takes, getting started. **Your end goals may change along the way, but you'll never know unless you get going. . . .**

And don't stop.

KNOW WHAT YOU DON'T KNOW

In my last book, *The Power of Broke,* I wrote about how entrepreneurs need to stay hungry in order to succeed, how we have to have a certain mindset that leaves us feeling at all times like our backs are against the wall, how we sometimes need that extra push to use every resource, every muscle, every piece of instinct and intuition available to us and find a way to leverage them—because, hey, let's face it, when there's nowhere to go but up, up, up, you kick into a higher gear and get it done. Even after you've made it, you've got to keep digging, keep reaching, keep moving about the planet with a sense of desperation, like you've got nothing to lose and everything to gain. Like you've got *no choice* but to hit your goals, one after another, because failure is just not an option.

(Remember: get started . . . *and don't stop!*)

Notice how I said, the *power of broke* is a state of mind. **The power of *rise and grind* is a state of *being.*** It's not enough to let that *power of broke*–type sense of desperation drive you . . . you've got to know where you're going. You've got to have a map you can follow. But you've also got to know when it's time to recalibrate your route. **Picture a little Waze app in your head that tells you to go north instead of south, or left instead of right—because what might have been the best route for you to take before is now jammed with other people. Or maybe there's been a road closing, an accident, or some other obstacle waiting to slow you down.**

But it's not enough to just know where you're going. You've got to make progress every single day. That's why I'm constantly learning and reimagining my approach to business and life. Yeah, it might look like I have my act together, but that act is still taking shape. My end goals are changing up on me all the time. My internal Waze app is constantly rerouting me and steering me out of trouble. I don't always know exactly where I'm going. **All I know, end of the day, is that there's a whole lot I don't know**—so I try to keep an open mind and grow my game and improve myself every way I know how.

Live your life in this way and you'll find the power to do anything, to get past anything, to become anything. You'll come to know that our success is in our court, and that we *rise* to meet our challenges and *grind* our way to the top . . . or not. Either way, it's on us.

Every time we get up in the morning ready to hit the ground running, it's on us.

Every hour we keep pushing before finally powering down and collapsing into bed at night, it's on us.

Every time we set a goal, it's on us.

Every time we *look at* our goals and hit the reset button because it's starting to look like we might miss our target, it's on us.

Every extra set at the gym, every extra mile we log on our morning run, it's on us.

Every follow-up call we make to a potential client or customer or partner, it's on us.

Every New Year's resolution we set and *keep,* it's on us.

Every fight we set out to win, every obstacle we shove out of our path, it's on us most of all.

....

POWER FACT: A *U.S. News & World Report* poll shows that 80 percent of our resolutions fail by mid-February. . . . *Something to keep in mind as you power past Groundhog Day and try to stick to your goals— remember, when you watched the ball drop on New Year's Eve, you didn't resolve to be like everyone else. Stand apart. Get it done.*

....

My whole life, I've learned from the people around me. I've grabbed at the behaviors I wanted to model, and rejected the approaches I wanted to avoid. One of the first times I did this in a structured way, as I mentioned earlier, was when I read Napoleon Hill's *Think and Grow Rich*—probably one of the most impactful books I've come across. That book is as relevant today, as *timely* today, as when it was first published—all the way back in 1937. Which is probably why it's one of the bestselling books of all time, and why people are still drawn to it. Why I thought to read it at fourteen years old, I'll never know. How I got through it with my dyslexia, I'll never know. But I heard people talking about it, so I set my mind to reading it . . . and I did. It took me a good long while, probably a couple of weeks, but I got it done. Can't say for sure what I was able to grab at in a full-on way, but what I took in stayed with me. Then, about a year later, I went back and read it again. The year after that, same thing. I'm still rereading it, after all this time—maybe not every year at this point, but every couple of years, at least. A lot of times, I'll throw my dog-eared copy in my bag when I travel.

Whenever I read that book, I get to thinking about Andrew Carnegie, the great nineteenth-century steel magnate, who inspired Napoleon Hill to write *Think and Grow Rich,* and who introduced him to the Fords and Rockefellers of the world. Carnegie to this day is considered one of the richest Americans ever, ever, ever. He was all about the grind, man. But he was also all about philanthropy, and sharing knowledge, and giving back. In fact, it was Carnegie who famously said, "Man may be born in poverty, but he does not have to go through life in poverty"—a quote I should have probably used somewhere in *The Power of Broke,* but I'm making up for it here.

Long as I'm on it, I want to shine a light on Carnegie's great legacy, which at the end of his life was mostly about sharing his wealth of knowledge with the world. He's known as the father of our modern library system, and he helped to create opportunities for people who might have been born without any advantages. Books were everything to him, which is one of the reasons I take special pride in setting my thoughts down on paper and sharing what I know and what I've learned with others looking to get and keep ahead.

Back to Napoleon Hill: third time I read *his* book, I started writing down my goals. That was my big takeaway. And do you want to know something? I'm still doing *that,* too. **Every day, I start off reading a list of goals I vow to meet.** I read them like my life depends on it—because, let's face it, it does! I see where I am on each goal, and where I need to be, and then I start to think what I can do *this very day* to meet it. I rise. I grind. Most days, I make my forward progress. And if I don't, I'll rise the next day and get after it again. And I don't just *read* that goal. I visualize it—something else I've been doing since I was a kid. I close my eyes and picture what I want to make happen—because, hey, you can't hit a target you don't see.

....

POWER FACT: According to *Inc.,* 59 percent of the action items on our to-do lists never get done.... *That adds up to a mess of stress and worry at the end of each day, which in turn can lead to a whole lot of sleepless nights, which is why* Inc. *editors suggest in that same study that you log your important tasks in your calendar instead.... Knock 'em off as you move about your day, and leave those to-do lists for your next trip to the grocery store, the hardware store, the mall.*

....

I've also learned to keep my daily list of goals manageable. That doesn't mean I sell myself short or hold something back. No way. But at the same time, I don't pile on each and every target, each and every objective that comes into my head. That would be self-defeating, right? I'll usually have eight or ten goals I'm working on at any time. Some of them are long-term goals, and some of them are short-term goals. Some of them are to-do-list-type goals, and some have to do with ongoing projects I'm just looking to advance in some way. Some of them are pie-in-the-sky, and some of them are low-hanging fruit, there for the taking. Some are health related—like wanting to lose a few extra pounds, or work on my stamina, or avoid processed foods. Some are family related—like wanting to spend more time with my daughters, the loves of my life. Some are business related, or philanthropy related, or relationship related. One thing I've found is that if I pile on too many objectives in one area, I get a little lost in the clutter, so I try to mix it up.

Some of my goals are super specific—like the one that says I want to cash a check for $102,345,086.32 by such-and-such a date. You may think that's crazy, to visualize a check of that size all the way down to the penny. But think about the power in this approach. We need to *see* something if we expect to believe it. So I make sure to look at that number every damn day! That's the essence of visualization, and that's why I stick to that number—although, got to be honest, it would be a pretty good day if I could cash a check for *half* that amount. Just sayin'.

Here, let me share a couple of current goals with you, word for word, so you can see the level of detail I bring to the task. Feel free to borrow or steal any of these for your own life! You'll see I also like to throw some motivational stuff in there, too, to help keep me energized.

Health

6 Packs are made in the Kitchen!!

I will get down to 170 pounds by June 1st by losing 2 pounds a week, drinking 8 bottles of water a day, Bone Broth, 1 fruit, 1 Green drink a day, no fried or fatty foods or red meat.

I will eat all that I am going to eat for the day before 6 p.m. unless after I work out or run.

I will eat only healthy snacks, grilled foods, vegetables, chicken and fish.

I will drink only "green" drinks, iced tea, protein shakes and water. Anything else is poison to my body.

I get out of my body what I put in it! I must eat super clean and monitor my health with regular check-ups.

Cancer and diseases feed off sugar and carbs. I will not give disease any reason to live off me. I will abolish the intake of poisons and increase my alkaline intake. Every meal I eat will have a lean protein, vegetables & good fat in it.

Alkaline and working out is the key to life!
  –I will walk 10,000 steps a day
  –I will do cardio in my early morning workout
  –I will weight-train in the evening
  –I will complete 200 push-ups a day when I am on the road, in increments of 20

Constant improvement of my health will allow me to stay in my family's lives longer and will give me the tools to be a more productive person.

The point is, whatever I'm shooting for, whatever I'm hoping to achieve . . . I set it up so it's always front and center. It's *right there*.

As you can see, I put a clock on those long-term goals. Most of them expire in six months, all on the same day, because I find that if I have this looming date on the calendar, it keeps me focused. And the way it works out, I usually accomplish two or three of those goals before time runs out on me, so I keep ahead of the game. The rest, I'll be 30 percent there, 40 percent there, maybe 60 percent there, and when that happens I reset and start in on them again, with another six-month timeline. I tell this to people, and they tell me it must drive me crazy to keep missing my goals like that. They think I'm setting myself up to fail. But I don't see it that way. I think of the incremental progress I've made. I think, *Okay, I've accomplished 60 percent of what I set out to do in this one area, so I'm more than halfway there.* I see any forward progress as a win.

One thing to keep in mind, as you start in on keeping your own goals: avoid setting negative ones. It doesn't do you any good to write down a long list of the things you *won't* do or *shouldn't* do. Keep focused on what you *will* do, what you *should* do.

But as we all know, your plan is only as good as your ability to execute on that plan. One of my favorite boxers, Mike Tyson, once said that everybody has a plan until they've been punched in the face. Then all bets are off. This is true. Planning is essential. Setting goals is essential. But you need to have a plan B, a plan C . . . sometimes, all the way down to a plan Z. And you want to have these backup plans in place before you really need them. That's why I'm always resetting and recalibrating my goals, be-cause what might seem like a good idea or a sound approach when I'm starting out doesn't always work out that way once I get going.

Of course, focusing on your long-term goals every day can be tough, especially given the never-ending stream of distractions—

text messages, Facebook status updates, emails, etc.—pinging us
all the time. Now, I'll be the first one to admit I love social media
as much as the next guy. Facebook, Twitter, and Instagram—I'm
into it all. It's how I connect with my fans. But email, that's a
different story. Not gonna lie, it can be a challenge to keep up,
especially since my dyslexia makes long, wordy emails that much
harder to process. So I've developed a few tricks to keep myself
sane as I try to manage the daily flood of emails:

1) I've let my team know that the best way to reach me if
   there's something urgent is via text instead of email.

   There's just no time to respond to each and every
   email immediately, but I've got my phone set to chime
   or vibrate whenever I receive a text message from an important number.

2) I've learned not to reply to a group email right away.

   I know I wrote earlier that I like to act on an email
   immediately, but that strategy doesn't really fly in these
   cases. There tends to be a lot of fluff in group threads,
   so I try to let the chain play out before weighing in. A
   lot of times, my point will be made by someone else, or
   maybe a question I might have asked will be answered by
   someone else, so it pays to hang back for a bit and let the
   conversation ride.

3) I'll set aside certain times throughout the day to respond
   to email.

   I don't see how people stop what they're doing every
   time a new email pops into their in-box, so I've gotten
   in the habit of checking in at set intervals throughout
   the day, or whenever I've got a bit of a breather, and get
   through what I can in the time I've set aside.

Basically, I try to think like my friend Chris Sacca when it comes to sorting through the pileup of electronic messages. In the ongoing debate over how much time to spend on "offense" during the workday, and how much time to spend on "defense," Chris looks at his sent messages as his offensive maneuvers, and his in-box as his defensive maneuvers. I've started taking the same approach—I'm in attack mode with what I put back out into the world, and on my heels with what comes back to me and lines up for my attention.

The point of all this is just to let you see what I'm up to, the ways I power up and press Play. **I'm not so full of myself to think my way is the only way.** I'm just here to collect all these different approaches, all these different states of being, and let you, the reader, see if any of them might work to build your own grind. Go ahead, set your goals in whatever way works for you. I won't be offended. Just make sure you set them. Because it doesn't matter if you're starting your own business, or punching a clock for someone else, or trying to eat healthier, or training for a marathon—you won't get anywhere if you don't have a destination in mind.

What do you say? Are you with me?

BE INSPIRED

CREATE A CARNIVAL

TYLER, THE CREATOR
Rapper, Artist, Impresario

WE ALL KNOW the old saying: there are two types of people in this world—people who wait for things to happen, and people who make things happen.

And we all know the old joke that says there's a third type—people who sit around and wonder what's happening.

Well, Tyler, The Creator, the groundbreaking rapper, music producer, event promoter, and clothing designer, fits right into the second group. The dude is only twenty-six years old and already he's carved out a place for himself in the music, fashion, and entertainment industries. Impressive, right?

How he grew up was key—as is the case for a lot of outside-the-box people, his neighborhood shaped him, his circumstances defined him. Tyler Gregory Okonma grew up in and around Los Angeles, raised by a single mother. He's got a younger sister, but Tyler was eight when she came along, so he'd already gotten into the groove of his routine. Many of his interests and habits were typical of an only child—similar to how things were with me. He spent a lot of time on his own, learned to amuse himself, be alone with his thoughts, but at the same time he was keenly aware of the energy of his community, the light all around. Also, he bounced around a lot, had gone to twelve different schools by the time he graduated from high school. That kind of childhood can force you to look inward and embrace the creative spirit most folks don't even take the time to acknowledge.

Tyler was drawn to music at a very young age. Music can be a kind of safe haven, when it feels like you're on your own—an outlet, a place to put your hopes and dreams. And keep in mind, Tyler didn't just *listen* to music—he *studied* it, made himself a part of it. He read the credits, started following certain artists, learned about hooks and rhymes and beats, back when he was just four or five years old. That was still *Barney and Friends* territory for most kids in Tyler's day, but he was out there on that cutting edge, even then. At seven, he was drawing and designing his own album covers—he'd take the CDs out of the case, and come up with a whole new concept, with imaginary song lists and everything. Don't think it ever occurred to him other kids weren't wired in the same way. This was just who he was, how he was.

In my case, I made a study out of my passion for music, too, but I didn't have Tyler's musical talent, didn't have his artistic talent, so I studied what my favorite hip-hop artists were wearing, where they were shooting their next video. To me, it was all about the style, the culture. To Tyler, it was a little bit of everything. The culture was a part of it, but it was mixed in with the music, the vibe . . . the scene. All those elements came to him at once, which I guess explains the way he sees the cultural world even today.

According to Tyler, he was an outsider-type kid—didn't have a lot of friends, didn't play with toys, watched a lot of television.

Cartoons, especially. Oh, and he loved maple syrup. Was crazy for the stuff. Don't know why he shares this detail with me, but here it is. Maybe that's what gave him all his energy, because looking on it seems like Tyler crammed about thirty hours of activity into a typical day—still does.

"I was writing raps at seven years old," he tells. "And when Myspace was happening, I'd take the beats I was making and upload them, and they were really bad, but I would post them on forums and word would get around. After a while, a lot of the music websites wouldn't post my stuff, so I was like, All right, I'll make my own website. That's all it was, a way to get my stuff out there. And through that, I was able to meet all these random people in Los Angeles who were into these things I wanted to be a part of, like this little magazine collective, because I was a really big fan of *VICE* magazine at the time and thought there could be a way to capture some of that. My beats were still pretty weak, but we started rapping over them, and we liked what we were putting out. Looking back, it was kind of gross, but at the time we all liked it."

This right here is important—and it cuts straight to the root of Tyler's success, because it shows us how he refused to give up on what he loved. It didn't matter to him what the marketplace said about his music. He only cared about putting his music out into the world. It wasn't about the money, just then. It was about the joy.

WHY NOT?

One of the things I love about this guy is how he takes what he's doing, what he's into, and he puts it out there. Doesn't matter if it doesn't fit into any mold. Doesn't matter if 99 percent of the people who come across his music tune him out. Tyler's thing is to create—why else would he make it part of his name!—and he doesn't spend too much time thinking about what others think of his creations. In this way, and in so many others, he's like my idol Prince—he makes the music that matters to him. He was born to share his deepest self with the world, and it just so happened that the Internet made that possible. Out of that, Tyler's career was born—only it wasn't a career just yet, at least not in the moneymaking sense.

Over time Tyler got together with a group of like-minded friends who shared his interest in music, art, photography, fashion . . . even cars. It happened in a crazy-organic way. He was a senior in high school, working at the local Starbucks, at a time when the music industry was imploding. The big record labels, they didn't know what they were doing, couldn't figure out how to make money in this new era of digital music, and at the same time magazine publishers were closing their print editions. It felt to a kid like Tyler like his whole world was moving online, and he embraced the shift. He understood that online world. It was a part of him.

"The thing with me," he says, "**I never let what other people are doing or aren't doing dictate what I plan on doing.** I didn't let the fact that the trajectory of magazines at the time wasn't looking so good push me into wanting to start my own magazine, or the fact that the record labels weren't making money push me to want to make whatever type of music I was making at the time. And my sound, it wasn't necessarily a popular sound, but there was this good group of us and we were just doing our thing. None of these people would post our music, but we had our own website, so people could come to it or not."

Looking back on that time in his life, Tyler doesn't see that he was working *toward* a long-held goal. He was just

doing what he loved. That's when your *grind* doesn't seem like a grind at all, even when it occupies your every waking thought, because you can't imagine going about your days in any other way. His thinking was, Why not?—while all around him people were thinking, Why?

Music was at the core of everything Tyler did, but it wasn't everything he did—no way. Ask him how much time he spent on his music, though, and what you get back is a great example of the nonstop grind you'll need to carry if you're looking to pop in a creative field. "There was always music playing in my head," he tells. "I was always arranging songs, writing raps, trying to figure out notes. I couldn't turn it off." There was no clock to Tyler's work—only, he never really thought of it as work. The music, the designs, the ideas running through his head . . . it was all an extension of who he was. He couldn't shut them off if he tried. The ideas just kept coming, and he ran with them—didn't matter what time of day it was, or how much work he'd already put in that day. When the spirit moved him, he up and moved.

....

POWER FACT: In the last ten years, there's been a 510 percent increase in the number of independent musicians who consider making music to be their full-time job. . . . *The barriers to entry have changed in the music industry—what's getting in the way of your success, in your field?*

....

That Starbucks job, it didn't last much beyond high school, and it went away because Tyler was able to recognize it for what it was: a job. Nothing against the good, hard-working people working a minimum-wage gig. That's Job One, for a lot of us. But in Tyler's case, his boss could sense his heart wasn't in it, that he wanted to spend his time putting something unique out into the world, instead of punching a clock and going through the same motions as everyone else. And yet, it was a decent job, and he needed the money, so he doesn't think he would have quit, had his boss not gone ahead and made that decision for him.

The spot Tyler was in reminded me of a similar spot I faced when I was just starting FUBU and still working at Red Lobster. I'm not a big believer in the idea that you should quit your day job when you're trying to start a new business. If I had quit my job with the very first tie-top hat I sewed, I'd have been out $150,000 in wages, because that's what I made, all told, from staying on at Red Lobster for another five years. That doesn't even count the health coverage and the free food I used to get, so there were benefits all-around. My hours were flexible. I didn't take my job home with me. I was spreading the word, meeting great people at the restaurant, so I was getting paid to network. I was also learning sales, how to manage money. Another way to look at it: I would have had to sell over $2 million in FUBU gear just to take home that same $150,000 or so in salary, so it was absolutely in my interest to keep that day job going for as long as possible.

This debate comes up all the time in the pitches we hear on *Shark Tank*. Yeah, if you're looking for a $1 million investment, or whatever the case may be, you damn well better be working this thing full-time. But other than that, when you're doing a start-up, the bottom line is you're probably going to have to make it happen on your off-hours, on top of your regular work. I went to Red Lobster, got there maybe four o'clock in the afternoon, left at midnight or so, went home and sewed hats until three, got up at six, checked the answering machine, delivered the hats people had ordered, and got back to work. I did that for five years—that was my *grind*, baby!

Tyler's situation was a little different, though, and to hear him tell it he regrets that his Starbucks job was taken from him before he was good and ready to let it go.

"At the time, it kind of sucked, getting fired," he says, "but looking back I realize it's the greatest thing that could have happened, because it let me focus on my music and my label and everything else I had going on."

The *everything else* was mostly this wild idea Tyler had to stage a carnival for all these friends he'd connected with in the Los Angeles music and arts scene—a carnival that would grow to become Camp Flog Gnaw, one of the coolest music and arts festivals on the scene. It started out as a kind of backyard deal— meaning Tyler just wanted to throw a little party. He'd put out his first mixtape, and there was a whole lot to celebrate.

"There was this street in my neighborhood, Fairfax, and that's kind of where I grew up, and I wanted to throw a block party for my birthday," he says. "I just wanted to get one of those carnival rides, have a bunch of people come by, play some music and give stuff out, but the city said no. They said it was a stupid idea, wouldn't let us do it. So instead of crying about it, we went out and found an empty lot in downtown Los Angeles, across the street from the Nokia Theatre, brought in a Ferris wheel, maybe a swing ride, a Zipper ride, and brought a bunch of artists in to perform. That first year, I think we had maybe twelve hundred people, but it just kind of grew from there."

That's the understatement of the year. His annual Camp Flog Gnaw carnival just kind of grew from that first homespun fair, and it gets bigger and bigger every year. People fly in from all over the world to take part, and no one's more surprised at how all this energy flows to this one place. This past year, the festival was held over two days for the first time, attracting more than

30,000 people. That's huge! It's a powerful tribute to Tyler's vision, but at the same time it's way bigger than Tyler's vision. It's taken on a life of its own.

That's the thing about Tyler, The Creator—he doesn't wait around for someone to give him the green light. That's not how it goes, for most people. Though to be fair, sometimes you don't have a choice. With us, at FUBU, we needed store owners to carry our clothes. With a lot of entrepreneurs, they need an industry, or at least an investor, to buy in to what they're selling. **We tend to walk around thinking someone else is holding the keys to unlock our success.** Not Tyler. He walks around doing whatever feels right. If it works, it works. If it doesn't, he might just keep on doing it anyway, because he doesn't look at his music or his art or his fashion through a business model. People will either spark to what he's putting out there, or they won't, and he's cool with it either way. He doesn't see his music, or his various sidelines, as any kind of money grab. He does what he does because he loves it.

It makes me think of that expression *it's not personal; it's just business.* Only with Tyler I think it's flipped. *It's not business; it's just personal.* If you studied the entertainment empire he's managed to build—and it now runs to his own record label, Odd Future, and a sought-after career as a music video director—you'll see that the common thread is the joy in the doing. He's one of those guys you've never heard of until you've heard of him . . . and then, you can't remember a time when you didn't know who was. His music is everywhere. In just a short time, he's become one of the most listened-to, most respected artists in the music business, and the thing of it is, he'd do it all for free. I have to believe his fans can sense this about him. His music, his clothing, his artwork . . . it all comes from a pure place. The bottom line is at the very bottom of his mind.

KEEP PLAYING

One of the lessons I draw from Tyler is the way he rejects the notion of failure. "I don't like that word," he tells. "I like learning what doesn't work, but when something doesn't work I don't see it as a failure. I see it as a lesson."

In other words, our failures are only failures if you let them beat you down.

"Look," he says. "I can't get a song on the radio to save my life. I may not be on the radio, but I'm somewhere else. It's the same with my clothing line, Golf Wang. We couldn't get our stuff into stores, so what did we do? We set up these pop-up shops in every city we hit on tour, and we tied it in to the music, made it an event. We figured it out."

Tyler applies that same determination, that same *grind,* to how he spends his days. He gets up, seven o'clock or so, and immediately gets dressed and gets to it. First thing, he'll probably go to his keyboard and start messing with some new hooks that might have come to him during the night. That time on the keyboard lets him find some new piece of music, or frees his mind to wander and zone out and start thinking about all the other stuff lining up for his attention. You can almost see Tyler's keyboard as a kind of productivity tool. That meditative, freeing mindset is what produces the music that always seems to reach him through the keys.

So he plays. And plays.

At some point, late afternoon, he starts to think he needs to get out of the house—to get outside himself, too. So he'll hit up some friends and go to an art show, or maybe they'll head out to the park and skate. Once, when I called him, he'd just gone to the park to sit in a tree for a couple of hours—just, you know, to think. That's how this dude is wired; he creates space for himself throughout the day, either at his keyboard or up in a tree, for inspiration to find him. And the thing is, it does. It almost always does.

Like me, he sets goals—but he didn't get the idea out of a book, he came to it on his own. His goals are also fluid. If he hits his target, that's great. If he misses wide, he'll take another shot tomorrow. Coming up short doesn't seem to bother him, the way it would gnaw at me. "My thing is, you get there slowly," he says. "Setting goals, that's a way to keep focused, but if I don't get there by tomorrow, I know I'll get there next week. And if it's not next week, it'll be next month, or next year. But I keep that goal in mind, and eventually I get there. That's just how it works out. I keep going for certain things I want, whether it's a car, or whether I want this song to have this kind of impact, or whether I want the carnival to reach a certain capacity by a certain year. It all depends."

One of the things that strikes me about Tyler is that he's old-school when it comes to keeping organized. He doesn't use a note-keeping app to keep track of his thoughts or projects. He doesn't put these little reminders in his smartphone. *He writes stuff down.* Me, I did my version of the same thing, writing all these little notes to myself throughout the day, which I'd stuff in my pockets and sort through each night when I got ready for bed. Tyler keeps his notes in a book, which he carries with him at all times—and it's like a lifeline, to hear him tell it. It's a sketchbook, notebook, appointment book, all rolled into one, and he fills it with drawings, lists, rhymes, notes for chords, important reminders, whatever. Oh, and there's also this: he uses all these different-colored markers to highlight what he's writing and drawing in all these different ways, so if you flip through the pages you're hit by all these bright, vibrant colors. "There's something about all these colors and the saturations that make what I'm doing seem real," he says.

Also, he stays hungry. Whatever fire was lit inside him when he was seven years old, writing his first raps, it's still burning there. He's got a theory on this, in fact. "I don't think people know what they want in life," he observes. "They might know what they want in terms of, you know, 'What's your dream car?' They might shoot a three-pointer and think they're successful. It's like when you hear a rapper and you're like, Damn, his early stuff was sick. You wonder what happened to him. That's where I get thinking, Okay, whatever that thing is they were working for when they were just starting out, they didn't have it yet. . . . But then they start making money and they get that car they want, or that girl, or that jewelry, or whatever it is that they want, they get that tangible thing. They lose that spirit that they had going for them, because that's gone. I mean, they have that now, so there's no reason to go hard anymore. That happens to a lot of people. They hit a ceiling. Me personally, I don't think I'll hit that ceiling because what I want I can't grasp. It's intangible. That's me always wanting to make tight clothes or always wanting to make really sick music or find these chord progressions that just make my heart melt, or things like that."

No, that's nothing you can grab—but Tyler, The Creator keeps grabbing at it, keeps reaching, keeps creating.

"Look," he says, summing up, "you just can't get complacent. You get that tangible thing you've always wanted, and you look up and realize it's not that fulfilling. That's when things can get really dark. That's when you start drinking or doing drugs and everything goes downhill, because you're lost. You don't know what you want. When you're lost you're roaming. And when you're roaming, your bill goes up. *It's not good.*"

No, it's not.

Tyler's Grind Checklist

✓ listen to the music in your mind—what moves you matters . . .

✓ climb a tree—there weren't a whole lot of opportunities for me to climb a decent-size tree when I was a kid, but there's something about the way Tyler finds the peace and quiet he needs up in a tree, looking out at the world, that I find really exciting . . .

✓ if you love carnivals, go ahead and build a carnival—or in other words, pursue the goals that are meaningful to you, without worrying how they might pay you back or advance your career . . . sure you should probably worry *a little bit* about these things, but don't let your worries keep you from chasing what moves you . . .

✓ love what you do—when there is joy in your work, it's not really *work,* is it? . . .

✓ learn to look at your failures as lessons in disguise . . .

✓ find a group of people who share the same passion and look for ways to ignite each other on your journey . . .

✓ understand that no doesn't always mean no—sometimes, it just means not yet . . .

✓ put your business model second—this one doesn't always work for a lot of us, but it worked like magic for Tyler because it gave him the freedom to do his own thing, even if his *own thing* didn't promise any kind of return on his investment . . .

✓ write stuff down—we live in digital world, but there is a power to be tapped in the simple act of putting pen (or pencil!) to paper and setting down our thoughts, our goals, our visions . . . the music that lives inside us all . . .

....

For more information on Tyler and how he uses the
Rise and Grind mindset, check out

www.DaymondJohn.com/Rise/Tyler

BE ON TASK

CELEBRATE YOUR DIFFERENCES

LOLA ALVAREZ
Mom, Advocate, Attention-getter

HERE'S A STORY that has nothing to do with making a living in business, but everything to do with the *business of living.*

It starts with a point of connection: I do a lot of work with an incredible organization called Understood. They provide free online resources for parents of children with learning and attention issues. I started working with them a couple of years back when I first talked publicly about what it was like to grow up with dyslexia, and it's been a great thing to connect with other people facing a similar deal. It's a gift, really—a gift that gives both ways, because I'm lifted by the stories of all the families I meet, just as I hope they might be lifted by mine.

Now, my story is way different than the stories of most of the young people I meet through this group. Back in my day, there were hardly any resources at all available to kids like me in a school setting, so it was on me to kind of figure it out for myself and work through it. The same was true for Lola Alvarez, one of the motivated, selfless young moms I met through Understood, who grew up in Mexico City dealing with some of the same issues. Her mother was dyslexic as well, only it was never diagnosed, never discussed. To Lola's mom, reading was a chore, not worth the trouble, so she didn't even bother. She dropped out of school by the time she was a teenager. To Lola, reading was just as hard, but she wasn't willing to give up on the idea. Still, she had a rough time of it. Around first grade or so, she started seeing the other kids latch on to reading and some of the other concepts being taught in class, and it felt to her—and her teachers—like she was falling behind. And she was, but no one made too big a deal about it. It was just sort of assumed that Lola wasn't meant to be a student—you know, in an apple-doesn't-fall-too-far-from-the-tree kind of way.

As Lola told me how it was for her growing up, I was taken back to how it was for me in school as well, when my teachers thought I was lazy or making trouble when really what I was doing was worrying over why the reading assignments came so easy to everyone else in the class, why it felt to me like I had to work twice as hard to learn half as much.

....

POWER FACT: **By fourth grade, many black and Latino students are already as much as three years behind their white counterparts in academic readiness and performance....** *That's a stat that comes from President Obama's My Brother's Keeper initiative, in which I was honored to take part, and it tells me we have to work extra hard to ensure that all of our young people, especially boys and young men of color, are given every opportunity to lift their lives and overcome the built-in barriers to their success.*

....

It ended up that Lola had to repeat second grade, and the thinking was that since she'd seen most of the material, she'd have an easier time, but that's not exactly how it went down. She continued to struggle. The teachers, they didn't know what to do with a kid like Lola. Her IQ tested well above average, even a little on the high side, so people naturally started thinking she was careless, or maybe lazy.

"Those were the two labels they attached to me," Lola remembers, "because they could see I was smart and I still wasn't able to perform at the level of the other kids. The whole time I was little I used to ask myself, 'Why did God make me so dumb?'"

Sadly, that's how a lot of kids who were facing these types of challenges were made to feel in those days. We were put in this frustrating bind that left us questioning our worth, left us feeling inferior, and *less than,* and in Lola's case these challenges were only part of the story because things were tough at home. Her parents were divorced, so here again she was slapped with another label, as the child of a broken home. So naturally the teachers and administrators at her school decided Lola's underperformance in the classroom was just her way of acting out, seeking attention as a kind of counter to all that uncertainty and confusion at home.

For a short time as her parents were splitting up, Lola lived with her grandmother, next door to a kind, patient woman named Olga, who was a retired teacher. "I don't know what I would have done if I didn't have Olga to teach me how to read," Lola recalls. "And to write. And to memorize my times tables."

That's how it goes for a lot of us: **we depend on the kindness of people outside the system to help us figure out the system**. And a lot of times, that kindness comes from someone outside our own families, as well. That's one of the things

I've come to appreciate through the work of organizations like Understood—the enormous value of taking advantage of *all* available resources, and of *being* an available resource to kids and families in this type of need.

Sometimes, it takes a godsend to see you through.

WALK THE PATH YOU'RE MEANT TO TAKE

But this isn't a story about how Lola Alvarez overcame her own learning disabilities—or "learning differences," as we've taken to saying. And it's not a story about the kindness of the retired teacher who just happened to live next door. I mean, it is and it isn't, because Lola's experiences as a child play a big part in the story I want to share about her. They were foundational, as she came to have children of her own, who also wrestled with learning differences. And *that's* where her *rise and grind* kicked in, bigtime. *That's* the story I want to tell here, because the way Lola was able to set up her three sons to succeed, when they were all wired in such a way that it would have been so easy for them to fail . . . well, it struck me as heroic. It struck me as the ultimate *grind,* to play this particular tough hand in such a winning way— not just for one child, but for all three of her children, all at once.

....

POWER FACT: According to WebMD, 25 percent of people with dyslexia also show signs of attention deficit/ hyperactivity disorder, or ADHD.... *When it rains it pours, right? Only here a lot of parents face a perfect storm of struggle with their "differently abled" kids, so if you find yourself dealing with this issue, be prepared to deal with a few more.*

....

Lola first noticed that her oldest son, Esteban, was having difficulty in second grade—and looking back she believes she might have missed some of the earlier signs. She gets mad at herself now, when she thinks of all the time she let pass while she was looking away from what was right there in front of her—but in all fairness, we parents don't always see our children as clearly as we might.

(I'm ashamed to admit it, but I made the same mistake when I saw my own daughter struggling with some of these same issues, even though I should have known better—me of all people.)

"We've moved eleven times," she explains of that time in the life of her young family, "so I just thought Esteban wasn't settled, that he was a little less mature than some of the other children, so I had already made him repeat preschool one more year, thinking he would never know."

Finally, after Lola and her family moved to New Jersey, Esteban's difficulties in school were hard to ignore. Here at last, Lola recognized them for what they were, and she saw herself in Esteban. "We were the same, I was realizing," she says, "and his younger brother Pablo, I could see he was the same as well."

This is where Lola's *grind* really kicked into high gear. Each night, Lola would spend hours teaching her two boys what they should have learned in school that day, reinforcing the lessons she collected from their teachers and patiently reading and rereading with Esteban and Pablo until the words began to make sense. On some nights, it felt to her like she was starting from scratch, as if the boys hadn't even gone to school that day. To hear her tell it, the house was basically put on pause and turned into a schoolhouse after the dinner dishes were cleared. And forget working with Esteban and Pablo so they could get ahead; this was just what she needed to do to keep them from falling behind. Each morning, she was up early, usually before the sun, making sure her boys had everything they needed to face another difficult school day. **It sometimes felt like there was no time for anything else, that's how crazy-making and all-consuming it was to keep her sons on track.**

Meanwhile, Lola's days were filled with advocating and arguing and agitating the folks at school to give her boys the services and extra attention they so desperately needed—just like my mother had to do for me, when she was trying to convince my teachers that I wasn't just dogging it in school.

"When Esteban was in fifth grade, and Pablo was in third grade, that's when it all kind of came to a head," Lola says. "That's when I knew there was something definitely going on with them that didn't have anything to do with all those times we moved, didn't have anything to do with them maybe being a little less mature, or whatever. So I went and demanded they be tested for ADHD. They didn't have a name for it when I was a child, but they had a name for it now, and my son Pablo's teacher at the time, who'd already had Esteban in the third grade, she just turned to me and said, "Mrs. Alvarez, you're just going to have to come to grips with the fact that God gave you two lazy boys."

There was that label again: *lazy.* The same label that had dogged Lola when she was a child. The same feeling that she was being written off, or set aside. She heard that word and it was like a flare went off. Right then, Lola knew that she and her husband would have to make a change. It was the middle of the school year, but they pulled the boys from public school and never looked back.

"We were lucky," Lola allows. "My husband, he had a good job, so I didn't have to work and we could afford to pay for a better school, and this school was a part of our parish, so we knew the priest, we knew the community, we knew the boys."

"Right away, we began to see a change," Lola remembers.

"Both of them, because the Catholic schools are very small, they were able to receive individual attention. They had the resources they needed to be successful, so that was another way we were lucky. Esteban even had a math teacher who told him he was quirky and smart like Albert Einstein—also, dyslexic! She actually put up a poster of Einstein in her classroom, so Esteban could be reminded how special he was, to never let anyone ever tell him different."

But Lola recognized that the supportive environment she was able to find for her boys in this new school setting was only one piece of the puzzle. She also needed to put in place systems and routines at home to reinforce the good habits they were finally taking in at school. For example, she ran her household on a color-coded system, so that each child would know immediately which backpack was theirs, which cubby was theirs, which lunch bucket was theirs: Esteban was blue; Pablo was green; and Jose, the youngest, was red.

"They were taught to be very organized," Lola says. "Everything had its place. **My husband used to joke that our house was like a museum. He laughed because even my spices were in alphabetical order. But you have to be organized like that if you want to be at your best.** It's like a coping mechanism."

Lola instilled her fierce work ethic in her boys, including a strict sense of order and routine. With a little help from the folks at Understood, she was able to keep her kids to a tight schedule. She'd use the alarm built into her watch to set reminders for herself throughout the day—and, as the boys got older and technology caught up to her needs, she started programming her smartphone to do the same. One of the things she had to track carefully was Jose's medications: in addition to his own set of learning differences, Jose is epileptic, so there were all these little reminders plugged into their days as a family to keep them on task. There was a time and a place for everything.

These days, the older boys are in high school, and they've done such a good job looking after themselves that Lola has been able to return to work as a paraprofessional, helping autistic students in her own school district—the same school her son Jose attends, which means she gets to drive him back and forth each day and spend a little extra time with him, reinforcing the good habits she learned for herself and helped to put in place for his older brothers. And so even as her kids grow up and gain a certain level of independence, the *grind* continues at home, same way it did for me as I got to the end of my high school experience.

It's amazing to me that a person who'd devoted so much of her adult life to the care and teaching of her three sons with ADHD or dyslexia would seize the first opportunity to work outside the home with other children in need . . . but to Lola it was an obvious and necessary next step. This was what she was good at. This was what she *knew*. And now that her boys were a little older, a little more autonomous, she could take what she'd learned as their mother and put it into play for the benefit of others.

One of the heartbreaking things I learned from Lola is that there's a kind of stigma associated with ADHD and dyslexia and other learning differences in the Hispanic community. I guess I knew as much, from my own time growing up in Queens, but it was surprising to hear that this is still the case today. "It's very hush-hush, if a family member struggles in this way," she says. Even little Jose's epilepsy diagnosis wasn't shared with family members back home in Mexico. Why? Because any illness or disorder is seen as a sign of weakness—maybe even a source of shame, even in this supposedly enlightened age.

Luckily there are people like Lola determined to do something about it. "That's basically my dream," Lola says, "to help change the education in my country, and to change the culture and bring all this advocacy to this issue. Here in the United States, we're a lot further along on this than we are in Mexico, but culturally, the Hispanic community still has some work to do on this." This is just Lola's opinion, of course, but she's earned the right to speak her mind on this, so listen up: "As parents of these children," she says, "it's up to us to look at the positive, because there are so many people who are not blessed as I have been blessed. I thank God for the children I have. Nobody's perfect. **We have all been gifted with some sort of talent, and in the same way we have all been given some sort of difficulty.** With me, when I was a girl, it was asking that question I told you about. Over and over, I would ask myself this question: 'Why did God make me so dumb?' I wasn't dumb, I know that now, but it took having children for me to learn the answer, why I was this way. It's not that God made me dumb. It's that He was making me stronger, because God knew what he was sending me. He knew the children He was sending to me, and He was preparing me to fight the battles necessary to raise three successful young men."

Lola's Grind Checklist

✓ find a way to prioritize your time so that you're fully available to meet your family's needs . . .

✓ consider the resources available to you and make sure you're putting them to full and effective use . . .

✓ learn from the struggles you might have had in childhood and put those lessons to work for you so you can help your kids struggle a little bit less with the same issues . . .

✓ wake up earlier than your children (or your staff) to get your
   house (or your office) ready to meet the demands of the day . . .

✓ speak up—meaning, don't be afraid to ask for what you need,
   and to advocate for the needs of others . . .

....

For more information on Lola and how she uses the
Rise and Grind mindset, check out
www.DaymondJohn.com/Rise/Lola

FOUR

MY EARLY RISING

I'VE TOLD DIFFERENT parts of my story a bunch of times, a bunch of different ways. But there is also a lot from my life that I haven't talked about, at least not publicly. Each time out, for a new book, speech, or interview, I try to tailor my story to whatever themes are on the table, and since we're talking about time management, motivational strategies, and developing a core work ethic, I'll keep the focus here—and, while I'm at it, I'll take a look at how we all come to develop our own routines, in our own ways.

Probably the earliest example of me learning the relationship between time and money was when my mother took out a mortgage on our house. She did it because I was starting high school, getting into different (and, probably, *bigger*) kinds of trouble, and she knew that if she didn't find a way to spend a little more time at home watching over me, I might take a turn down a wrong road. She borrowed $80,000—enough to buy her some time to maybe let go of one or two of her jobs. It was a powerful lesson, because up until that time **I never really understood that we all have options when it comes to money.** All I knew was that you had to work your butt off for it, and now here I was learning that you could also take something you've already worked your butt off for and let it work for *you*.

The lesson didn't change my day-to-day just yet. It was more like something to file away for later. But it did change how I was able to run around the neighborhood. It did make me more accountable to my mother for how I spent my time. It did push me to appreciate the sacrifices she made for me, to keep our lives pulsing. And it did inspire me to hustle like never before so I could get to the place where my mother was at and let my money start making *me* money.

In my mind, back then, I couldn't get there fast enough.

My grind back in high school was all-out, on either side of that school bell. **I set it up in my head like I was in a race, and I had to scramble to make as much as I could, quick as I could, because I'd be out on my own before too, too long.** That $80,000 my mother took out of the house? I knew we'd run through *that* money before long as well—so I guess I was scrambling to keep ahead of that day, too.

I had a lot of hustle jobs, and a lot of legit jobs. For me, my quality of life and my hopes for my future were tied up in that balance. The hustle jobs were the opportunities I made for myself, like shoveling snow, or fixing up bicycles so I could re-sell them. Later on, it was buying and refitting a van so I could shuttle commuters around the neighborhood, and then double-dipping on that van and using it to haul a shipment of Super Soakers or maybe a couple dozen boxes of T-shirts I'd buy at a deep discount down on Delancey Street, and then pulling up at flea markets or concert venues and selling the merch for a profit. The longest-running of my legit jobs was that gig at Red Lobster, which I held for years. Soon as high school was over, that meant waking up at six o'clock in the morning, getting a head start on all my side deals, then heading to the restaurant and staying on through the late shift some nights.

The idea, once I graduated high school, was to take a year off before going to college. At least, that was the plan. I'd struggled as a student, and thought I could use the time to build a little stake, maybe decompress from all that studying, maybe even grow up a little bit so I'd be in a better position to succeed in an academic setting. A year seemed about right. Honestly, I didn't think I was ready to go to college—it was a little overwhelming, especially with the way I struggled with my dyslexia. So instead I put together all these different plays, and I was running around the city like crazy, trying to keep the money coming in. I was into all kinds of things. The comparison I always make, when I tell people how I started out in business, is to Ralph Kramden, from *The Honeymooners*. Remember that show? He always had some kind of scheme going, some kind of long-shot play to lift him from that crappy little apartment and his job as a bus driver, to a life of ease. That was me, with all these different hustles. **My thinking was to keep throwing in on all these different plays and hope a couple of them might stick:** T-shirts, hats, Super Soakers, livery service. I went in to each hustle thinking it would be my ticket up and out, thinking it would somehow move from a Ralph Kramden–type deal into a straight-up business. If it made sense on paper, if I could fit it into my days, if my wallet could handle any kind of start-up investment . . . I'd go for it. For a while, I even had a crash car business. I'd buy a beat-up clunker for $5,000 or so, put a couple thousand into it, and then sell it for $10,000. I couldn't do the work myself, but I had a shop I did a lot of work with, and those guys took care of me.

One hustle always led to the next, so on the one hand things were going great. There was money coming in, my time was my own, I could head into Manhattan at night and party like the city was mine and still haul myself out of bed in the morning and start back in on my grind. Problem was, that one year I meant to take off from school soon ran into a second year, and then into a third year. I hadn't really moved the needle too much, as far as my bank account was concerned. It's like I was stuck. So that was the other hand. I was making money, but I wasn't making progress, and as I began to realize this it started to weigh on me. It didn't happen all at once, but I could see I'd lost some of the bounce I had when I first got out of high school. I started to feel like a loser, because I didn't really have anything going. I guess I was realizing more and more that all these side deals, all these hustle plays, they weren't sustainable. I'd make money on some, lose money on others, and live and hope and dream in the spaces between. And the whole time I was still clocking in at Red Lobster, but I couldn't see myself working a gig like that for the rest of my life—not because there was anything beneath me in the work, but because I wanted so much more for myself.

Meanwhile, my friends from the neighborhood were going every which way. A lot of them were in jail. Some of them were halfway through college. Some of them were just nowhere. I put a mirror on myself and saw that I fit into this last category. I hadn't really moved forward since graduation. I was treading water, walking in place . . . whatever. Plus, I was partying harder than ever before, spending money harder than ever before. Don't get me wrong, it was a great, good time, but it was too much of a great, good time. Like my man Tyler said, when you're lost, you're roaming. And when you're roaming, your bill goes up. That was me in those days. There was no end to it, no *endgame*. It felt like I didn't have any momentum, any plan.

That pile of cash I'd been building? I looked up one day and noticed it had dwindled all the way down to nothing. All I had, other than my steady paycheck from Red Lobster, was what was coming my way on the next deal.

....

POWER FACT: A recent Gallup survey shows that eight out of ten children polled are determined to be their own boss.... *Kids want to call their own shots, right? I know I did, and here we see that kids today are more entrepreneurial than ever before—the same survey reported that four out of ten kids want to start their own business. Future sharks unite!*

....

Go ahead and try to find a structure to my days, to my routines back then, and you'll come up empty. If I had to wake up early to meet somebody or make a pickup, I'd set my alarm. If I could sleep in, I'd sleep in. My body clock was set to hustle time —meaning, I wasn't disciplined or smart enough to know that I needed to set myself up for success. I thought I could go chasing it instead. Basically, I was making it up as I went along, working my way through all these different styles of working, all these different ways of doing business, and after a while I got to feeling like I was swinging and missing way more than I was making contact.

The low point probably came when I told myself I could be some kind of event promoter. It was just another one of my get-rich-quick schemes, only this one ended up costing me. I had this idea that I could rent a boat, hire a deejay, and run a summer party cruise from one of the docks in lower Manhattan. You know, the Circle Line had always been popular with tourists and day-trippers, so I figured I would just add some booze and some music to the mix and sell tickets to all my friends, and to all *their* friends. I had dollar signs in my eyes, so I borrowed about $10,000 to hire out the boat, and another couple grand to hire a deejay named Kid Capri. (He is *still* the man!) I also took out some ads on the radio, put out a couple of fliers, and that put me even deeper in the hole. After that, I sat back and waited for all these people to turn up. But they never came.

Best-laid plans, right? Only here I thought my plans were dead-on; it was my execution that was off. Truth was, I didn't know anything about party promotion or marketing, didn't know anything about limiting my risk or exposure, didn't know how to price my tickets, and didn't know anything about anything. Most of that debt I put on a credit card, so now I was stuck with these ridiculous interest payments, and I just couldn't see my way out from under.

Maybe I should have taken my own advice and practiced the power of broke here—thinking things *all the way* through before spending money I didn't really have on a scheme that didn't really make a whole lot of sense.

IF YOU CAN'T GET YOUR ASS TO WORK, GET YOUR ASSETS TO WORK

It was around this time that I started the first of my FUBU businesses. A lot of people, they think we were some kind of overnight success, but it took us a couple of times to get it right. When we hit it big, the press played it up like we were these four street-savvy, fashion-forward kids from Hollis, Queens, who'd just happened to burst on the scene. We couldn't help but play to that image, too—told ourselves (and anyone who'd listen!) it was good for business, good for our brand. But early on, FUBU was more of a hobby than a business. Long story short: I'd buy a shirt for $10, spend $20 on a custom embroidery job, and then sell it for $30 or $35—not exactly a winning business model, but it was something to stoke the flames, a way to meet girls and travel with my friends on the hip-hop circuit. And it was clear to all of us this wasn't a moneymaking enterprise, but we loved how it justified and kind of subsidized the good times we were chasing.

Nowadays, of course, I look at different factors when I'm ramping up a new business. My goals now are much more about the bottom line than they were back then, but they're also about empowering my staff, creating an environment where folks want to come to work, and putting good things out into the world. But when you're just starting out, you take your motivation where you can find it—and here we didn't set the bar too, too high.

Remember how I wrote earlier that most of the successful people I meet in life learned to fail early? This was a little like that. We weren't failing big, but we just couldn't get out of our own way. First couple of times out, wasn't a whole lot of money changing hands, but we were taking our lumps and learning from our mistakes.

Those three years, sinking more and more into a funk, feeling more and more like I was stuck at the starting gate . . . eventually, that's what helped me get back the *grind* I had in high school. I got it in my head that I was down so low there was no place to go but up—so I started climbing. I was twenty, maybe twenty-one, and thirty started looking like it was right around the corner. Thirty was like this giant marker on the road of life—that's how I saw it. If I didn't get my act together, didn't get my bank together by the time I hit thirty . . . well then, I knew I'd never break out of that funk I'd been swimming around in those past couple of years.

This was where the one big-ticket asset we had—our house—changed the game on me a second time. My mother decided she wanted to live in Manhattan, but she also wanted me to stay on in the house and take over the payments—kind of a shape up or ship out motivational strategy. She said, "Daymond, you been helping to pay the bills around here since you were twelve years old. You'll be fine."

And I guessed I would be—but, got to admit, there were a couple of weeks in there when I couldn't see my way to *fine*. I had all that credit card debt hanging over me, and college at this point was feeling like a pipe dream. Like so many kids from similar backgrounds, **the further out I got from that one year off of school I'd planned on taking, the less likely it was that I'd ever go back**. So I looked at all the options spread out before me and decided to put the house to work in a whole new way. We already had that mortgage, so I didn't want to take more money *out* and have to service all that additional debt. Instead, I decided to turn the place into a little bed-and-breakfast. Remember, this was back in the days before Airbnb, so there weren't too many people renting out single rooms on a short-term basis. I knew there were local ordinances telling me this kind of thing was against the law, but I was flying under the radar. Small-timers in my neighborhood, we didn't always pay attention to that kind of stuff. My thinking was, if I was breaking the law, someone would come around and tell me. Until then, I could let out a mess of rooms, at $75 per week, and be able to at least cover the mortgage payments. For my own peace of mind (and, for my sanity!), I would also rent a couple of rooms to my friends, and they'd kick in toward the mortgage, too. Everyone paid me in cash, so if the city caught up to what we were doing I could just say my tenants were my friends, and whatever money was changing hands between us was for household expenses.

POWER FACT: With the rise of short-stay booking services like Airbnb and VRBO, *Research and Markets* expects the category to represent $190 billion in annual global bookings by 2019. . . . *We were on to something back in the day, and now it's even easier to vet potential renters and collect rents.*

I took out an ad in the *Village Voice* and put up a bunch of fliers around the neighborhood, and people came calling. (Guess that was my version of an early Kickstarter campaign, huh?) At $75 per week, the rent was attractive even back in 1989 or so, and the room came with kitchen privileges and full use of the common areas throughout the house. The setup worked great, there was money coming in to cover my nut, but it got a little crazy after a while. Check that: it got *a lot* crazy. Got to where the place started looking, smelling like a frat house. Really, it was like a scene from *Animal House* in there. People were coming and going all the time, and there was usually an extra person or two crashing on one of our couches, and on some nights it was just impossible to find a quiet corner in the place just to sit and chill.

Looking back, I think my experience running those room rentals was key in developing my own management style. It taught me how to deal with people, how to manage them—*and* how to manage my own expectations of them. If someone was late on their rent, I had to hear them out on it and decide if I wanted to let it slide for a couple of days or toss them out. If someone lost his job, it was on me to either cut him some slack or bust his chops. If one dude wasn't getting along with another, it fell to me to broker some kind of truce . . . or not.

Also, renting out those rooms gave me great insight into how other people approached the *rise and grind,* because most of the

people living in the house had their own deals taking shape. They
had jobs, classes, routines they meant to follow. My FUBU guys
were with me: Keith took the room downstairs, Carl was in one
room, and Jay was in another. Then for a long time we had our
friend Skeeter tucked into another room. Keith was managing
an apartment building in uptown Manhattan, and his hours were
basically nine to five. His mindset, too. That meant he'd grind
all day, and when he got home he'd want to relax. Wouldn't
exactly call him a slacker, but his head was someplace else—he'd
be the first to admit it. That was just his way. Carl was working
at a factory, so his grind lined up with his shift—only there was
room in *his* day (and his mindset) to throw in full-tilt on our
little clothing business. And Jay was just back from a tour of duty
in Operation Desert Storm and going to school at the Fashion
Institute of Technology (FIT), so his time was the most flexible
of all of us, and thanks to his military discipline he was always
looking to fill it in meaningful ways. In between all our comings
and goings we'd all meet at the house and get to work on selling
our T-shirts and hats.

Around the time it hit me that I wasn't headed in a positive,
purposeful direction, I decided to get serious about what we had
going on with FUBU. I started getting up with the sun each
morning and sewing and tagging a bunch of hats by myself. I'd
answer any orders that had come in overnight. The other guys,
they'd spend a little time on the business on their way out to
work, but I was at it hard most mornings until about noon. Then
I'd hit up Red Lobster and work until midnight, and when I got
back home we'd sit around for another couple of hours making
more hats and tallying orders. Talk about a *grind,* right? This
went on for about three years straight and, after a break, we hit it
again for another couple of years. It's not like I was the only one
working it—Carl and Jay, they were right there with me, filling
in the time between shifts and classes. Even Keith, once he saw

we had a good thing going, a chance to make some serious paper, he was in there cranking with the rest of us. **No matter what time we came home, what time we had to leave in the morning, there was always something to do.** We set it up so everyone could play to his strength: we had someone who was good at design, someone who could sew, someone who could handle marketing, and on and on.

YOU ARE YOUR HANG

When I could find a free moment to myself (usually on the subway), and when I wasn't busy rereading Napoleon Hill's book, I'd reach for motivation from other sources . . . books, videos, audiotapes. This was my version of college, I guess. The late 1980s, early '90s were a big time for inspirational content, so like a lot of folks I was trying to step up my game by tuning in to all these self-help gurus. Stephen Covey's *The 7 Habits of Highly Effective People* was just out around then, and a lot of people were still being stoked by the work of people like Jim Rohn and Dale Carnegie. Me, I found a lot to like in some of the stuff Tony Robbins was putting out—his book *Unlimited Power,* especially. One of the things he always talked about was how we mirror the behaviors of people around us. You know, **if you spend a lot of time with a bunch of losers, you're bound to start thinking and acting like a loser, too. If you spend time with winners, you'll develop a winning mentality.**

Makes sense, right? It did to me, but it took seeing the way my roomies were doing their thing for the message really sink in. My FUBU guys, they were all right. We had one another's backs. We pushed one another forward. But some of my tenants, some of the guys on the fringes of our group, on the outside looking in . . . well, it wasn't always clear that we could rely on them to do the right thing. We had one guy living with us for a stretch, he was in the air bag business—only to call it a business is to make it seem like he wasn't breaking the law every time he made an "acquisition" or a "deal." What this guy would do was patrol the neighborhood looking for parked cars equipped with air bags. He'd break into the steering wheel, say, and remove the bag without setting it off, because of course once the thing deployed it was useless.

POWER FACT: Larry Page and Sergey Brin of Google met on a campus tour at Stanford, before they even enrolled at the school. . . . *The story goes that these two didn't exactly hit it off at first, but out of this one chance meeting they formed a connection that set the world spinning on an entirely new axis, transforming the ways we access information online. The lesson? In good company there is opportunity.*

Now, the dude wasn't pinching those air bags just to make trouble. He was selling them into a pretty healthy after-market. Auto-body garages would pay him $100 or so for each air bag, which they'd they turn around and sell for $200 or $300, so in some cars with the driver and passenger and side-panel air bags he could make $400 . . . for about five minutes of work.

There was an art to snatching those air bags, it turned out. This guy showed us all how he did it, tried to recruit us into his operation, but that was not my thing. That's not how my boys and I leaned. So this guy didn't stick around long—it wasn't cool to hang with him, and even though there was a time right after high school when I would have found something to admire in this hustle, we weren't about cutting corners. It was trouble enough just trying to get things going with FUBU—we didn't need to pile on any extra trouble on top of *that*.

Tony Robbins was right: you are your hang, and I still carry that lesson. That's why I still hang with my boys from back in the day, but I also hang with billionaires, Fortune 500 executives, tech-savvy millennials, small business owners who don't know the meaning of quit. **There are all these different levels to my game these days, but wherever I'm playing, whoever I'm playing *with*, I've got something to learn each time out.** The people around me, their good habits rub off on me; their positive routines become mine—same way I like to think *my* good habits, my positive routines, might rub off on them.

One of the things I've noticed is that there seems to be a generational divide in the way successful people go about their days. The older, more traditional executive types in my circle remain somewhat tied to the concept of a workday. The more they've accomplished, the more wealth and influence they've accumulated, the more likely they are to *power down* at the end of a conventional business day. To most of them, there are work hours and there are after-work hours. That doesn't mean they ever truly stop thinking about how to drive their businesses forward, but they do set aside their phones as they head home to spend some time with their families. The younger entrepreneurs don't really pay attention to the clock. They work when they can, when they must, when they feel like it—and in a lot of cases that adds up to pretty much all the time. Like their old-school counterparts, they never stop moving their business forward, and even when they leave the "office" they keep plugged in, often in a full-on way

Long as I'm on it, let me just say that one of the things I've noticed is that younger people are more and more connected to the idea of doing good. It used to be that the focus was all about

"What have you done for me?" and now it's all about "What have you done for the planet?" So even though their phones are always on and they're wired in all kinds of weird ways, the new generation of entrepreneurs and game-changers seems to have its heart in the right place.

Another trait I see from the people in my life who make it their business to light a fire for others—people like Tim Ferriss and Jay Abraham, who were profiled in my last book; and Gary Vaynerchuk, who is profiled in this one—is an authenticity that cuts through the work itself. They're genuine, and **when you're passionate about your work, when it really feels to you like you're on a mission to change people's lives for the better, the *grind* comes easy**. They aren't watching the clock, or even worrying too much about how they might get paid. All of that falls away, and their sole focus, their sole motivation, becomes standing as a kind of lightning rod for new insights and strategies—taking in what they can, quick as they can, and putting it back out into the world.

The same is true for entrepreneurs who really believe in their product. They see themselves on a mission to change the world, improve the quality of people's lives, keep their employees working . . . whatever the case may be. For them, too, it's not a bottom-line pursuit. It's an integrated enterprise. They're so wrapped up in the entirety of the operation—from conception to execution, from selling to fulfillment—that the money they make is almost beside the point. What drives them is keeping all those people who work for them employed, seeding the world with whatever it is they're selling, and growing their business, and the *grind* that finds them in pursuit very often doesn't feel like a grind at all.

These days, I like to ask the people who work for me to describe themselves or their goals in two to five words. My answer up until recently has been "I'm on a quest"—because, hey, that's what drives me. That's *still* what drives me, although lately I've started telling people I'm "building something massive." Back in the day, I would've had a different answer. "Show me the money!" Or, "Don't count us out!"

There's no chore in the work when you're doing something you love, putting good things out into the world, creating opportunities for others. That's not something I could always see as a kid back in high school, or just after. That's a realization I had to come to in time—and now that I have, it's a message I try to put back out there, every chance I get. It's not always an easy message to take in, when you're scrambling to get and keep an edge, but I try to remind people of the power of the long view.

Passion wins! And if it works out that your passion can also bring about meaningful change and grow into a sustainable business . . . well, then you're good to go.

ITEM, LABEL, BRAND, LIFESTYLE

In my second book, *The Brand Within,* I wrote about the four stages of brand development—*item, label, brand, lifestyle*—and made the point that every designer, retailer, and manufacturer looks to go through these stages as they grow their product, their service, their company. Not every company makes it through all four, but the successful ones manage to hit 'em all. Miss one, or start looking for shortcuts, and it'll come back to bite you in the long haul. I also shared a similar lesson in my online virtual academy, "Daymond on Demand." Point is, there's a life cycle to a successful run in business. What's hot one season is not so hot the next, and it's on our cutting-edge visionaries to keep reinvigorating the brand to keep things popping. The same holds true for our personal brands, and for our individual careers. We've all got some kind of expiration date on our backs. Fly too close to the sun for too long, and you're bound to get burned; soar under the radar for too long, and you'll be unnoticed; find the right balance between flying just high enough, at just the right velocity, and you might just stay up there forever.

Our *grind* has a life cycle, too—because a lot of times when we shift gears and move to a new phase in our careers, we shift our *grind* as well. We bend our days and our routines to the new demands in our new environment, and change our habits in anticipation of the demands to come.

Understand, I've had to change my game to keep pace with shifts in my career, as I've gone from the scrappy kid hustling up every odd job he could find; to this hard-driving twenty-something, with a headful of dreams of making it big in the fashion world, sewing T-shirts and hats with my boys every spare minute we had; to this straight-talking urban fashion designer keeping it real for FUBU customers; to "the People's Shark," this straight-talking fashion-executive-turned-entrepreneur who's still keeping it real, betting on my potential partners as much as I am investing in their product or service. And by the way, it's not like I've abandoned the core business that got me started. We're still making FUBU gear, same way Under Armour is still making performance athletic garments and Amazon is still selling books.

So, yeah, my brand has evolved, and my grind along with it. **In a lot of ways, I'm working harder now than I ever have.** My *grind* has become *a part* of my brand, my lifestyle. It's who I am. And I'm not the only Shark who feels this way. My great friend Barbara Corcoran tells me she can't remember a time in her life when she's worked so hard, not even when she was launching the real estate business that made her rep and her fortune.

....

POWER FACT: Americans take about 488 million business trips each year, according to the Global Business Travel Association. . . . *Lately, it's starting to feel like I'm accounting for about half of those trips—that's how much time I've been spending away from home, away from my comfort zones and routines.*

....

As hard as I worked back in the day, that's nothing compared to the hours I'm putting in now, when I'm on the road a couple hundred days each year. Vegas, Sydney, Hong Kong, Paris, Cincinnati . . . wherever there's a deal to be made, or a group that wants to bring me in to talk about entrepreneurship or small business opportunities, I'm all over it. And as anyone who travels for business can tell you, the road has a way of dialing up the grind.

Yeah, I'm hitting it *hard,* but I've made a little bit of money along the way so I'm able to travel in style. The first time me and my boys went to Vegas for the MAGIC show—a key fashion industry trade show where we wrote our first big orders for FUBU—we were scrambling to catch a bunch of standby flights. (Shout-out to my mother, who was working at American Airlines at the time!) To save cash we were squeezing into a tiny-ass hotel room that also doubled as our showroom. Thankfully, those days are gone, and now I'm staying in nice hotel rooms or stylin' Airbnb houses on the beach, but it's still a wearying thing, to be away from home and living out of a suitcase for long stretches. What's different about how things are for me now is that most times I can schedule my trips around whatever else I've got going on. I can be home for my daughter's birthday, say, or set it up so I can spend a couple of hours with her before bedtime before heading out of town, maybe catch a red-eye flight home so I can be there when she wakes up in the morning.

It's gotten to where I *own* **my schedule, and my schedule doesn't own me**—an essential difference that only came into play for me in success. And better believe I've worked hard to move past those days where I'd be hanging out at airports, twiddling my thumbs on a long layover just to save a couple of bucks on flights, or searching for the most budget-friendly motel I could find on the outskirts of town.

But that's why we *grind*. **We keep pushing—ever forward, ever harder—until we get to that place where we can maybe smooth out the ride a little bit, which in turn makes it a little easier to keep pushing.** So as I set these thoughts to paper here, I'm reminded of where I was when I was just starting out, and I try to keep that perspective in mind as I consider where I am, and look ahead to where I'm going.

BE ON EDGE

LIFT THE WEIGHT OF WORRY

GARY VAYNERCHUK
Serial Entrepreneur, Marketing Expert, Influencer, Ball of Energy

ONE OF THE great side benefits to being on a show like *Shark Tank* is the way it's opened a door for me to meet and hang with some of the leading minds in technology and innovation. And it's through that open door that I met my friend Gary Vaynerchuk, one of the most forward-thinking people I've been blessed to know.

Gary's got his fingers into just about everything. First and foremost, he's one of the most insightful, commanding influencers on social media, with about five million followers on Facebook, Twitter, and Instagram combined. But it's not just the *quantity* of people who plug in to what Gary's saying online; it's the *quality,* because his followers tend to be influencers themselves, so the level of his engagement is just through the roof. What that means, basically, is that when Gary posts something, lots of people stop what they're doing and give it some meaningful thought—and, typically, that thought leads to some type of meaningful action, which in turn leads to some sort of equally meaningful *reaction*. That's kind of what influence is all about, isn't it?

But Gary's influence doesn't end on social media. He's also a megaselling author—maybe you've read *Crush It!* or *Jab, Jab, Jab, Right Hook,* two of my all-time favorite business books. Maybe you've seen him speak at some global tech conference, or checked in to his daily vlog for his insights and strategies. Or maybe you've seen him on Apple TV's *Planet of the Apps* reality show, with Jessica Alba, Gwyneth Paltrow, and will.i.am—a kind of *Shark Tank* for app developers.

Through his company VaynerMedia, he advises dozens of Fortune 500 companies on digital and social media strategies, so he has his fingerprints in just about every nook and cranny of the Internet, on just about every platform, in just about every industry—whether you see them or not. His notorious "jam" sessions at the South by Southwest conference each year are a highlight—that's when he puts on his impresario hat and pulls together these free-form think tank sessions with top executives from cutting-edge companies, and everybody just sits around and spins all these fantastic notions about the coming innovations in technology and commerce and trends in social media. Really, this guy's reach is incredible—and he moves like a million miles a minute.

Gary's backstory is just as amazing as the front-and-center story that his millions of readers and followers have come to admire. He was born in the Soviet Union and immigrated to the United States with his family when he was just two or three years old. At first the entire family was squeezed into a studio apartment in Queens—nine people in all!—and out of those humble beginnings he somehow developed the hard-core, hard-charging work ethic that still drives his days. When his family moved to the New Jersey suburbs a couple of years later, Gary started his first business—a lemonade stand. (It's the American dream, baby!) But Gary didn't run that stand like a cliché. He didn't phone it in or sip away the profits. No, he cleaned up. When the weather was right, he wouldn't close shop until he'd pocketed a couple hundred bucks, and then he started making even more money selling baseball cards—because hey, why not? By the time he was fourteen, he was working in his family's retail wine business—a business he would rebrand and reinvent when he got out of college.

That's really where Gary made his name, in the wine industry, after growing that company, now called the Wine Library, into a $60 million business, mostly by tapping the emerging power of e-commerce. I'll set aside the details of Gary's stunning rise to becoming one of technology's leading angel investors and a trend-stamping voice on digital marketing, because that's his story to tell. I want to tell a different story, one that really gets to the heart of what keeps him grinding.

Hang around with Gary long enough and you get to where nothing this guy does or says or sets into motion surprises you. He's a straight talker, comes right out with what needs to be said instead of what people might want to hear, and he's one of these guys who believes everything is possible, so you learn to expect the unexpected when he gets going on a topic. And yet when we sat down to talk about the ideas behind this book, his responses blew me away.

So what motivates a world-class motivator like Gary Vaynerchuk? Well, he doesn't like to talk about it, but he opened up to me at one of my salon-talks at Blueprint + Co, the new co-working space I launched in Manhattan in February 2017. Gary happened to be the very first guest I invited to visit with our members, and I asked him to talk very specifically about the way he framed his days—knowing that the couple hundred passionate, purpose-driven entrepreneurs in the audience would be hanging on his every word.

I started as basic as you can get: "Tell me what you did when you got up this morning."

What's interesting about this drill is that Gary thought to even share it with me at all, especially in response to a simple question about his daily routines. Most people, you ask them how they start their day, they'll tell you about their morning workout, or what they like to have for breakfast. Maybe they'll mention all the blogs and newspapers they read, the people they check in with on social media. But not Gary. From this one open-ended, softball-type question he gave me one of the bravest, most deeply personal answers I've ever heard from someone in a public setting. He could have offered up some easy, saccharine answer, because I'm sure he'd been asked a version of this question a whole bunch of times. And there would have been wisdom in response, and experience, and maybe even a laugh line or two. But instead he went another way.

It feels to me like I should set this up with a warning: Gary's answer was pretty dark, which surprised me a little because he puts out such a positive energy, but the people in the room were so moved by what he had to say I want share it with you, right out of the gate.

"ENOUGH WITH THE DRUMROLL—GET ON WITH IT, DAYMOND!"

"The one constant in my life," he said, "is that I still have nightmares. I used to have nightmares when I was a kid, and it was a recurring nightmare. In my dream, my family and I were flying back to Belarus, and the plane would crash. Every time, different people from my family, usually one to three people, would survive. It was very dark, very disturbing, and parents today would find out their kid was having this same recurring dream and send him somewhere to see what was wrong with him. I must've had that dream fifty times, from the time I was in maybe second grade until I started middle school. And everything was so clear to me in those dreams. There'd be one or two or three of us who would survive this horrible crash, and we'd be walking through the snow, and it was very, very weird.

"I've never really talked about this before, but you asked me this question in a very interesting way. **You asked how I start my day, and you'll want to know how I end each day, and the answer is the same: perspective and gratitude.** That's true from when I first started having these dreams as a kid, all the way to today. Perspective and gratitude, that's what drives me. That's what I'm about. Every morning, I wake up and I force myself to think like I used to think after one of these nightmares. Every morning, I pretend that my mother or my wife or one of my children has died. Every day, I do this. I did it just today. I let my mind go to this dark, dark place and feel what I would feel if this is what happened. When I go to sleep at night, I do the same thing. And it doesn't just flash through my mind, this thought. It doesn't just register and then disappear. No, it fills my whole body. What would it be like if my four-year-old son got hit by a car while he was crossing the street? I force myself to think this way, to feel this way. But I'm very in tune with myself as I do this. And I promise you, if you're in touch with your feelings, and if you're able to trick yourself into feeling in this way, it really hurts. I tear up just telling you about it now, but if you allow yourself to go there, you get to the place where nothing else matters. It keeps everything you're likely to face in perspective."

Wow. I was really moved when I heard that, because nothing matters in this world if we don't remember what's important, or where we come from, and nothing matters if we don't find a way to give thanks for the blessings that come our way.

Let me tell you, Gary wasn't the only one tearing up as he told me this. I was sitting next to him on the stage, and I was trying not to cry in front of all those people and I could see the folks in the audience wiping their eyes, trying to process what they were hearing.

Pretty powerful stuff, don't you think? I mean, who *does* that? Who willingly puts himself in that kind of frame of mind, to jump-start each day? Who thinks to summon his deepest, darkest fears—to stare them down and confront them in a determined way? Later on, I actually caught myself trying to imagine the same kind of nightmare for my own family, and I couldn't do it. Right there on the stage, as Gary was sharing this gut-wrenching trick of the mind, I tried to call up these horrifying images, and then I stiff-armed them right out of my head. It was too painful to think about, too depressing, too chilling . . . just *too much,* you know.

But Gary Vaynerchuk doesn't think so. Each day, he goes to this dark, dark place as a way to keep himself grounded and focused, to tap into those feelings of gratitude and perspective that have come to shape him. **This *mortality-check,* above all, is his *grind*. It moves him, defines him, and propels him forward.**

"I think you need to know how to breathe," he explains. "And this helps me breathe. My family makes me breathe. The health of my family, that's big for me. And the truth of it is, three of my four grandparents died before I was born, or just after I was born. I never knew them. We have a small family. I just haven't dealt with a whole lot of death, not of people close to me, and I guess I'm curious how I'm going to play it out when that starts to happen, so maybe this is just my way of looking at that, and dealing with that."

POWER FACT: Did you know that Pablo Picasso, at three years old, survived a devastating earthquake in Malaga, Spain, and moved with this family to a nearby cave while the community recovered? . . . *His younger sister was actually born in that cave, and I mention it here as a reminder that sometimes a childhood trauma can offer a lifetime of inspiration to a survivor, and in exceptional cases it might even spark a streak of genius or creativity.*

And so for a while after we talked I kept coming back to this idea of holding a candle to your deepest, darkest fears and seeing what you can see in the flickering light. I even tried to put myself through some of these paces another couple of times, just to see what it was about the exercise that motivates Gary and keeps him striving, but I didn't have the stomach for it. Didn't have the heart for it. Oh, man, it just tore me up inside, to think in this way.

Look, not *every* strategy works for *every* person, right? That's what makes us individuals—we're each cut in our own way. But even though Gary's approach wasn't for me, I think I understand what it is about these dark thoughts that can push a person forward. With someone like Gary V., maybe, it comes down to a sense of being in control. He's always telling me that he's got the business part of his life down. "I'm a beast at business," he says. Or, "I will always be successful in business." No doubt. But what wakes him up some nights, what *keeps* him up some nights, is the part of his life he *can't* control—that none of us can—and that has to do with the health and well-being of his family and the people close to him. I'm guessing that this is just his way of coping, because while he might not have the power to prevent some horrible tragedy or disaster from striking, the one thing he *can* do is steel himself for whatever sadness might come his way. The heartbreak that inevitably hits us all, *that's* the great unknown—so when he spends a little time thinking this way each morning, and a little time each night before turning in, he's bracing for the worst and reconnecting to the idea that he can pretty much handle anything that gets thrown at him . . . *anything.*

UNDERSTAND THE EQUATION

The takeaway here, for me, is that **there is a positive side to emotions that we think of as being purely negative—like fear, worry, or sadness**. The *weight of worry* I'm referring to in the title to this chapter is the weight Gary forces himself to carry each day, by putting himself through these tough paces. It's a worry that's strengthened him, he suggests, a worry that continues to strengthen him, as he keeps working that same muscle. That's where someone like Gary lives and breathes, when he's staring down those black moments. That's where he survives and thrives, by reminding himself in this primal way that nothing can touch him if he's able to harness the gratitude he feels for the love and blessings of his family, and the perspective he gains from understanding how small everything else can seem in comparison.

The flip side, the positive stuff, that's a cakewalk to someone like Gary Vaynerchuk. For him, it's all about keeping it fundamental.

"You know who talks to me about hustling, and finding the right balance in their lives?" he says. "It's the people who aren't happy, the people who make things too complicated. They want their business to be bigger, or they want to make more money, but then they complain that they're not spending enough time with their families. My answer to that? Spend more time with your family. They tell me they want their business to grow. My answer to that? Work harder. Put in the time. This is binary stuff. It's basic."

Here again, the central message is one of perspective. "I tend to think in extremes," Gary explains. "People talk all the time about finding a work-life balance, but that balance is not the same for everybody. And it's different at different times of your life."

What he means by that, I think, is that there's no set formula. **It's fluid. It's individual.** But whatever the balance, it helps if you're someone like Gary, who can squeeze a week's worth of juice out of a single day. It helps to live your life in ultrahigh definition, and move at a million miles an hour, with the volume cranked up, like Gary does. This is a guy who encourages the people who work for him and alongside him to play music during the day . . . *loud*. It's a way to ratchet up the energy and keep things pulsing, and if you step onto the floor of any one of Gary's places of business you might think at first you were at a club. There's sound and fury—a wild mix. Now, there's a lot going on in the offices of the Shark Group, where I now spend most of my time when I'm in New York. There's music, too. But we're nowhere near the level of bass that Gary seems to like to operate at.

Another example: he's a whiz at multitasking. Probably, he doesn't even think of it as multitasking, because he manages to integrate it all into one. He'll think nothing about flying cross-country for a single meeting, and he'll use the time on the plane to read, write, and catch up on his social media feeds.

Point is, Gary knows how to *grind*. And maybe it's because of his killer work ethic that he doesn't have a whole lot of love for people who go around thinking this or that job is beneath them. Remember, this is a guy who went out and promoted his wine business by printing up his own fliers and trekking out to New Jersey's Short Hills Mall and slipping them underneath all the windshield wipers on the parked cars.

"People today, they're too fancy," he tells me. "Look at yourself in the mirror. If you have ambitions to win, you're fancy. If you think you're so big, so important that you don't have to do a certain job, you're fancy. If you see something that needs doing and you hand it off to someone else instead of doing it yourself, you're fancy. So that's another thing I tell people that they don't necessarily want to hear. Stop being so fancy.

"And stop running around telling the world how hard you work, how you hustle, because I see you. *We* see you. There's a picture of you on Instagram playing Ping-Pong at four thirty in the afternoon, so don't tell me about hustle. People don't understand what hustle is. I took one vacation in my twenties. One, for the whole decade. And I'm not saying that to boast, because I should have taken one or two every year. I've learned. But don't tell me about hustle."

Fair enough, Gary. Fair enough.

Gary's Grind Checklist

✓ take time each day to appreciate what you have and where you come from . . .

✓ confront your fears—that trick of the mind Gary plays on himself each morning might be too dark, too painful for many of you to try at home, but you can dial it down a notch and force yourself to think through the worst-case scenarios that lie in wait for you in your career or in your business . . .

✓ juggle!—basically, this means we need to learn to walk and chew gum at the same time, because there just aren't enough hours in the day to get everything done if we try to tick them off one by one . . .

✓ delegate at your own risk—if you're out to connect with your audience or your customers in a genuine way, you can't hand the job off to someone else, because people will see right through you . . .

✓ work–life balance is all about perspective—it's not the same for everyone . . . we all move at different paces, live at different speeds, play our music at different volumes . . .

✓ don't talk yourself into believing that a job or a task is beneath you . . .

✓ always remember to count your blessings, but keep in mind that you can't always count *on* them . . .

....

For more information on Gary and how he uses the
Rise and Grind mindset, check out
www.DaymondJohn.com/Rise/Gary

BE HONEST

PAY YOUR DUES

BRIAN LEE
Serial Entrepreneur, "Honest" Engine, Game-changer

I'M DRAWN TO people like myself who grew up with a kind of paycheck-to-paycheck mentality. Doesn't matter if it was handed down to them by their parents and grandparents, or if they came to it on their own . . . the working stiffs of the world are my kind of people. Nothing against the good folks who were born into money or privilege or opportunity, but they seem to be cut from a different cloth than those of us who come from more modest beginnings . . . just sayin'. And, even if we're able to connect on a deal or find common ground in a social setting, there's always a disconnect when it comes to how we started out.

Here's the thing: when they come out of that kind of hardscrabble background, people just don't shake that drive to succeed, even after they've succeeded beyond their wildest dreams.

In my last book, *The Power of Broke,* I spent a lot of time looking at the ways we push ourselves to succeed when we have no other option but to succeed—at the *power* we can find in desperation. My feeling is you kind of need to have your back against the wall, no place to go but up, in order to discover the will and wherewithal to truly succeed. That doesn't mean you can't find those things if you come from a place of advantage; it just means that disadvantage isn't necessarily a deal-breaker—and, if you play it right and smart, you can find a way to turn your hardships into assets.

What doesn't kill you only makes you stronger, right?

All of which takes me to my friend Brian Lee—a wildly successful entrepreneur you might never have heard of, although I'm betting you've heard of the companies he's started. Brian's the visionary behind LegalZoom and ShoeDazzle, and together with the actress Jessica Alba he's launched The Honest Company, a megasuccessful household products line built on the concept of ethical consumerism—meaning they only sell holistic, natural stuff that's good for you.

I'll get to all that in a bit, but for now let's take a look at Brian's backstory, because that's where I find our true points of connection. His parents came to this country from South Korea when Brian was just a toddler. They arrived with two kids, two pieces of luggage, and $500, determined to start a new life for their family—the classic version of the American dream.

"My dad really started from ground zero," Brian tells. "He started out working in a furniture factory during the day, and he was picking oranges at night, just hustling. My entire childhood was really just watching my father rise and grind. It made an impression."

Brian believes he was hit by his father's entrepreneurial streak, as well as his unshakable work ethic. He watched his old man hustle and sweat to make a life for his family, and move from that paycheck-to-paycheck mindset to finally being able to establish himself and build a stake. Out of that, Brian was able to take in some of the tools he'd need to do the same. Growing up, Brian would grab at his father's example and make it his own, in little kid ways at first—like on Halloween, when he'd come home from trick-or-treating, bunch his candies, four to a Ziploc bag, and resell them the next day to the kids in school for 25 cents.

"That's how I used to buy Star Wars cards, with those quarters," he says. "I was always trying to come up with an idea to make a buck, some way to create something out of nothing."

GET OUTSIDE YOUR PERSONAL ZIP CODE

Selling candy to kids the day after Halloween is a little like selling ice to Eskimos, but Brian found a way to make it work—and he would ride that entrepreneurial streak straight into a winning career. It took him a while, though, and during that while Brian started to think he might never match his father's success. You see, by the time Brian graduated from high school, his father was running one of the largest stainless steel factories in the world, and just figured Brian would follow him into the stainless steel business. But Brian had a different thought entirely: he wanted to be a rapper.

Got to be honest, when Brian shared this little detail it just about knocked me out. I'm sure he had some chops, even if he didn't quite look the part, which only goes to show you that you can't judge a book by its cover. **You can be meant to do something, called to a certain type of work, that on its face might seem to be completely outside your personal zip code, but that's what makes this country great.** You can do anything, dream anything, *become* anything . . . even an Asian rapper. Weren't a whole lot of Asian rappers back in the 1980s, but Brian was inspired by Kool Moe Dee and my boy LL Cool J, and this was the life he imagined for himself, so he reached for it. I can't help but respect the dream, and the fact that

Brian didn't see color or race when it came to music, couldn't understand why he should be counted out on this before he'd even given it a shot.

Only, it didn't exactly work out the way Brian had planned.

"I told my parents I didn't want to go to college, and it was a big, big troubled time," he says. "When I told them I was moving to New York to become a rapper, my dad was like, No one's going to listen to an Asian rapper."

His father was right, of course, but it took Brian a while to concede the point—six months, in fact. That's how long he and a buddy tried to make a go of it in New York. They got as far as making their own mixtape, as far as hanging out in front of all the music industry buildings they could identify in Midtown and pressing that tape into the hands of people headed in and out of those buildings all day long. Wasn't exactly a winning strategy, but they kept at it, hard—and still, they couldn't catch a break for trying.

Looking back, Brian seems to see this side trip to New York as a formative experience. It taught him how to fail, and he got it out of the way early—one of the lessons I try to teach when I talk to aspiring entrepreneurs. **You're only as tough as the ways you've been toughened.** And here it just worked out that *it just didn't work out.* In Brian's case, he was young enough to regroup, and hit reset—no biggie when you're in your early twenties and just starting out, but maybe a tough one to get past when you're older, with a mortgage to pay and mouths to feed and fit with braces.

Six months later, Brian was back in California, back in his parents' good graces, going to college at UCLA. He studied business economics, and as graduation approached he decided to apply to law school—not because he wanted to be a lawyer, necessarily, but he figured another three years of school would give him time to figure out what he did want to do. Plus, college was a great good time, and he figured law school would keep the party going.

"This is going to sound terrible," he says, "but I never had a strong work ethic in school. I have a very strong work ethic outside of school. I just wasn't that interested in the content. There were some classes I loved, but they were very few and far between. It was more about what was happening outside of school for me."

(You know, I spend a lot of time speaking on college campuses, and it's remarkable to me how many times I hear this same thing from students today. It always leaves me thinking we should be doing a better job matching the curriculum to what students actually want to do when they get out of school.)

Brian didn't apply to a lot of law schools, mind you. Just one—UCLA, where he knew the lay of the land. Happily, he got in, and three years later, when all his law school friends were signing on to high-paying jobs as first-year associates, he thought he'd give that a try, too. So he signed on at a big-time law firm— and, as he says, "I almost shot myself in the head."

....

POWER FACT: The Small Business Association considers any company with fewer than 500 employees a "small" business. . . . *Hey, by that measure, more than 99 percent of American businesses fall into this category—a huge number, but a reminder that the great majority of our companies remain nimble and able to adapt to changes in the marketplace.*

....

His colleagues were incredibly smart and talented, Brian recalls. But he couldn't find any joy in his work, and I think it felt to Brian like he was out there in the field, picking oranges like his father, just to make a buck. It was grunt work, to him—pure *grind,* but without the joy. Even so, he hung in there for a couple of years, had a hard time looking away from a decent salary, but during that whole time he was thinking of an exit strategy, something else he could do that might fill him with a sense of energy and purpose as he set about his days.

Now here's where Brian's story gets a little confusing, so stay with me. One of his best friends from law school was working in a building across the street in downtown Los Angeles. His name was Brian Liu—see what I mean about confusing? The two Brians would get together almost every day for lunch and scheme about ways to escape the world of corporate law—a classic example of two aspiring entrepreneurs taking the lead on offense!

"Every time we got together we were like, There's got to be something else we can do," *our* Brian says. "The first idea we came up with was something we called LawGarden.com. We'd be a bunch of stay-at-home attorneys that would be available to answer questions online for ninety-nine cents a minute. That was the idea, but it never came to fruition because there were a lot of legal barriers, in terms of being able to offer legal advice in all fifty states. It just wasn't workable, but it pushed us to start thinking that those barriers wouldn't apply if we were just creating legal documents."

That was the genesis of LegalZoom, which Brian started out of his condo. What he and the other Brian had figured out was the power and reach of the World Wide Web, and here they'd hit on a way to make wills and trusts and other standard legal documents available on this new thing called the Internet. Remember, this was back in the late 1990s, when people were still reluctant to share personal information on the computer, when there was no such thing as online banking, when hardly anyone was thinking of encryption and firewalls and identity theft issues.

One of the biggest challenges facing innovators like Brian is getting people to understand their product or service, but before they can even *understand* what you're trying to sell them you have to be on their radar. That's the great hurdle we faced back when we were launching FUBU—we could have the hottest designs, but if people weren't aware of our clothes, we were nowhere. In our case, we were able to chase down LL Cool J, who was also from Hollis, Queens, and who was already a superstar. Once LL started wearing our stuff, people started to notice, and Brian knew that if he and the other Brian wanted to drive people to their service they needed a celebrity spokesperson.

Trouble was, they didn't have any money to hire one.

"This was right after the O. J. Simpson trial," Brian tells, "and Robert Shapiro was world-famous. Everyone knew his face, and it was a face people had come to trust, so I cold-called him. Got his number from information and called him at like nine or ten o'clock at night, thinking nobody would be in the office. I had my voice message all planned, all written out. But he picked up the phone. He said, 'Hi, this is Robert Shapiro, how can I help you?' The first thing I said to him was, 'Robert Shapiro, the attorney?' Not exactly the best way to begin my pitch. He said, 'Yes,' so I said, 'Well, I'm Brian Lee and I have a business idea I'd like to run by you.'

"Of course, he just said, 'I'm not interested,' which is what anyone in his position would have said. But I knew he was about to hang up on me so I yelled, 'Wait, how do you know you're not interested if you don't hear me out?' I was just trying to keep him on the line. And at that point he said, 'Okay, you've got two minutes,' and in those two minutes I told him the whole idea for LegalZoom. And at the end he said, 'You know, I hear about a hundred ideas every day, and I actually really like this one.'"

One of the things I love about that story is that Brian had his whole pitch written out. I've done that from time to time over the years—and, got to admit, I've sometimes felt a little foolish, writing out a whole script for myself, but it can really pay off. It forces you to think of what you might say in this scenario, or that scenario, almost like one of those Choose Your Own Adventure stories we used to read as kids. But as much as you might want to prepare ahead of an important phone call like this one, there's also great value in being nimble enough in your thinking to go off-script, as the situation dictates—like here, with this late-night phone call—so be prepared to improvise.

Of course, Brian never expected Robert Shapiro to actually *answer* his phone, and when he did it was because Brian had already taken the time to write down his key proposal points that he was able to make some kind of impression. So even though he had a script he intended to follow, it wasn't meant as part of a conversation. He'd just thought he'd leave a carefully worded message. He'd thought through what he wanted to say, and internalized it in such a way that he was able to deliver a decent pitch—maybe not in a scripted, polished way, but it got the job done.

SEE THE OUTCOME YOU WANT, BE THE OUTCOME YOU WANT

It took a couple of months even for a whip-smart attorney like Robert Shapiro to do his due diligence and sign on the dotted line, and in that time the financial markets took a dive. The way it worked out, the day the two Brians and their third partner—Eddie Hartman, who handled the technology end of things—had their very first venture capital meeting, the NASDAQ tanked. The dot-com explosion pretty much exploded in their faces, but they went to the meeting anyway. When they got there, the guy they were pitching opened the door and said, "What are you doing here?"

Brian said, "We had a meeting. We're here to pitch you on our dot-com idea."

The guy said, "Don't you know what's happening in the market?"

Brian said, "Yeah, Internet stocks hit a little speed bump, but we still believe in our business."

The venture capital guy, he didn't agree—but he did take the time to sit with Brian and his partners and try to convince them to get their jobs back at their respective law firms. It just about scared the crap out of Brian, but he was determined to press on with their business plan.

In the end, they were able to finance their start-up with $50,000 in loans from their parents, and this was where Brian's *grind* kicked in for the first time. Oh, he'd worked hard before— you don't get through law school and land a job with a top firm without putting in those hours. But he can't remember a time when he worked *so* hard, for *so* long.

"I was working all the time, because the office was in my condo," he says. "There was no thought of what you were doing that weekend. There was no thought of a vacation. It was just work, work, work. For three years. I couldn't even afford to take a girl out to dinner."

This right here is one of the killer dilemmas facing entrepreneurs just starting to get a business off the ground: when you work from home, and there aren't enough hours in the day to get through your to-do list, and there's no money to hire additional staff, you run the risk of burning out. That's what me and my boys were facing back in the day with FUBU, when all we could do was live, breathe, eat, and sleep the business, and whole days would go by when we didn't even leave the house! I don't care what kind of *go-hard* person you are, there's just no way to move a project forward without taking a step back from time to time. Brian was able to figure this out, over time, but those first three years were a nonstop treadmill. The pace was unsustainable—and now that he's reached a certain level of success, he's in a position to structure his days in a more manageable way.

For example, one of his personal rules is never to schedule any meetings or phone calls over the weekend—that's family time for Brian, these days. It's sacred. And he'll never miss one of his kid's school functions—also, sacred. **"I turn my phone off when I get home," he says.** "That's been a big help to me. I'll turn it back on to check email before I go to sleep, but for those three or four hours, it's family time, and that's incredibly important."

But that's today. Back when he was just starting out, Brian couldn't really afford to step away from his desk. I mean, he and his partners were investing everything into this LegalZoom start-up. Robert Shapiro was out there talking to the media, promoting the service, but for the first couple of days when the site was up and running they didn't get a single order. Brian and his partners were sweating bullets that whole time, thinking maybe they'd misread the marketplace, big-time. But then, middle of the third day, they got an order from some guy in Miami who wanted to buy a will.

Brian remembers the moment like it was yesterday. "The guy asked us when he could expect to receive the document," he says, "and we were like, right away, sir. I mean, that was the whole idea, and to have it validated through this one sale . . . it was honestly the best fifty-nine dollars I ever made in my life. Just knowing our system worked, and we had a real customer outside of my mom, my dad, and my sister. It was real proof of concept."

Okay, so as we all now know, LegalZoom went on from there to become a runaway success, and after a while Brian had an itch to start something new—this time, he was inspired by his wife, who just loved to buy shoes. He just couldn't believe how many pairs she had and how much they all cost. He had friends in the shoe business, had a basic idea on the cost of goods, and knew a profit margin when he saw one, so he started thinking of some kind of online shoe business. By this time, Brian and his partners had hired a full-time CEO to run LegalZoom, so he was free to look at other projects, and here with the launch of ShoeDazzle it was the same formula all over again: find the right celebrity to push the brand (Kim Kardashian, in this case), work like crazy, put your idea out into the world. Only this time around, he was able to power down at the end of each day and over the weekend to spend that all-important quality time with his family.

Pretty soon, though, he started feeling that now-familiar entrepreneurial itch, and ended up getting connected with Jessica Alba to talk about her idea for a lifestyle company focusing exclusively on safe and effective products. The idea didn't really resonate with Brian at first, but he sparked to it eventually. Here again, it took some inspiration from his wife, who was leaning more and more to household products that were safer, healthier, better for the environment. He went by his gut on this—same way he did when he pushed ahead with his first two companies.

"I wish I could say I looked at a lot of data before coming to these decisions," he says, "but at the end of the day it's just gut. It comes down to your instincts."

Like LegalZoom and ShoeDazzle before it, The Honest Company was a huge success, and Brian's finally in a position to run his businesses in ways that focus on efficiency and allow him to free up the quality time he's determined to make a priority for his family.

Here are just a few time-tested strategies Brian has put in place to keep things on track:

- **run structured meetings, on fixed schedules**

    "I meet with my staff every Monday morning," Brian shares. "Then once a month I'll meet with the team leader in each department."
- **read the newspaper, first thing**

    "I read the *Wall Street Journal*. I read the local paper. I need to know what's happening in the world."
- **find time to make breakfast for the kids**

    "That's my happy time every morning, and it's actually a really great time for me to meditate on the day ahead. Cooking is very relaxing for me, and when I'm in the kitchen like that with my family I can zone out and think about all the things I have to do that day."
- **hire strong management and let them do their thing**

    "You're only as good as your team, right? It's incredibly important to have that second layer of management below you, so the executives can really execute. In an ideal world, only the most drastic fires will reach you. In a big company, most of the heat shouldn't rise all the way to the top, unless it's a true issue."
- **seek mentors**

    "I have a lot of people I talk to on a regular basis, people I talk to all the time, people who have been there and done that."

Brian finds motivation everywhere he looks. "There are so many things that inspire me every day," he says. "To work, to try something new, to make a difference. Whether it's the charities I'm involved with, the schools for my kids, or my employees at work, if you keep your eyes open, there's inspiration all around. I try to draw from that each and every day."

One of the things that surprised me when I sat with Brian on this was how much he loves the hustle and bustle of starting a new business, same as me. You'd think someone who's ramped up three crazy-successful companies might be inclined to sit back and chill, but he seems to thrive on the thrill of the chase that finds you in a start-up environment.

"I'm always looking for the grind," he says, a line that really gets to the difference between people who make it to the top, and those who don't. "At the end of the day, that's what drives me. What's the next cool thing? Where's the future headed? Wherever we're going, whatever's about to happen, I want to be a part of it, and I want to make an impact."

Brian's Grind Checklist

✓ don't be afraid to chase your dreams, even if they're a little crazy and out there and everybody you know is telling you you're out of your mind . . .

✓ if you can find a way to fail *early*—meaning, before you've got kids and a mortgage, or employees and killer operating costs, go ahead and do so . . .

✓ carve out some uninterrupted family time, away from the office, and do this in a disciplined way—follow Brian's lead on this and shut off your phone if you have to . . .

✓ take the time to write down your pitch before you find yourself in the unexpected position of making your pitch . . .

✓ know that if you're cold-calling someone and get it in your head that all you're doing is leaving a message, you might be

surprised when the person you're pitching actually picks up
the phone . . .

✓ trust the instincts of the people around you—in other words,
if your wife loves to buy shoes, or use organic products, be
open to opportunities that confirm what she's been trying to
tell you . . .

✓ be prepared to pay your dues—grind hard (but not *too* hard)
when you're first starting out, and then give yourself permis-
sion to slow your game (but not *too* slow) once you begin to
achieve some success . . .

....

For more information on Brian and how he uses the
Rise and Grind mindset, check out
www.DaymondJohn.com/Rise/Brian

BE ON POINT

BARK ONCE FOR A BIG IDEA

KRISTINA GUERRERO

Outdoorswoman, Former Air Force Pilot, Shark Tank *Partner*

HAVE YOU EVER reached for a product or service believing it already existed?

Have you ever come up with an idea that strikes you as so basic and obvious, you're surprised to find out nobody else has thought of it?

That's kind of what happened to my amazing business partner Kristina Guerrero, who without really realizing it, without really meaning to, has managed to take a bite out of the $60 billion pet food industry. It's just a tiny bite, for now, but I'm betting that's about to change. What happened was she was out backcountry skiing with her dog Dunkan, at the top of the mountain, when she realized the big guy might be a little hungry—and out of that one moment, where need bumped up against inspiration, came the seeds of a business.

"He was more of a grazer," she explains of Dunkan, "so he wouldn't really eat before we went out, and now we were about six miles in and I didn't have any food for him. At least, I didn't have the *right* kind of food for him. It's not like he was about to go hungry, but when we're at home I made sure he would always eat healthy. I ended up giving him a burrito, while I had a PowerBar, and that was when it hit me that I should find a meal bar for dogs that I could carry around with me."

A couple of things you should know before we get going on Kristina's story. One, I'm a dog lover, so as soon as I saw Kristina's pitch, I was pretty much sold. It was such a great concept, one of those lightbulb-over-the-head ideas you start to think you should've come up with yourself. And two, I'm on the board of the Petco Foundation, which does amazing work in the area of animal welfare, so I'm always looking twice at products and initiatives that seek to make a difference in our pets' lives.

Okay, back to Kristina and Dunkan . . .

Dunkan did just fine with that burrito, but Kristina kept thinking there had to be some company out there selling the doggie equivalent of a Clif Bar or PowerBar, something you could carry around when you're out and about with your best friend and a bowl of food isn't really an option. She went online, tried every search term she could think of, and came up empty. She asked around at local pet stores and among her dog-lover pals . . . still nothing. She couldn't believe that something as simple as an individually wrapped, healthy meal bar for active dogs didn't already exist.

Now, I should mention here that **Kristina wasn't looking to start a business—she just wanted a convenient way to feed her dog when they were out on the trail.** I should also mention that Kristina, like everyone else you've met in this book, doesn't do things halfway. When she goes, she goes hard. And when you're the kind of person who sees a need and looks to fill it, like Kristina, things start to happen. Her direct, aggressive approach to problem-solving, her relentless work ethic— she comes by these traits naturally, but they were sharpened and refined by her military experience. You see, Kristina got it in her head at fifteen years old that she wanted to go to the US Air Force Academy, and so she made it happen—same way she makes most things happen.

IN THE LINE OF DUTY

Growing up, Kristina wasn't happy at home, didn't always get along with her father, and she was looking for a way up and out. The Air Force was a dream, but it was a dream within reach, and it turned out the discipline and demanding requirements of the academy really suited her. After graduating, she became a C–130 pilot, going on to complete three combat tours, including deployments in Operation Enduring Freedom, in Afghanistan, and Operation Iraqi Freedom. And she wasn't just going through the motions, logging her time behind a desk: she was flying missions, fighting the good fight, and every here and there she'd give herself a little pep talk—you know, one of those "what doesn't kill you makes you stronger" mantra-type lines we talked about way back in the beginning of the book.

To hear Kristina tell it, she found her grind—or maybe her grind found her—when she started at the Air Force Academy, located in Colorado Springs, Colorado. "In my head I set it up that, whatever moment of extreme difficulty I was in, whether it was physical or mental, I told myself that the long-term returns were endless," she recalls. **"I knew that by staying in and keeping in the game, I would do something great with my life, and have the freedom to choose my own path.** That was true in the academy, and it was true in the line of duty."

That path took Kristina all the way to her thirtieth birthday, when she decided to leave the service and get her master's degree in occupational therapy. "My idea was to move into a life of service on the home front," she explains of her decision to set off on the next good and noble chapter in her life and career. So there she was in Colorado, with all this rich experience, all these hard knocks, and she decided to take that uncompromising mindset she'd gotten in the Air Force into the great outdoors. She was big into backcountry skiing, hiking, biking . . . the full Rocky Mountain adventure experience. That was the stuff that brought joy to her days, the way she decompressed outside of the pressures of school and work. But here's the thing: that day on top of that mountain, when that lightbulb went off in her head about a single-package travel meal for dogs, she didn't think to carry it forward. And it's not that she didn't think she *could* develop the idea into a business; it just never occurred to her to try. It wasn't her thing. She finally had that master's degree she'd been chasing, so that was her first and foremost focus, career-wise. Still, this was an idea she just couldn't let lie. She kept finding herself kicking it around. At first, she tried to pawn it off on some of her friends in business school—people she thought might be better equipped or better positioned to make it happen. But those efforts never went anywhere, because most of her friends were all bark, no bite—you know, wannabe entrepreneurs who talked the talk but who didn't seem to have the drive or the grind to start in on a start-up.

Finally, after just a few months, that first lightbulb moment lit another one. That's how it happens, right? You rub two sparks together and next thing you know you're on fire, and here Kristina decided to go all-in on the idea herself—with the help of her boyfriend (and soon-to-be-husband), who just happened to be a food scientist. (Note to readers: if you're looking to create a food product, it's a good idea to marry a food scientist!) She came up with a name and slogan for her product: TurboPUP—the Complete K9 Meal Bar. Then she registered the business, started messing with formulas and recipes, and pretty soon a business was born.

YOU ARE WHAT YOU EAT (OR, YOUR DOG IS WHAT YOUR DOG EATS)

Looking back, Kristina can see the benefits of her military training in the way she approached her start-up business. "The Air Force doesn't exactly tell you, 'Okay, you're going to accomplish this objective by doing A, B, and C,'" she reports. "No, the Air Force says, 'Here's the goal, here's your team, figure it out.' So for me the goal was clear. I knew what I had, and I knew what I wanted, so I had to figure it out, that's all. I didn't have any kind of culinary background, but I had my boyfriend at the time, so that was my team. And I didn't have any kind of business background, so I joined a bunch of entrepreneur groups for veterans, and that was really the spark for me. Just the chance to learn from all these other veterans, and to embrace together what we had done, what we were hoping to do, that was such a great catalyst."

All Kristina had going for her at this early stage was what may or may not have been a winning concept—she still had to develop the product, and turn it into an *actual* winner, and for that she leaned heavily on her live-in food scientist. By this point they'd moved to Oregon, where they were living in a tiny studio apartment. Yet somehow they managed to turn their entire kitchen area into a working laboratory. It wasn't exactly the industrialized food preparation lab you need in order to get going on a project like this, but Kristina had learned from her time in the service to make do with what she had. Here we have a *power of broke* meets *rise and grind* kind of story, because she was at this thing all hours of the day. Whatever free time she had, she filled it with this right here. She experimented with hundreds of recipes, hundreds of concepts.

One of the first bars her boyfriend came up with didn't exactly fly with her target customer. "Our dog wouldn't give it the time of day," Kristina remembers. "He just wouldn't eat it. So, of course, we had to come up with something that dogs would actually like, right? Otherwise, what were we doing?"

Going in, Kristina thought it might take just a few months to develop a recipe, but it took almost two years. She wasn't frustrated by the delays so much as she was fascinated by all there was to learn. During that time, she immersed herself in all the various standards and requirements, and studied the trends in the pet food industry. Her guiding principle was to come up with a product that was healthy and made with natural, human-grade ingredients. It would be 100 percent American sourced, 100 percent grain-free, and 100 percent natural. Her read on the market was that active dog owners pay good and close attention to what they feed their active dogs, the same way they pay good and close attention to the foods they put into their own bodies, so she was less concerned with keeping the cost of her product down than she was with keeping the quality high.

Soon, with a recipe finally in hand (something Dunkan would actually eat!), she was able to start selling her bars out of her kitchen, handling most of the fulfillment and shipping herself. Her TurboPUP brand was a long way from being a scalable business, but at least she was in the marketplace, getting a great response from customers and positioning herself for a push into some kind of mass distribution.

"I never really saw this as a mom-and-pop business," she shares. "The people who do that, and who do that well, I'm all for it. Good for them. *Great* for them. But my thing was to really make a living out of this, and to get there quickly, and I didn't think we could do that by doing door-to-door."

All along, when friends and contacts learned of Kristina's TurboPUP product, people kept trying to steer her to *Shark Tank,* which had very quickly become a kind of Holy Grail opportunity for small business owners. Kristina was familiar with the show, but she wasn't looking for that kind of an assist, that kind of exposure. Still, it kept coming up, and it worked out that the show was looking to feature veterans in an upcoming segment. Kristina found out about it through Syracuse University's Institute for Veteran and Military Families, where she'd been receiving some invaluable business guidance.

POWER FACT: More than 30,000 companies apply to *Shark Tank* each year.... *Only 200 applicants are brought in to tape a segment, and just over 100 of those segments make it on the air—but, hey, you never know.*

"I have this weird, twisted belief that if you get nudged three times to do the same thing, it must mean something," she says. "My motto is, if a door is open, I'm gonna walk through it." And here was this door, not opened wide just yet, only opened a crack, but there were all these people in her life, people she admired and trusted, telling her to push her way through.

So she did—tried to, anyway.

Sure enough, the *Shark Tank* producers were into Kristina's story. For one thing, her business was unique—and perfect for television. The dog lovers out there would be all over it. For another, they found her military background compelling and perfect for a veteran-themed show. For her part, Kristina wasn't really looking for the publicity the show can offer, or even for an investment partner. But she knew enough to recognize an opportunity, so she reached for it—never expecting anything to come out of it, but reaching just the same.

Well, it turned out that Kristina's reach was exactly in line with her grasp. The way it works, when you're invited onto the show, is that there are no guarantees. We make that clear, all through the process. Forget that you might not get the deal you want from me or any of my fellow Sharks—your segment might not even make it on the air. And even if it does make the cut, the pitches are edited down to just ten minutes or so in the finished broadcast, even though they can run an hour or two, sometimes even longer in the studio.

What Kristina had going for her here, other than what she *already* had going for her with a killer concept and an inspiring story, was that she wasn't counting on or even really expecting a deal. A lot of folks, they come on the show, and there's *everything* riding on their appearance. They're nervous, because the stakes are so high, and their lack of confidence comes across in their pitch. Or maybe they're desperate, and that comes across, too. But Kristina, she was cool, calm, chill. She didn't *need* to be here; she was here for the ride.

"Somebody gave me a great piece of advice as I was getting ready to go on the show," she says. "They said, 'Just manifest the best possible outcome.' So I prayed to the higher power and told myself I was going to have faith that the best possible outcome is going to happen when I'm out there, even though I had no idea at the time what that best possible outcome might be. Whether it's getting an investment, or not getting an investment, getting on the air or not getting on the air, I kept telling myself that the best thing will happen."

INVEST IN THE PERSON, INVEST IN YOURSELF

Kristina came to *Shark Tank* with her other dog Odin, Dunkan's running buddy, seeking $100,000 for a 20 percent stake in her company, slapping a $500,000 valuation on her business. My fel-

low Sharks thought that number was high, based on current TurboPUP sales—and so did I, frankly.

Even so, I took one look at Odin, and I was sold—and right
away, I put on my Petco Foundation hat and started thinking
how this simple product could really be a boon to the health and
wellness of active dogs. But I also liked the *grind* in this woman. I
looked at her and said, "Obviously you don't sleep, just like me."
And I liked the potential in her business and brand, so I offered
her the money for a 40 percent stake. One of the things she said
in her pitch that struck me was how her friends all joked that
she'd come up with the name for her product. They said it was
because she only knows two speeds: *turbo* or *off*.

I was also taken by her military background. My thinking
was, A woman who has done three tours for our country will not
go to sleep on this. She was in it to win it . . . and now, so was I.

In the end, we did a deal for $100,000 at 35 percent, and
we were both thrilled—Kristina, for the investment, and the
chance to learn whatever it was I had to teach her about ramping up her business; and me, for the chance to help take this
powerful woman to a new level, and maybe make a little money
besides.

And now here we are, a couple of years into our partnership,
and it turns out I've got a lot to learn from Kristina as well. She's
a new mom, and I'm a new-and-improved dad—her daughter,
Madeline, was born just a couple of months before my youngest
daughter, Minka. Got to say, I'm a little bit in awe at how Kristina's able to balance work and play and parenting. I know how
tough it is to make time in my schedule just to hang with Minka,
and here I see Kristina keeping all these balls in the air, and
growing her business (*our* business!), while still being the primary
caregiver to little Madeline—pretty inspiring.

If I had to come up with one word to describe Kristina's

work ethic, I'd say she was *efficient*. Really efficient. There's not a bit of wasted energy with this woman. That's something she picked up at the Air Force Academy, the ability to see a straight line to her goals and to walk that straight line, no matter what. She's always looking for ways to get the most out of her time, the biggest bang for her buck. When she started the business, for example, she used to go to a lot of trade shows, but after a while she thought the "hand-selling" that was happening on the floors of these shows was a lot less effective than connecting with customers online. She was also recognizing that she could move more product as the public face of the brand, making television appearances or sitting for newspapers interviews, so she started chasing news outlets for media coverage.

....

POWER FACT: 76 percent of so-called mompreneurs used their personal savings as a primary funding source . . . *What I take from this stat is that women are often passionate about their new businesses, and willing to bet on themselves.*

....

These days, Kristina continues to run the business from her home—to keep a lid on costs, but also to be fully available to Madeline and do the mommy thing. That freedom to choose her own path we talked about earlier? Well, it came to light in a big-time way. After conceiving the business and throwing in with me, Kristina moved with her new husband to Oregon, but they started to realize their lifestyle was unsustainable in the Pacific Northwest, so when Kristina became pregnant they started looking at other parts of the country, eventually settling on a move to Vermont. "We were headed for trouble if we stayed out in Oregon," Kristina says. "Financially, it just didn't make sense, and we figured out there were a lot of companies in Vermont that could use a food scientist, so we packed everything we could fit into our two cars and drove across the country when I was nine months pregnant."

When Kristina was wrestling with the decision to move, she told me, she had a vision of her life going forward when the path before her was both clear and uncertain. And she looks back on that vision as an authentic, defining moment. "I knew what was going to happen if we stayed in Oregon," she says. "We were screwed. No doubt about it, we were screwed. And I also knew that if we moved to Vermont, there was like a fifty percent chance we were screwed. So we just thought, Let's go for the better odds."

FIND ORDER IN CHAOS

One of the ways she's managed to stay on point, to balance the many different aspects of the TurboPUP business—alongside the business of parenting—is to assign certain routines to certain days of the week—a straightforward, elegant approach to task management.

"I try not to make appointments on Mondays," she shares, "because on Mondays, I have to fulfill all the orders from the weekend. Plus, the house is like a tornado after the weekend, there's laundry everywhere, and that's the day I just have to catch up on everything."

Tuesdays, she's on to long-term planning, and she also makes time to see and ride her horse. (Oh yeah, forgot to mention—she has a horse.) Wednesdays, it's back to fulfillment. Thursdays, it might be new product development. Fridays, she's back to the stables again, and maybe finding time to work on marketing or promotion.

It's a smart way to compartmentalize the many facets of a small business, and to keep things manageable. "It's not set in stone to the point where if it doesn't happen on this daily schedule it's the end of the world or anything," she allows. "But unless there's something crazy going on that I have to get to, I try to stick to this routine."

Another of Kristina's secrets to finding order in chaos, she says, is working out, which helps to keep her centered and focused. And her workouts are no joke: she used to do a lot of weight lifting, but when she got pregnant she shifted gears and started doing mostly cardio work. She mixes it up—swimming, running, cross-country skiing, snowshoeing. Other days, she does the StairMaster thing, or the elliptical thing, or the back-country skiing thing, or the mountain climbing thing.

I like to multitask when I work out, maybe return a couple of phone calls when I'm on the treadmill, return some emails, but Kristina doesn't do that. She says, **"My time at the gym is my 'me' time. I don't want anything messing with my 'me' time. That's my gift to myself."**

Kristina compartmentalizes her social and professional networks, too. She's got a group of friends and contacts from her entrepreneurial journey. There's a group of pet lovers, a group of young moms, a group of military-based pals. She's learned to lean on one group or another, depending on what's going on in her life.

"That's really been one of the keys for me," she says, "having all these different people in my life I can lean on for different things. It's like, no offense, but I would never call one of my friends who doesn't have kids to ask them for advice about parenting. And I wouldn't ask someone who's not in business for advice on my business. My best friend in the whole world, I met her at the Air Force Academy, and as much as I rely on her, I'm not going to her for help with TurboPUP."

That life of service Kristina set out to live on the home front? Already, she's helped to create an entirely new product category that makes it easier for dogs—and their owners—to keep fit, healthy, and active, and she earmarks a certain percentage of the proceeds to go to various nonprofits, very often in support of veterans groups. And even though she didn't initially set out to start a business, today she's determined to grow TurboPUP into a recognized and trusted brand. (Right now, her meal bars are available online at www .turbopup.com and at specialty stores around the country.)

And I'm sure she will—same way I'm sure this determined young woman will do anything she sets out to do. Because, hey, when your grind is as on point as hers, anything (and, *everything!*) is possible.

Kristina's Grind Checklist

✓ put yourself in position to receive a new idea—doesn't mean you have to climb to the top of a mountain to reach for the sky, but be on the lookout for an idea that just might change your life . . .

✓ lay a solid foundation—can't think of a better building block than a military background, but even we civilians can de-velop good, purposeful habits and learn to move about with military-like precision . . .

✓ know that strength leads to strength—meaning, if you at-tack your days with a relentless passion, if you attack your goals with relentless precision, you're bound to get a strong result . . .

✓ don't quit—think how easy it would have been for Kristina to pack it in after her dog rejected her first recipes, but she kept at it because she believed in herself . . .

✓ if you're looking to develop a formula or recipe for a new food product, it helps to be married to a food scientist . . .

✓ if you're planning to start a family, look for business opportunities that allow you to work from home or keep a flexible schedule—this one's easier said than done, I know, but if you keep it in mind as you start in on your career or launch a new business, you might make certain choices along the way to help you make room for the demands of parenthood in your busy schedule . . .

....

For more information on Kristina and how she uses the
Rise and Grind mindset, check out
www.DaymondJohn.com/Rise/Kristina

FIVE

A DAY IN THE LIFE OF A SHARK

I'M TRAVELING SO much these days, I'm afraid I might lose my rhythm, my sense of routine . . . my mojo.

I'm not alone in this—a lot of folks are working their *grind* away from home. It's easy to get off your game when you're traveling, but there's never a better time to refocus or refigure your routines than when you're on the road. And, if you're looking for an in-your-face reminder of how hard you're working, how dedicated you are to whatever goals you're chasing, how single-minded you can be in the pursuit of even the most remote possibility . . . look no further than your travel receipts at the end of each year.

Hey, there's a good chance you're traveling as you read this. I know in my case that I tend to get most of my reading (and audiobook-listening) done when I step away from my day-to-day—my *writing,* too! But for every good habit that finds you on the road, there are all these drawbacks that can trip you up. So I thought I'd spend some time going over some of the positive behaviors I've tried to put in place to keep my days running smooth, no matter where I am. To do so, I'm about to give you an up-close-and-personal look at a typical day from my typically crazy travel schedule—though as I sit down to write it all out I'm noticing that it's really more like thirty-six hours, if we're being technical about it.

But you know what? Sometimes when you're on the road and grinding hard the days meld together and it all starts to feel like one giant day anyway, so stay with me. . . .

ROAD WARRIOR

On Wednesday, April 5, just as I was putting the finishing touches on this book, I left New York for one of those reverse red-eye flights to California. It's not the most convenient flight on the departure board, but I find the evening and late-night hours to be the least disruptive when I'm flying East Coast to West Coast: It leaves me with a full day to work in the office before heading to the airport, and allows me to hit the ground running when I land in sunny California first thing the next morning. (Okay, so maybe I'm not *running*, exactly, after a late cross-country flight, but you get the idea.) That time zone change can trip up your body clock if you're not careful, but I find that if I'm breezing in and out of town for just a day or two, mine never really notices the shift. I usually don't wear a watch these days, so there's no need to reset a clock. I rely on the locals (and the GPS-synced clock on my cellphone) to get me where I'm going on time and in one piece.

This time out, I was headed to San Francisco, where I'd hop a car for the hour-and-a-half drive to Napa for a speech I was due to give the next morning. The plan was to do my speech, finish up in the late morning, and then head back to San Francisco to catch a flight home—what folks like me who travel for a good chunk of their living call a quick hit. The idea is you fly clear across the country, take your meeting or make your presentation or do whatever it is you're there to do, and then double back before anyone at home even notices you're gone. So how do I stay alert, on my game, and productive under these crazy circumstances?

Here, let me break it down:

- **Wednesday, April 5, 8:00 p.m.**—*depart New York for flight to San Francisco*

  Like I said, this is a tough time of day to fly from New York to California. There are pluses and minuses to it, but I tend to think the good outweighs the bad. On the downside, I'm never sure how much to sleep and how much to just plow ahead and try to be productive on the plane. There's this trapped block of time, free from distractions, so my instinct is to get things done while I'm in the air, but I know I have a long day ahead of me, and I also know that folks on the ground waiting to hear from me on this or that are conditioned to assume I'm offline when I'm flying, so I try to take advantage of that and hide out for a bit.

  The way it usually works is I board early and try to catch up on emails and texts while we're getting ready to take off. There's usually a half hour to play with when you're just sitting on the tarmac. Then I'll spend the first half hour or so of the flight catching up on the reading I have to do, before drifting off—that's kind of what happened here. I had a lot of pages to go over in this book, some new material I had to write, and I made some good progress . . . for a while, until I hit a kind of wall. There's something about the white noise of the plane, the whoosh of air travel that always rocks me to sleep—same way I tend to drift off when I'm on a train. It's like I lose myself in the rhythm of the engines and then I'm gone.

[Getaway Takeaway #1: Plan to take advantage of your travel time by catching up on your reading or focusing on a long-term goal.]

- **Wednesday, April 5, 11:30 p.m.**—*arrive San Francisco, depart for Napa Valley Marriott*

Another trapped block of time is the long car service ride from the airport, but here it was around midnight in California, three in the morning back home, and I was dragging. I'd catnapped on the plane—though nowhere near enough that I could step off feeling refreshed.

I was traveling with Danny Estrella, my audio-visual guy who accompanies me on a lot of my speaking trips. Danny's a top deejay in his own right, one of the best sound and tech engineers out there—a talent he puts on full display as an entrepreneur through his Music 2 the Max event-staging company.

One of the things I like to do on these long car rides is create some videos I can post on social media, so I had Danny hold the GoPro while I recorded two separate bits of content. In the first, I riffed on the importance of keeping it "green" when you're on the road. I'd just stayed in a Westin hotel a couple of nights before, and spent some time reading about their effort to protect the environment. I was inspired by the way certain companies give back and take the lead on important social issues, which more often than not comes back to help their bottom line. So I did a one-minute call-to-action type video, just off the top of my head—something we could chop up at a later date and blast out. Then I did a short riff on appreciation, because I'd just received an amazing bouquet of flowers from Carlos Santana, thanking me for reaching out to him to include his thoughts for this book. It pushed me to think how we can make a big impact on people with small gestures of kindness, and how we should make an effort to show our gratitude and share our blessings and pay them forward. So I talked about *that,* too.

Somewhere in there I also found time to read over my goals, which is something I do to start each day—and since it was a little unclear when this long day began and when it would end, this seemed as good a time as any.

Usually I'll also try to pile up a lot of the interview requests I get and schedule them for when I'm traveling. Why? Because there's a lot of trapped time on the road, and I'd much rather fill the time doing press when I'm away from the office. Think about it: **When I'm in New York, I've got a whole staff I need to check in with, all these different projects I need to catch up on, meetings I have to sit in on with my team, so why would I want to take time away from *that* if it's not absolutely necessary?** I also want to get home and spend some time with my family. So whenever a reporter reaches out for an interview, or even if someone just wants to pick my brain on something that's not directly connected to one of my businesses, I'll ask them to hit me up when I'm on the road, when there are fewer demands on my time—that way I can give them the time they deserve without taking anything away from the time *I* deserve.

[Getaway Takeaway #2: You can always carve out a few minutes *somewhere* to stick to your daily rituals, even if it's in the backseat of a moving car.]

....

POWER FACT: When people set and identify specific goals, it leads to higher performance 90 percent of the time. . . . *Do the math, people!*

....

- **Thursday, April 6, 1:30 a.m.**—*check-in, Napa Valley Marriott*

    Sometimes when you arrive late to your hotel room, all you want to do is crash, but if you've got something the next day you need to be ready for, that's not always an option. So what did I do when I got to my room? I shaved my head . . . natch. Why? Because I was feeling that "five o'clock stubble" you hear people talk about—only it was damn near five o'clock in the morning (New York time) and the stubble was on my head, not my face. I wanted to look *good* the next morning when I did my thing, and I knew I wouldn't feel like shaving when I got up, so I got it out of the way. While I was at it, I laid out my suit and my shoes for the next morning, and ran the iron over the shirt I planned to wear. That's how I handle chores and the daily maintenance of living—I identify what needs doing, then I just get to it. This way, nothing piles up for later.

    I should mention here that I didn't take the time to do my usual push-ups, or to check my emails one final time, because I don't like to do either of those things within an hour of turning in. Exercise gets me amped up in such a way that it's sometimes hard to fall asleep, and there's all kinds of research to support the fact that the light from a cellphone or any electronic screen can mess with your body clock and sleep cycle when you're close to bedtime.

By two o'clock I was in bed, and as my head hit the pillow I took the time to pray before nodding off. I don't usually pray out loud, and I don't drop to my knees, but I find that a few moments of peaceful prayer and reflection really helps to ground me at the end of each day. One of the things I do when I pray is to reflect with intention. I spend a lot of time thinking of how to tap the power in the people around me, how to send out these ripples of appreciation for the good that has come my way, the opportunities that have come my way, and hope that somehow those ripples will reach to some other shore.

[Getaway Takeaway #3: Remember to seek stillness, no matter what else you've got going on.]

- **Thursday, April 6, 6:00 a.m.**—*time to rise and grind*

I had set the alarm the night before, but I got up on my own anyway. That's how I'm wired. My body knows what it's got to do—only, I don't always trust it, so I call in the alarm for backup. First thing I did when I got up is iron a couple of other items, because I still wasn't sure what I wanted to wear. I didn't want to head out to this morning's event looking all disheveled and tired! Next I tried on a couple of outfits, to see what went with what. A lot of times I'll be bouncing around to six or seven cities on the same trip, and I've got to look smart and sharp for different types of meetings, press interviews, formal presentations, and all kinds of social events. On longer trips, that means I'll pack a traditional black suit, with a black tie—**basic black is appropriate for just about any occasion, and with a white dress shirt, a white T-shirt, and a couple of belts, I'm good to go.**

I can get away with a bunch of different looks. I got my start in the fashion business—so, right or wrong, people have come to trust me on this. I've developed a certain personal style, so I can be comfortable and maybe even a little trendy wearing a classic FB ball cap and a hoodie. But I can also pull off a classic power suit, set off by a pair of diamond stud earrings, so I tailor my look to wherever it is I'm going, whoever it is I'm meeting. You are what you wear—or, at least, you are whatever *statement* you're trying to make with your clothes.

Still, if you want to know the truth, **I probably spend more time worrying about what I eat when I'm on the road than what I wear.** That's why the protein packs are key. I'm getting up at four or five in the morning to catch a predawn flight, and my stomach's just not up at that hour. That's way too early to eat, right? (Or I can just get rid of that comma and that question mark and make an entirely different point: "That's way too early to eat right.") That's why, when I travel, I always pack my vitamins and a shaker bottle with five protein packs, so that if I'm racing straight to my hotel or the venue where I'm speaking or whatever, I can get some nourishment without having to take the time to have a sit-down meal.

Today I was doing an event, so as I chose my suit, I took the time to call my two older daughters. My oldest, Destiny, was stuck in the Atlanta airport due to nasty weather, so I was able to call around and set her up with a rental car and help her sort through the mess she was in. And I was happy to do it, too—because when you're a long-distance dad like I am, you grab at whatever time your kids can throw your way, even if they're just reaching out for a little help.

[Getaway Takeaway #4: Looking sharp and feeling

sharp keep you thinking sharp, so the time you put into your appearance (and your diet!) when you're on the road always pays great dividends.]

....

POWER FACT: Brigham Young University research-ers report that workers with unhealthy diets are 66 per-cent more likely to show a drop in productivity levels than healthy eaters. . . . *You are what you eat, after all.*

....

- **Thursday, April 6, 8:20 a.m.**—*arrive at venue*

    Whenever I turn up to give a talk, I meet with the organizers to go over their agenda . . . and mine. I mean, I'm traveling all this way to talk to these good people, carving out all this time, so I want to make double sure I hit all the right notes for them, while at the same time covering the ground that's important to me. I'm there at the pleasure of the host or sponsor, so it's important for me to understand what they hope to get out of the deal.

    After freshening up, I sat back down and studied this questionnaire I always have my hosts fill out, which is like a "cheat sheet" for me as I get ready to do my thing. If it's a company that brought me in to speak, it'll tell me who their competitors are, where their market lies, what new products they've got coming out. Basically, everything I need to know will be written down for me on this docu-ment, so I can go over it all one final time and internal-ize it and then have it come back out of me in a way that doesn't feel rehearsed. I don't work from a script, so every time I give a talk it's different, but I do have certain beats I want to be sure to hit, certain slides I might want to put

up to illustrate a point, so that's what I tend to study during these final few minutes.

It's written into my contract that I need thirty minutes
of "alone" time before I hit the stage—that's the time I
need to get my head around what I want to say, and get
in the zone. That time is sacred to me, man. I try not to
let the outside world interfere, which means I don't look
at my phone to make sure I'm not distracted by texts or
emails or the news and trending issues of the day.

[Getaway Takeaway #5: It's not enough to just *do* your
homework . . . you've got to find the energy to get what
you learned across.]

....

POWER FACT: Organizations are tapping the
power of public speaking to engage their employees more
than ever before. . . . *Recent studies show that companies
invest approximately $720 million annually on speaking
programs—a number that's expected to double in the
next few years.*

....

• **Thursday, April 6, 9:00 a.m.**—*offer keynote address*
The deal when I come in to deliver one of these keynote addresses is I commit to spending two hours. Most
times, that means I talk for an hour, and then I give them
another hour immediately after for a question-and-answer
session, a meet-and-greet, maybe take some photos and
sign some books. On this morning in Napa, I ran a little
long. I knew this because I had Danny in my ear for the
whole second half of my presentation, telling me we were
hitting our marks about ten minutes late, but it felt to me
like I had a good momentum going and I couldn't think

what to cut from the rest of my talk. So I just kept going, figured I would tack on a little extra time to the meet-and-greet. I wanted everyone in that arena or auditorium to find a meaningful takeaway in all this, right down to the very last question.

[Getaway Takeaway #6: You've got to give to get. . . . In my case, this comes from years of me being on the other side of the equation, as the guy who brings in the talent to motivate or educate the troops. . . . That means I always try to give value when I'm brought in to give a keynote address, because I know that if I don't, I won't honor the time of all the people who came out to hear me speak.]

- **Thursday, April 6, 2:00 p.m.**—*lunch meeting with* Shark Tank *partners*

  After grabbing a few winks in the Uber on the way back into San Francisco, it was lunchtime, which for most people living the *rise and grind* mindset usually means one thing: a lunch meeting. Hey, you've got to eat, so might as well use that time productively. I won't bore you with the specifics of my meeting, but I do want to make the point that whenever I travel I look to double-dip on my time in another city. To me, that doesn't *just* mean sightseeing, although I will take the time to soak in the local attractions whenever possible. No, that means reaching out to connect with colleagues and partners and fellow influencers in all these different markets, to see if we might get together. There's nothing like a face-to-face meeting to move things along on a project, and here when I booked this gig with the reinsurers, I made sure to reach out to my partners in the Bay Area to let them know I was coming to town.

[Getaway Takeaway #7: I'm a big fan of double-dipping. You can't always be in two places at once, but when you're on the road you can often knock off two or three objectives on a single trip.]

....

POWER FACT: **Ray Kroc was a traveling salesman when he came across the McDonald brothers' unique design for a milkshake machine, inspiring him to pursue a partnership. . . . *You never know where or when inspiration will hit, so keep your ear to the ground and your eyes open as you travel.***

....

• **Thursday, April 6, 3:30 p.m.**—*return calls and emails from hotel room*

   By this point, it's 6:30 p.m. on the East Coast, the butt end of a full day at my Shark Group offices in New York, so I take the time to call and check in with my team. I had planned on this, so my office was waiting on my call, and I spent a couple of minutes to check with a couple of different people running a couple of different projects.

   Then I tackled my email, the plan being to get through as many emails as I could before heading down to the hotel gym at five o'clock, but there was an urgent piece of business I had to respond to with one of our *Shark Tank* producers, and also a note from my daughter that I had to do some follow-up on, so that took some time away from my task. Still, I knew I had to stick to my schedule if I was going to get in a workout, so when five o'clock came around, the laptop got powered down.

   [Getaway Takeaway #8: My daily planner usually

goes out the window when I travel, but wherever possible I try to frame my days with set meetings at set times.]

- **Thursday, April 6, 5:00 p.m.**—*workout session, Sheraton Four Points gym*

  I was looking down the barrel of another long flight, so I wanted to be sure to get my cardio in before heading back to the airport. It sometimes feels like I'm fighting a losing battle, trying to eat healthy and keep fit when I'm traveling, so I make an extra effort to get it right. I walked on the treadmill for forty-five minutes, returning as many calls as I could. Out of the corner of my eye, I was watching the CNN news feed.

  For me, the perfect hotel gym is quiet, without a whole lot of activity. That way I can hop on the treadmill for a couple of hours and make a bunch of calls. If it's a busy gym, where talking on the phone doesn't make sense, I'll do my push-ups, lift weights, use the machines . . . but I'll cut my workout short. I'll go hard for a half hour or so, but since I'm not able to multitask like I am on the treadmill, I'll need to get back on the phone. I can't be spending all day working on my Greek-god physique!

  [Getaway Takeaway #9: Workouts at home are great, but you may find that when you're away from home they matter most of all.]

- **Thursday, April 6, 6:30 p.m.**—*call to Heather and Minka*

  I set it up with Heather that I would call home at nine thirty her time so I could catch Minka right after her bath, and just before bed. We FaceTimed for a half hour or so, and it was a good and blessed thing. Really, this time with Minka is the most delicious time in our lives.

Doesn't matter if it's long-distance, or if I'm right there in the room with her, this right here is the sweet spot of my day. Since she was born, I've been shutting things down at work earlier than I used to so I can make it back to the apartment in time to give her a bath and spend a precious hour or two with her before she goes to sleep. If I need to go out, or meet someone for dinner or whatever, I always try to push it to after her bedtime, because I don't want to miss these moments, and when I'm on the road I'm always grateful for the technological assist in keeping connected to my little girl. Seeing her face on a computer screen isn't the same as the real thing, but it's a whole lot better than missing out entirely.

[Getaway Takeaway #10: Thank God for Skype and WhatsApp and FaceTime and all the other ways we can keep connected to family when we travel.]

....

POWER FACT: **A Pew Research Center study reports that 47 percent of Americans surveyed believe Internet access and cellphones have had a positive impact on their interactions with family, while only 4 percent report a negative impact....** *These connections are never more important than when you're on the road, so keep your phone charged and make a special effort to check in at home.*

....

- **Thursday, April 6, 8:05 p.m.**—*arrive at San Francisco airport*

    After a shower and a room-service dinner (salmon, and lots of ice water to keep me hydrated on the long flight), I Ubered my way to the airport, getting there just about a half hour before my scheduled departure time. A lot of folks, they might think I was crazy to cut it this close, arriving to the airport, but I'd been traveling so much I had the whole airport thing down. Also, I hate wasting time at the airport, so I try to avoid it at all costs. Time is money, right?

Once on board, I managed to return a bunch of emails before we went wheels up. I also checked my social media feeds and put up a post or two, and pulled out the book pages I was working on so they were within easy reach. Then I watched a little bit of television, just to rest my mind for a stretch, before starting in to read. Within a half hour, I was out—and I didn't wake up until someone got on the PA system and announced that the flight crew was preparing the cabin for landing.

[Getaway Takeaway #11: Yeah, the early bird catches the worm and all that, but those worms can get pretty slippery if you're totally beat, so make sure you're well rested when you travel. Even if it's just a power nap, grab your sleep when you can.]

- **Friday, April 7, 5:30 a.m.**—*arrive in New York*

    It was tomorrow already when we touched down at JFK, but I didn't reach for my phone as soon as we landed. I do that sometimes, but I figured everyone I knew, everyone I was doing any kind of business with, was still asleep. When I did finally power up my phone, it was to read over my goals and get going on my day. It wasn't until I was actually sitting in an Uber that I started to work my way through the messages that had somehow lined up in wait for me overnight. I have a system for plowing through my emails, I should mention. I erase anything from an email address I don't recognize, because

I've got a thing about viruses. What that means is, if we don't already know each other, you'll have to reach me through other channels. Next, I erase anything I'm cc'd on, because I've come to realize that if there's something I need to respond to on one of those threads, it'll come back to me before long. That usually just leaves me with a few questions I might have to answer on an ongoing piece of business, maybe a few appointments I have to make or confirm. I also used the time to leave a few voice notes for my team. These voice notes are a great time saver, especially with my dyslexia. A message that might take me ten or fifteen minutes to write out, I can knock off in under a minute, without worrying over my spelling or my grammar.

[Getaway Takeaway #12: Know how you work and what works best for you. If you're the type who needs to plow through your in-box all at once, then go for it. If you're like me, and you've got your own system for pruning those messages so you're only dealing with front-burner stuff, then go for that instead.]

- **Friday, April 7, 6:30 a.m.**—*return home*

  Minka was still asleep when I got back to the apartment, so I slipped quietly into bed and tried to catch a few winks before she woke up. A half hour later she came bouncing into the bedroom and started climbing around on my head—it was like I'd never left. If I'm there when she wakes up in the morning, and if I'm there to put her to bed in the evening, I could be jetting all over the planet in between and she might never know the difference.

  [Getaway Takeaway #13: Be it ever so humble, people, there *is* no place like home, and the thought of rest-ing my head on my own pillow after a long journey is often enough to help me power through those last difficult miles.]

....

POWER FACT: In our mobile economy, Americans are on the road more than ever before. US workers took more than 450 million business trips in 2016.... *Almost 40 percent of those trips were to attend a conference or an event.*

....

So that about covers it—only the play-by-play I've just offered doesn't *really* reflect the crazy whirlwind frenzy that seems to find me whenever I'm on the road for one of these quick-hit trips. The power, the urgency, the nonstop pace . . . it feels like there's no let-up when I'm in the middle of it. And then, when I'm finally back home in New York, it just keeps going. My day wasn't really *done.* It hadn't even started, really, seeing that it was still only about 8 a.m. (or 5 a.m. California time). It was time to *rise and grind* again, and I was ready to get to it. Now, when I set it all down on paper and relive this long day in a beat-by-beat sort of way, it seems like it must have been exhausting—but, got to admit, it didn't feel that way as the day was unfolding. Really, it was an absolute joy. I tell that to people and they look at me like I'm putting one over on them, but that's the God's honest truth. There is no burden in what I do. There is no sense of drudgery, or feeling like I'm dragging, or wishing that the pace of my life could just slow down. I never catch myself thinking it should be someone else's turn to rise and grind and "make the donuts." Not at all. And I suppose it's possible to look on and find these little points of pause in my day, where I could have easily taken some time for myself, maybe pulled back for a bit. But I love what I do, so it doesn't even occur to me to take a time-out—never has, never will. I'd rather be rising and grinding.

SWIMMING WITH THE SHARKS

Speaking of a day in the life, one question I often get is, "What does a typical day on the *Shark Tank* set look like?" So before we move on, let me give you a little peek behind the scenes. Days on the set of *Shark Tank* are the ultimate rise and grind, to say the least. When we're shooting I'll get up at five thirty and head straight to my trailer. I'll check out my wardrobe, figure out what I'm going to wear. I'm in the makeup chair by seven o'clock in the morning. It takes about an hour to make me look beautiful, and during that time I'm going over production notes, maybe talking to some of my fellow Sharks, or calling in to my staff back in New York. By then it's already ten, eleven o'clock on the East Coast, so I want to check in.

....

POWER FACT: According to *Fitness* magazine, people who wake up before 7 a.m. report lower stress levels
than those who sleep in.... *The message here: rise and
grind!*

....

Keep in mind, when I say I spend some time looking over my notes, we don't receive any information on the people coming in to pitch us. We don't get any background, or supporting details, or anything—we hear each pitch cold. And as I listen to each pitch, I go through my mental Rolodex, trying to think who I know, who I've worked with, who might be in a position to help me advance this idea, either with distribution or experience or whatever. I write notes to myself to remind me of the points I'll want to consider (sales history, market trends) in case I want to pursue a deal, but it all happens on the fly. There's no such thing as a heads-up in the *Shark Tank*.

The last thing I do before we're called to the set is pray. A lot of folks are surprised when I share this with them, but I find that offering up a few words of prayer, alone, is a great way to ground me before the long shooting day gets going. **It pushes me to reflect on what's important in my life, to be thankful and mindful of the many blessings that have come my way, and to honor the fact that what we're doing on *Shark Tank* is helping to inspire millions of people—not just the folks who come on the show to pitch their ideas or their businesses, but the folks at home who look on and are encouraged to start believing in themselves.**

We shoot from nine o'clock in the morning to about one in the afternoon, when we break for lunch. The goal is to knock out five pitches in that time, if we can. Some of the pitches run short, and some of them run long, so we'll hit or miss our mark, depending. Then we're back in our chairs by two o'clock and we go at it again until seven, maybe eight, when we break for the day.

On some nights I'll head out to dinner with one of my fellow Sharks—or maybe we'll all go out together. Or maybe I'll have a dinner meeting arranged with one of my *Shark Tank* partners, or a client, or a friend or family member who happens to be in town, or maybe my agent.

I'll try to be home most nights by eleven o'clock, at which point I'll take some time to catch up on emails and put out any fires back home—making sure I give myself at least an hour or so from the time I power down on my phone to the time I go to bed, usually by one o'clock.

Next day, same deal. We'll shoot for eighteen days over the course of a single season, broken up into two nine-day sessions.

Most years those sessions happen in June and September, and most times it works out that there are a bunch of different events and media days in which the network expects us to participate while we're out in Los Angeles.

We don't shoot for nine days straight. We get a two-day break, so from time to time someone will arrange a nearby road trip for a large group of us—like, say, to Vegas or Disney or Palm Springs. Usually, though, we go our separate ways. Mark Cuban heads home to Dallas, for example. Me, since home is so far away, I'll usually stay in Los Angeles, especially if I've brought my family out, and I'll use the time to catch up on my sleep and take long morning walks on the beach.

There was a time in there when I swapped out those long walks for a two- or three-mile run, but those days are over. And it's not that running was hard on my knees, like it is for some folks. No, it's hard on my drinking. (Or maybe it's the other way around.) I say this as a joke, but that's one of the pitfalls of all that time on the road—there's usually a whole lot of partying. It always reminds me of that great line from Billy Joel in "Piano Man," when he sings about all those long nights in the bar while the businessmen slowly get stoned. (Hey, it's better than drinking alone, right?) All that partying, all those nights out, that's just the nature of my business, comes with the territory. Remember, I got my start in the clubs, slinging FUBU, chasing our favorite hip-hop artists, and I still find that I'm drawn to that environment. This isn't a good thing or a bad thing, but it *is* something I need to pay attention to, especially when I'm traveling and it becomes all too easy to shake the good habits I might be working on at home. Plus, I have to keep it real *and* realistic: it's when I'm out and partying that a lot of my business gets done—and, goes without saying, whenever you close a deal or find something to celebrate, it tends to come with a round of drinks.

Look, I'm not about to put it out there that I'm perfect. I

have my flaws, my weaknesses, same as most everyone else. So my thing is to be honest with myself about this kind of thing, and try to make incremental changes that might be helpful to me over the long haul.

Back in the day, when we all stayed in the same hotel, the temptation to go out and party with the cast and crew was hard to resist. Though in retrospect, Mark Burnett and his team of executive producers (Clay Newbill, Yun Linger, and Max Swedlow) must have known on some level that all that partying would result in the kind of camaraderie and friendships that have played a big part in the show's success.

But **even though the Sharks no longer stay in the same hotel, all of our "contestants" do.** For a time in there, they were known to get together in the hotel bar or lobby each night and go over one another's pitches. They'd give one another pointers: "Oh, Daymond won't like that." Or, "Kevin is gonna jump on you for this." Or whatever. They have no idea when they're going to be called on to the set, so they're at the ever-ready for those nine days of taping. Finally, they'll be told they're "on deck," and at that point they'll be put in some sequestered room away from the other hopefuls, but even then it could be a full day or more before they're called to the *Tank* to do their thing. It's such a stressful situation, I'm sure that camaraderie helps. **We tend to forget that these folks have put their lives on hold, just for the chance to make this one pitch.** They're looking to catch that big break. They're chasing a deal and a little shot of fame and fortune—can't help but respect *that*.

BE IN HARMONY

LIVE IN ABUNDANCE

CARLOS SANTANA
Rock 'n' Roll Hall of Famer, Legendary Guitarist, Spirit Guide

"AS SOON AS I wake up I take a deep breath, and before my feet touch the floor I'm very present and lucid and filled with thankfulness and gratitude for another day."

That's what multiple–Grammy winner Carlos Santana has to say when I ask him how he starts his day. He answers without hesitation, doesn't skip a beat, like the gratitude is *ingrained* in him. This is no surprise—to me, at least. I've known Carlos for several years, been working with him on a bunch of projects, and I'm always struck by his joyful spirit. Really, I don't think I've come across a gentler, more connected soul, and I was particularly interested in hearing what he had to say about how he plugs into the world each morning to face each new day. I wanted to know if the mindfulness and purity he shows as he moves about the planet is with him as he opens his eyes, if it's etched permanently on his heart—or if it's a state of mind he actually has to call to mind.

Turns out, it's a little bit of both.

"I just know that the more I give thanks, the more I live in abundance," he tells me. "The abundance of blessings, miracles, and opportunities. It's almost like I make a promise to myself every day. To say, 'Today, I will have another victory over myself, over my own fear, over my own guilt.' A victory over yourself, what Bob Marley calls 'mental slavery,' is knowing that your light will see you through."

That's a beautiful thought, don't you think? Empowering, too. But to hear it almost whispered from the lips of a man who can make music with such intense passion and ferocity you think his guitar is about to burst into flames . . . well, it's almost mystical, the way the hard and the soft play off each other.

FIND YOUR TRUE TOUCHSTONE

I'm guessing you probably know Carlos's band, Santana, or at least you'd recognize a bunch of his songs if you heard them. They had a whole string of hit records in the late 1960s and early 1970s—like "Evil Ways," "Black Magic Woman," and "Oye Como Va"—all with Carlos's signature blend of rock, jazz, blues, salsa, African rhythms, and Latin American music. There was nothing else like it on the radio, and his music still gets a ton of airplay. And then, in 1999, more than thirty years after he burst on the scene, he had the biggest commercial success of his career with the number one album *Supernatural,* featuring collaborations with then-up-and-coming young artists like Wyclef Jean, CeeLo Green, Lauryn Hill, and Rob Thomas of Matchbox Twenty.

That magic, that *light* Carlos talks about, has been coursing through him since he first picked up a guitar as a kid. But what strikes me about Carlos is that the virtuosity he exhibits onstage, his gifts as a musician, are not something he nurtures each day.

What I mean by that is, he doesn't seem to practice—at least not in the traditional way. When you listen to him talk about his daily routines, it's all about the music . . . but it doesn't necessarily follow that he spends a lot of time honing his craft. No, these days Carlos finds that his harmony comes mostly from the inside.

Before he even *gets* to the music in his life, Carlos concentrates on his core, his essence. Each morning, right after he takes that deep breath and fills himself with gratitude, he tries to reconnect himself to his dreams. It's a conscious effort, and sometimes those dreams are out of reach, but he reaches for them anyway. And then he reaches for his wife, Cindy—just a touch, Carlos says, a way to connect with her spirituality and light.

"I look in her eyes and thank her for loving me," he says. "For sharing her everything with me."

Next, he draws inspiration from five books he keeps by his bed; each one holds a special place in his soul, and in his heart. To Carlos, these aren't so much books as daily affirmations, and they ground him in clarity and courage as he navigates through life.

They are:

- *A Deep Breath of Life* by Alan Cohen
- *A Daily Dose of Sanity: A Five-Minute Soul Recharge for Every Day of the Year* by Alan Cohen
- *A Course in Miracles* by Helen Schucman
- *Daily Meditations for Practicing the Course* by Karen Casey
- *Quantum Success: The Astounding Science of Wealth* by Sandra Anne Taylor

He reads these books daily—not all the way through, obviously, but he jumps back in at the spot where he left off the day before, or maybe he'll flip to a page at random and start in fresh. The point is, he spends some time on them and sets himself for the day. And then, before he goes to bed, he reaches for those same books again. So the words and wisdom they contain are the first things he thinks about each morning and the last things he thinks about each night.

I love the way he describes what he's after here, framing his days with these books. Check it out:

"It's like when you get in the car, and you make sure the mirrors are all set," he explains. "You check the driver-side mirror, the passenger-side mirror, the rearview mirror. You make sure they're set just right for you, so you can see what's coming from the back, from the left, from the right. It's all aligned for you so you can protect yourself. What do they say when you're learning to drive, that you should know what's going on seven cars ahead of you, and seven cars behind you? That's what these books do for me, they help me to see what's coming, and to protect myself. They encourage me to be more mindful, and to invite myself to become like a divine observer."

Wow, right? This illustration of checking your mirrors and setting your car so you're good to go . . . . . . it's the perfect metaphor for what it means to *rise and grind*.

So this is how one of the greatest guitarists of his generation, or any generation, for that matter, starts his day. The music comes later. When he stops in at the office, he takes the time to give thanks for every prospect that crosses his desk, doesn't ever want to get complacent or take anything for granted. And he's not content to leave it to the people who work with him to determine how all these different opportunities might line up. Rather, he wants to keep connected to the possibilities that lie in wait for him, and to be the one to see where there's a deep or meaningful connection, where one person's vision might lead into another person's vision and create something truly magical.

What Carlos is getting at here, really, is the spirit of innovation. Here's how he puts it: "When you put peanut butter with chocolate, you get something more than chocolate with peanut butter." What he means, of course, is that a whole other kind of magic can happen when a pairing is right.

> **POWER FACT:** To commemorate the International Day of Peace, executives at Burger King and McDonald's teamed up to combine their signature sandwiches and sell a McWhopper for one day only, with proceeds going to the Peace One Day charity. . . . *Never underestimate the power (and reach) of collaboration, even among rivals.*

For a guy who lives and breathes music the way Carlos Santana does, it's also amazing that on most days he doesn't actually *listen* to music until he gets home from the office—at least, not in any kind of conscious way. He tells me the music is always in his head, that all the music he's ever played, all the music he's ever listened to, it fills his soul. But when he does finally sit down to listen to music, he does it with serious and joyful intent. He lets the music wash over him, become a part of him—the same way he takes in that feeling of gratitude in the morning.

Now, I've got to admit, I'm a little ignorant when it comes to understanding how you nurture a gift like Carlos's talent on the guitar. I can appreciate his brilliance—of the thousands of people who've taken up the guitar (maybe even the *millions*), critics and other musicians put Carlos in the top ten, all-time. But I can't begin to appreciate the work that must go into it. And yet, to hear Carlos tell it, that "work" is mostly done. I'm repeating myself, I know, but it really floored me to see that this giant talent didn't take the time each day to nurture that talent. Or, at least, he didn't take the time in ways I would've thought. Got to admit, when I reached out to pick Carlos's brain and get a sense of his daily regimen, I would've thought practicing the guitar would have taken up a good chunk of his time. You know, I had this picture in my mind that he was spending hours and hours each day, working on scales, strengthening his fingers, honing his chops. But that's not the case at all . . . not even close.

And when he does pick up his guitar, there is no clock on his session. He doesn't set aside this much time to play, or that much time to listen, or whatever. It's more organic than that. His *intuition* is what fuels his *grind*.

"I know how to play the guitar," he says. "I dream about playing the guitar. But I have played the guitar for my entire life, so I practice in a different way. I practice in a way where I can live in the music. Time disappears when I take my fingers for a walk with Jimi Hendrix or Marvin Gaye or my other sisters and brothers. That's exactly what I call it. I don't really practice. I call it taking my fingers for a walk with them. By the time I get back, from two or three hours with Marvin Gaye, my fingers know how to align with him so clearly. Every singer, they do what they do, and then I answer. I have to answer them in such a way that I don't step on their lines. They talk and I listen. So the time that I spend with my guitar, it's not as much as I did in the beginning, because my guitar has become pretty much like my tongue. I don't have to think anymore about enunciation or pronunciation. I trust my fingers to go where I want, and to go as fast as I want, and as deep as I want. All I need to do is let my fingers make it true and make it believable and make it honest.

"If I had to put a number on it, I'd say ninety-nine percent of the music I listen to comes from Africa," Carlos tells. "I learn the melodies. I learn the conga parts. I learn the rhythm. I take it all in, so that when these other musicians sit down to play with me in Paris, for example, their eyes get really big and they start to wonder, How the hell is it that this Mexican can play this music and be a part of this music? Well, that's because I love it like it is a part of me, and I learn it like it is a part of me."

And yet the thing is, when Carlos *learns* music in this way, he's not playing it on the guitar. He's not studying it, or teaching himself a new riff. He's simply absorbing it, as if through osmosis, imagining it flowing through his soul, through his fingers.

MAKE YOURSELF USEFUL

One of Carlos's big things is excellence—more than almost anyone else I know, he seems to truly appreciate the beauty of a thing well done or well made. For example, during basketball season, he and his wife like to watch the San Antonio Spurs on television. That's where you'll find them after dinner most nights, and if the Spurs aren't on they'll watch the Golden State Warriors or the Cleveland Cavaliers. Part of it is a deep appreciation of the skill, the excellence they put out, for sure. But it's the selflessness, the "team-first" mentality of the Spurs that really resonates. "The way they conduct themselves," Carlos says, "on the court, off the court, it is so elegant. Very quiet. They don't beat their chests like King Kong. They have a certain way they carry themselves on the court, a certain way they carry themselves off the court."

He counts tennis legend Arthur Ashe and jazz saxophonist John Coltrane as role models, which makes sense once he tells me it's because they too carried themselves with a certain dignity, a certain elegance.

"Excellence and elegance," he says. "Those words mean a lot to me. People who embrace those ideals mean a lot to me."

Carlos credits his mother with instilling in him the discipline he needed to find his way to excellence in his music. "My mother, she taught me that we might have been dirt poor here in Tijuana, but we were not filthy," he says. "We lived with pride, with purpose. She kept a clean house. She would come into my room, and I could be with my brothers and sisters, and she would say, 'Carlos, what are you doing?' She would say it like I was going to be in trouble. And I would say, 'Mom, I don't want to get in trouble. I'm not doing anything.' And she would say, 'I know. That is why I'm telling you, make yourself useful. Do something.'"

From his father, Carlos learned the importance of patience—in music, and in everything else. His old man was a mean violinist, so he knew what he was talking about, and Carlos knew enough to listen to him.

"Oh, it used to drive me crazy," Carlos remembers, "because when you're young, you want to go really fast. And my dad would say, 'No, slower. Do not be in such a big hurry. Play the slowest blues that you can play.' And he was right, of course, because when you play it really slow, you're very naked and raw and you can't hide. The more you slow it down, the deeper you go into a person's heart."

I AM NOT WHAT HAPPENED TO ME . . .

One of Carlos's most enduring contributions to the world didn't have anything at all to do with music. After he'd made that big second splash with *Supernatural* and found himself a whole new audience, he went public with a revelation. He told *Rolling Stone* he'd been abused as a child, by the father of a childhood friend, and he shared this difficult personal story because he felt called to do so.

"At first I thought, No, man, I can't do that," he recalls. "That was scary, raw, and embarrassing. But then I was like, Wait, this can help a lot of people. Because a lot of people, this happened to them. And it felt to me like it would liberate them, to hear someone like me talking about it. It would make it so they could go to the mirror, look into their eyes, and think, I am still pure and innocent. I am still the way God made me. I am not what happened to me."

....

POWER FACT: A report of child abuse occurs every ten seconds in the United States.... *I have such deep appreciation and admiration for my friend Carlos, for having the courage to shine a light this way!*

....

I am not what happened to me. That's a very powerful statement, and when Carlos was finally able to get his head around his own ordeal and find a way to power past it, he also found the will to make himself whole. To get there, he called on the healing power of prayer and spirituality, but also on the music, and to this day he finds that music can take him to a place of transcendence. The great takeaway here, for me, is that we all have our hardships, our issues. For some of us, it's abuse. For some, it's poverty or lack of opportunity. For some, it's learning or physical disabilities. The lesson I get from Carlos is that it's how you rise above that hardship, how you get past your issues, that shapes you.

"It is no longer in my fingers," he says, of the music. "It is in my breath. I take a deep breath, that is all. It is like when a woman gives birth, she must change the way she breathes. That is Lamaze. Their breath gives them strength. With me, with my music, my breath gives me strength, especially because I keep saying that the joy of God is my strength. So I take a deep breath and trust it to actually channel my lungs and in my brain. It's going to propel my calves, because when I hit a note, it comes from my calves, my heart . . . my cojones. You'll excuse me, but I have to make every part of my body feel relaxed. When you relax, you get a lot of strength. When you get afraid and tighten up, you immediately get tired and weak.

"Look, when I play, it is very physical. If I knew I was going to live to be ninety-nine years old, I would've taken better care of myself. But now I have a wife who takes good, good care of me. She makes me drink a lot of water. And she makes me do this and helps me do that. I trust that even though I'm seventy years old, I can get onstage and be like my brother Buddy Guy. I can have some seriously divine but mean intentions. And that's a good balance to have, some softness, but then you have to be mean, like a lion. You have to be able to bring a buffalo down with one stroke. Those things come from Albert King, Freddie King, and B. B. King. The three Kings. When I want to hit that note a certain way, hard and soft, all at once, I want people to go, 'Oh, dang.' I want them to think it's more than just one string, making that note. More than one person playing that guitar. I want them to hear my spirit."

Carlos's Grind Checklist

✓ try to wake up feeling thankful, and mindful, and joyful—because, hey, might as well greet the day with a song in your heart . . .

✓ immerse yourself in positive influences, surround yourself with positive energy, and keep a positive outlook . . .

✓ celebrate excellence and elegance in the work of others . . .

✓ as long as you're celebrating, go ahead and celebrate those small victories, too, because we get where we're going by taking small, affordable next steps . . .

✓ read (and reread)—tapping back in to a familiar passage on a daily basis is a great way to keep grounded, so seek out writers who inspire, enlighten, or speak to you in some way and keep their books by your bedside . . .

✓ trust your talents—yeah, practice makes perfect and all that, but sometimes you get to a place where there's nothing left to practice and you know your gifts will be there waiting for you . . .

....

For more information on Carlos and how he uses the
Rise and Grind mindset, check out

www.DaymondJohn.com/Rise/Carlos

BE TRUE TO YOURSELF

DO YOUR OWN THING

WENDY WILLIAMS
Talk Show Host, Working Mom, Plain-talker

HAVE YOU EVER flipped around the television dial and come across a person with so much positive energy it feels like she can reach right through the screen and shake some serious sense into you? Someone so refreshing and genuine you want to get her on the phone and just hang out, maybe get your nails done together?

That's probably how millions of viewers felt when they first encountered my friend Wendy Williams, after her syndicated talk show debuted in 2008. Folks in New York and in certain markets around the country already knew Wendy from her radio show—she'd been a top "shock jock" for almost twenty years, so she was good and comfortable in front of a microphone. But now that she was out in front of the cameras, she lit it up!

One of the ways Wendy separated herself from the crowded field of wannabe talk show hosts who try to get a show going every year was with her *grind*. You see, it's the custom in daytime syndication for shows to go on hiatus over the summer. Most shows stop airing new episodes in May and ramp up again in

September. That's how Wendy played it in her first season on *The Wendy Williams Show,* because that's how the folks in charge *told* her to play it, but by the second season she was at it full-throttle all summer long—not to get an edge on the competition, necessarily, but mostly because she was wired to work. Wasn't exactly a strategy so much as it was a symptom of her unstoppable drive, and it just worked out that Wendy's strength helped to pull in a whole mess of new and loyal viewers.

"I went stir crazy, being off the air for three months," she says now. "I'm a hustler and a grinder. I wasn't used to having all that downtime. It didn't occupy my mind enough. So for the second year, we put it in the budget to shoot until the end of July, so we were out there with all these new episodes while everyone else was in reruns."

That's how it's been ever since. Wendy does about two hundred shows a year, and it's not like *The View* or *The Talk* or *The Five* or any of those shows with a panel of hosts to help with the heavy lifting. No, sir—it's just Wendy out there, all on her lonesome, doing her thing. The show shoots four days a week, Monday through Thursday, and on Friday Wendy's usually jetting to one of her affiliate cities for a promotional event. Might seem glamorous to someone from outside the television industry, but that's a grueling schedule—trust me on this. **Don't know how she does it, but this woman turns up like a ball of fire, bursting with fresh energy, each and every time.**

Wendy's shooting days all start out the same way: the alarm goes off at five thirty in the morning. She hits Snooze a couple of times, until about five fifty. And then she spends the next ninety minutes getting her family ready to meet the day.

"Oh, please, I have a full glam squad waiting for me at the studio," she says, when I joke that she must be pretty low-maintenance, not to have to spend any time in the morning on hair and makeup. "So it's not like I have to get ready for the show before I leave the house. All I have to do is get in the shower, jump in my costume, which is a pair of leggings or, you know, something very random, no makeup. Then I throw on a wig and I head out to the studio, because that's where I get my stuff done."

What that means, in practice, is that Wendy doesn't have to deal with a lot of the early morning prep stuff that eats up a ton of time for working women all over the world. She's able to focus on her household, and her family, so that time in the morning is like a great windfall—and she makes good and full use of it. She's able to get her sixteen-year-old son, Kevin Jr., up and out the door to school, let the dog out the back door, get breakfast ready. Then she's off in the car with her husband, Kevin Sr., for the drive to the studio. They work together, so that makes for an interesting dynamic. "He's usually so tense in the head," she says of her husband. "He's management, you know, so he protects me from a lot of what's going on with the show. We might be going over the schedule and I'll see something and say, 'Wow, I didn't know I was going to be doing this or that.' So we talk through whatever we've got going on, and after that we turn up Nas, or we turn up the Wu-Tang Clan, and we zone out."

....

POWER FACT: There are approximately 4 million family-owned businesses in the United States, including about 1.4 million being run by a husband-and-wife team. . . . *Those numbers come from the Bureau of Labor Statistics, and they tell us that Wendy and her husband, Kevin, might be on to something. Couples who work together get to engage as professionals away from the office, and to interact on a personal level in the workplace—good things both, if you ask me.*

....

WALK THE TALK

Wendy grew up in Ocean Township, New Jersey, with the idea that her family had money, even though she realized later on that her parents were really stretching just to send Wendy and her siblings to college and keep them in nice clothes. "Oh please," she says now. "I thought I was a countess. We were driving around in Lincoln Continentals with that big wheel on the back, when we should have been driving in a Dodge Dart."

Out of that, she's learned to keep herself grounded. She shops for her own groceries—might not seem like a big deal, but when you're in the public eye (and especially when you've got a hit, long-running show on daytime television), it's damn near impossible to walk up and down a supermarket aisle without being stopped by people who want to talk to you, maybe ask for a picture, or an autograph, or whatever. I've seen this myself, since I started appearing on *Shark Tank*—and, like Wendy, I've chosen to embrace all that attention instead of running away from it.

"I love the community of it," Wendy says. "I love seeing the 'Wendy Watchers.' That's what we call 'em. **It's like taking my own temperature, know what I mean?** And that might sound corny, but in television they have all that research, all those surveys, those ratings that tell you how you're doing, but I like to check my own stuff, and the only way you can do that is by going to the drugstore and picking up your own thyroid pills. I don't get them sent to the house. I don't have someone get 'em for me. I go and stand in line with the people on a Saturday or Sunday, and they're like, 'How are you doing?' And I'm like, 'How are *you* doing?' 'Well, you know, my husband and I watch you all the time.' 'Oh, fabulous.' And it just goes on from there, so if I need a broom or cashews or some dog food, I just go and get it myself."

Wendy talks the talk—that's the main reason people love her

on television. She's real. She credits her mother for teaching her to be a well-rounded person and to appreciate the good things that come her way. "My parents have been married for like a hundred and fifty-five years," she tells me, in a way that doesn't make it sound like an exaggeration. "And my mother has always been a nice-looking woman. She always kept a nice house. Her dinners were always scrumptious. The house always smelled of Pine-Sol. And she had somebody come in once in a while, but not every day. Just a helper-outer person. But my mom, what I learned from my mom is that no matter how successful a woman gets, no matter how confident a woman gets, you can't have it all. You can't. Because you always have to be available to figure things out. Because when the dishwasher breaks, guess who handles that? So I've learned to keep my nails done, keep my waist tight, keep the dinner good, whether I make it or gather it, and to make sure the dishwasher is fixed, and then I get out there and work my job and make sure I have smart conversations when I come home."

....

POWER FACT: **According to the Craft and Hobby Association, 56 percent of US households have at least one member who crafts on a regular basis. . . .** *This can mean sewing, woodworking, painting . . . what have you. And what it can also mean is that even though we're becoming busier and busier, we're still finding time to put our world on pause and lose ourselves in a constructive way.*

....

Another lesson she took from her mother was to find happiness where she can—and to tune people out if they think what she's doing is corny. "Look," she says. "I love crafting. I just made this ottoman. I picked up a plain ottoman at Home Goods, but then I bought a cheetah print for it, and when I was finished I put it in my office. Crafting makes me feel good. It's how I unwind. And this was just a plain, stupid ottoman, and you might look at it and think it's stupid, but you know what? It's my stupid."

Now, before you go off thinking Wendy's life has been all peaches and cream and cheetah-print ottomans, you should know that she's had her rough spots. She's talked about these things publicly, but I don't want to step on her privacy and write about these moments here. Just know that **it's helpful to see the dark times people go through if you want to appreciate the ways they've come to live in the light**.

ADD YOUR ACCOUTREMENTS

These days, Wendy's household is undergoing a bit of a transformation—her kitchen especially. Her son has become a full-on vegan, while her husband is now a vegetarian. Wendy's not quite there yet with her diet. She considers herself a pescatarian, because she likes a nice piece of fish every once in a while—but she's careful to honor the dietary choices of the men in her life.

You might think that she's out there wining and dining at five-star joints every night, but actually she usually prepares dinners at home. Sometimes she cooks, and sometimes she "gathers"—that's a phrase she uses a couple of times during our visit, and I'm thinking I'll start using it, too. (Sounds so much better than "orders takeout," don't you think?) But it comes with a little footnote: "I'll gather something from our favorite vegetarian vegan places," she explains, "but then I'll add my own accoutrements. **I always have accoutrements.**"

Noted.

After dinner, Wendy likes to unwind with some "sane" television. These days, with what's going on in Washington, it's easy to get distracted by the chatter on our cable news shows, but Wendy goes in for shows like *Black-ish* and *New Girl*. One of her great not-so-guilty pleasures is to tune in to the Home Shopping Network, which she sees as a kind of comfortable escape from the grind of her day—and a great way to plug in to the tastes and trends that might be taking shape among her viewers.

Oh, and before we get too far away from the subject of dinner, let me also mention that Wendy's family is big into supplements. The only synthetic pill Wendy puts into her body each day is her one thyroid pill, but other than that it's all natural. Her son Kevin actually makes some of their supplements from scratch—Wendy lays in the raw ingredients and then he crushes them and mixes it all up and sets it into capsules.

"We're like the weirdo family, okay?" Wendy says. "All right, we're the weirdos, but you want to know what? We're happy, we're healthy, we love each other. What else is there?"

Words to live by.

Wendy's Grind Checklist

✓ do it yourself . . . even if you get to that stage in your life when you can afford to bring in reinforcements to help you with the cooking and cleaning and shopping, there's nothing like doing for yourself and your family in this way . . .

✓ believe in what you're putting out there . . . when you're on television, folks can see right through you, so keep that transparency in mind . . .

✓ find a hobby or a craft to exercise your mind and help you to put your life on a meaningful pause . . .

✓ make room in your life to accommodate the diet and exercise regimens of the people you love . . . you're in a position to reinforce their healthy habit so become a cheerleader for their extra efforts . . . even better, sign on to them in ways that make sense . . .

✓ dress for success, absolutely, but don't give it a thought if you're out running errands like a little less than a million bucks . . . you are who you are—embrace it!

....

For more information on Wendy and how she uses the
Rise and Grind mindset, check out
www.DaymondJohn.com/Rise/Wendy

BE NIMBLE

USE WHAT'S USEFUL

MICHAEL PARRELLA
Gym Developer, Marketing Beast, Opportunity Creator

GOT SOMEONE ELSE I want to introduce you to who counted Bruce Lee as one of his idols growing up. Forget how Bruce Lee inspired millions with the way he moved, with his insane strength and agility. What struck Michael Parrella was the way this man *thought*.

"The thing Bruce Lee pioneered," Mike says, "was to **use what's useful**. Instead of just being stuck with a traditional dogma of, 'Oh, this is the way business is done,' or, 'This is the way life is done,' his message was like, 'Do for you.'"

I'm a big Bruce Lee guy myself, but I'd never heard this quote until Mike shared it, and it clicked. *Use what's useful.* I like that—and I love the way Mike has come to embrace it as well.

You see, Mike is well known as someone who gets things done—in his own way, in his own time. Like when he gets up each morning. Most people I know, they open their eyes, shake out the cobwebs, throw off the covers, and have at it. Not Mike. He just lies there. For thirty, maybe forty-five minutes. "That's my quiet time," he says. "Sun's coming up, it's as quiet as anything in my house, and it's really the only time in my day where I can think without interruption, so that's become like my creative period."

Lately, there are a lot of folks waiting for Mike to get out of bed and start in on his day. There are his wife and kids, of course. There are the folks at the five gyms he owns and operates in the New York area. There are the hundreds of franchise owners who operate their own gyms using Mike's unique platform and concept. And there are the thousands of people who make those gyms a part of their morning routine and who look to Mike and his fitness methods to help them start their days in an innovative, invigorating way.

But Mike's got this *do for you* thing going on, so he takes his time.

GET THERE EVENTUALLY

There's a lot to admire about the way Michael Parrella has built his businesses, and the way he builds his days. We met when he brought me in to help motivate his troops—one of my favorite types of speaking gigs, because I'm invited in to see and experience all these different corporate cultures and to bring my own style into each environment. Only here it worked out that Mike motivated *me,* too. His story inspired me. I left there thinking I had to find a way to work with this guy, who brings so much energy and passion to everything he does.

Wasn't always that way, however, but before I tell you where Mike fell short when he was just getting started, let me tell you where he is today. He's riding high now that he's figured a few things out. He made his bones as one of the world's leading martial arts marketers, but most people know him as the founder and CEO of the wildly popular chain of iLoveKickboxing workout studios all over the country. Even if you've never been to one, I'm pretty sure you've driven by one of Mike's storefront signs and wondered what was going on inside. Well, what's going on are adrenaline-pumping kickboxing sessions that really let participants get their sweat on. They strap on a pair of boxing gloves and learn moves that work their cardio, their core, their upper and lower body . . . the full package. And they have so much fun doing it they can't help but come back for more.

And the iLoveKickboxing franchise owners, they get their sweat on, too. But it's worth it, because these gyms are insanely profitable—in part because Michael has created a successful turnkey system with the franchise and it doesn't cost a whole lot to open and operate one. Unlike most gyms, where an owner would have to invest in high-end cardio equipment like treadmills and ellipticals that need to be replaced constantly, the ILKB studios feature mostly gym mats and a bunch of heavy bags. They don't take up a lot of room, so franchise owners save on the cost of space, too. But mostly they're profitable because part of Mike's end of the deal is to get customers in the door—and to keep them walking in the door. It's the way he markets the fitness franchise and builds a sense of community among his participants and instructors that really sets his gyms apart.

....

POWER FACT: Gyms need to enroll ten times as many members as they can comfortably accommodate in order to turn a profit. . . . *Yet only 18 percent of members work out on a consistent basis, so if you can find a way to keep them coming to your gym, you'll give yourself an edge.*

....

The most compelling thing about Mike's success is that he didn't ride a straight line to the top of his field. This is the *fall-*

ing short part of his story. He started his first business in the early 1990s—a martial arts school located on the second floor of an office building on Long Island—with $7,000 in borrowed money. It wasn't much, but it was something. And soon he grew it into something more. So he opened a second location, and a third. And so on. After five years he was running five gyms, then he looked up one day and realized he'd spread himself thin.

"Managing one or two studios, and five or six employees, it's not a big deal," he says now. "But when you get to twenty, twenty-five employees, and four or five locations, it requires a whole new set of skills. It's like I'd built a house of cards, so it's not really a surprise that the whole thing collapsed on me."

Within a couple of years, Mike went bust. His house was in foreclosure. He'd run through his 401(k). His car was being repossessed—he had to park five blocks away from where he was staying, so the repo man couldn't find it! He found a way to tap into his neighbor's electrical lines, just to keep the lights on. And for food, he was living off the expired TV dinners his friend's mother was hoarding in the industrial freezer-lockers she kept in her basement. His rule of thumb was that he'd eat anything with an expiration date on the package that was less than two years old.

This right here was the *power of broke*—only Mike couldn't tap the *power* in it, not just yet. For a couple of years, he sank further and further into debt, deeper and deeper into despair. "When you're broke, and your business sucks, you don't even want to go to work," he reflects. "I had days where I couldn't even leave the house."

He'd been firing on all cylinders, and now he was scraping, and it was in this place of desperation that Mike found true inspiration. He found it not long after the death of his mother, when he got to talking with one of his friends about what it might say on his own tombstone after he was gone. **He'd been thinking**

about his legacy, about the footprint he was leaving on this earth, and out of that he actually began writing his own eulogy. He took out a yellow legal pad and got a page or two into it when he put down his pen and realized everything he was writing was crap.

"It was all bullshit," he says now. "It was how I wanted people to perceive me, but it wasn't how I actually was."

So he crumpled up his first draft and started in on a new one. This time he was brutally honest, listing all the things he wasn't good at, all the ways he'd failed, all the targets he'd set for himself and somehow missed.

"I'm writing this thing," he remembers, "and it was just horrible. I get to the end and I'm like, Man, I'm forty-one years old. I'm at the middle of my life, and what have I done? Half my life is gone, and what have I accomplished? And then I had this moment where I realized, Okay, I now have this opportunity to become the architect of my life. I am going to do things differently. I am going to rewrite my own eulogy."

....

POWER FACT: **If you want to keep sharp, studies show that the best brain-healthy foods include fish, berries, lean protein, beets, and walnuts. . . .** *I'm sorry, but I just can't stop thinking about Mike's TV dinner diet, so I thought I'd throw a couple of positive alternatives at you.*

....

It was the classic *glass half-empty versus glass half-full* equation, but here Mike put it in *life half-over versus life half-started* terms. His saving grace was that during those long, desperate days when he couldn't even find the energy or the courage to drag himself to work, he wasn't just staring at the ceiling watching the paint dry. He spent a ton of time online, reading articles on digital marketing. Reading books on motivation and mindset. Learning website development and HTML code. He was well aware of the pitfalls of the fitness industry. He knew all the statistics, the failure rates. But he also knew that the tried-and-true marketing approaches used by most gyms just weren't working for him, so he threw out the playbook and started developing his own. **The way Mike rewrote his eulogy was to rewrite his present.**

This was where his *grind* kicked in—but Mike is cut a little differently than most of the other people I'm introducing you to here in this book. His *grind* has more to do with his mind than his routine. His days take on a different shape, depending on what's going on, but what's constant is his determination to do whatever it takes to solve whatever puzzle he's facing. That's why those uncluttered, uninterrupted half hours are so important to him each morning, before he climbs out of bed and gets down to it. With him, hard work is a given. Extra effort is expected. With him, pushing himself physically goes without saying. The game-changer is his discipline in thinking through all these different approaches in the quiet of his bedroom until he finds what works.

In this case, the game-changer was realizing what *didn't* work, namely, the promotional model being used throughout the workout industry. This was his lightbulb-over-the-head moment. The practice of giving out free trial memberships had become the standard, default way of recruiting new members, but Mike wasn't buying it—and neither were consumers, apparently. "I learned from all that time online that nobody's giving away anything for free," he says. "Except in gyms and martial arts schools, this was the way it was done. It made no sense. So I decided I wasn't doing that anymore."

He started offering Groupon-type deals to get people in the door at his martial arts studios. They'd have to pay their way in, but at a discount—it went against everything his competitors were doing in the field, but Mike was down so low he was willing to try anything. Almost immediately, he started to see a turnaround. Members felt a sense of buy-in, a new level of commitment, from the very beginning, so they kept coming. They told their friends, and they kept coming, too.

Finally, it felt to him like he was back in business.

"Money only solves the problems that not having money creates," he says. "That's a line from John Carlton, a great motivator, and that really described my thinking at the time. I was really off base. I let people in my life who were really not on my team. They were more money motivated than I was. I made decisions that were not in the best interests of my business. I followed the pack instead of taking the lead. It took losing just about everything to realize that money wasn't what was driving me. What was driving me was the ability to change people's lives."

One of the ways he hit on to help do that was to develop the concept that would grow into iLoveKickboxing. He came up with a curriculum, a marketing package, and a platform and invited franchisees to join him on this journey. The idea, he says, was to build a kind of business in a box, a turnkey operation that would allow entrepreneurs like himself to stake their own claim in the booming field of health and fitness and maybe learn from some of his mistakes. He studied all the barriers to entry in the gym business and looked to eliminate as many of them as he could—that's what he found so appealing about the kickboxing workout: the cost of equipment was low. All you needed were some boxing gloves and some free-standing heavy bags and you were good to go.

His was a model that no one had ever really seen in the fitness world before, but remember, he had Bruce Lee's "use what's useful" mindset. He left it to others to "use what other people are doing, just because that's the way things are done."

BE A TEAM PLAYER

Mike's franchise owners get a lot more than just a business in a box. The ILKB platform includes training courses, tutorials, videos, and even in-person coaching on how franchisees can grow their business. One of the things Mike always tells them is to think like a superhero—but not one of those lone-wolf superheroes who believe they can do everything. No, Mike's thing is to be a part of a superhero team, like the Justice League of America or Super Friends.

"If you're part of a team," he says, "everybody knows how to fly, everybody can talk to animals, and everybody is invulnerable. When you're the CEO of a company, you start to think you can do everything. You think, I can sell. I can market. I can bookkeep. But what I realized was, I can't do all those things. In fact, I suck at a lot of those things. So I started finding people who had the superpower I didn't have, and looking for ways we could work together."

These days, Mike's got so much going on, he often has to remind himself to take time for his "team" at home—that is, his family. It's why he works, after all. It's what keeps him up nights, the worry that he's taking too much time away from his family, or that he can't fully relax when he's spending time with his wife and kids, because he's distracted by what's going on with work. And his "team" at home is what helps him sleep at night as well, because he's content in the knowledge that he's building a life and an opportunity for the people he cares about the most.

"The last ninety minutes of my day is not at all about my cellphone," he tells. "It's about time with my family. So there's nothing digital. It's time with my wife, our kids. It's sharing dinner, talking about what the kids did that day at school. For our younger kids, it's going over vocabulary words with them at the dinner table and seeing how many they can remember."

And in the morning, when he's gathering his thoughts for the day, he reminds himself that he's got it covered. "Take away my business," he says. "Take away my money, my career, and I know I can get it back again. I can always take care of my family. That's such an incredibly empowering thought. No matter what problems I'm facing, I know I can take care of them. If franchising became illegal, if kickboxing was outlawed, I know that I can get up tomorrow morning, take that forty-five minutes I need to get my head right, and I'll come up with the million-dollar idea I need."

Michael's Grind Checklist

✓ take inventory—I don't mean you should count up all the money you have in the bank or the cars you keep in your garage, but take the time to see *who* you are, and *how* you manage your business, your relationships, your commitments . . . be honest with yourself, and if you don't measure up, make some changes . . .

✓ when you give away something for nothing, you might just get back nothing in return . . .

✓ be careful about what you put into your body . . . yeah, Mike might have been able to survive on those nasty microwave meals for a time, but even though they didn't kill him they didn't do him any favors . . .

✓ if you get knocked down, get up again—remember that silly Chumbawamba song from the nineties? It's like that . . .

✓ empower the people around you . . . their success is your success . . . their failure is your failure . . .

✓ respect resilience—know that if you fail, you have it in you to recover . . .

✓ build a better mousetrap—just because things have always been done a certain way, it doesn't mean you can't find a better one . . .

✓ it's not *always* about the money . . .

✓ build a base of knowledge to fall back on . . . fire up the computer and spend your time reading, learning, growing, because when life throws you a lifeline—and it *will*—you won't be able to grab on if you're too busy twiddling your thumbs!

....

For more information on Michael and how he uses the
Rise and Grind mindset, check out
www.DaymondJohn.com/Rise/Michael

SIX

GRIND ALL NIGHT

MY *GRIND* DOESN'T always follow the clock, doesn't always follow the sun, and doesn't always follow a set schedule. That's why I still make time to hit the clubs—when I'm home in New York, or when I travel.

Some people don't get that about me, but it's who I am, how I got here. I spend a lot of time in the clubs—only, I'm not out there to party and dance and have a good time. I understand that appearances can be deceiving. I post a lot of pictures when I'm out and about, and in some of those shots I'm mixing it up with a social group.

The point, really, is to keep doing my thing in an environment that exposes me to as many different people, brands, and trends as possible, in the shortest time possible.

For a long time now, most of my club-hopping has been tied to work, tied to my *grind,* but that doesn't always come across on social media, and I've recently noticed that I get two very different reactions whenever I post that I'm out late at a nightclub.

There's one group of folks that seems to love seeing my pictures and videos of partygoers having the time of their lives. But then there's another group out there that might wonder what the hell an old man like me is doing out at some hip place surrounded by kids half his age.

So let me set the record straight, if you don't mind. Let's be clear, I'm still going to the clubs, and I'll probably *always* be going to the clubs—hey, I grew up in that world, it's where my roots are—but I don't go for the same reasons I used to go when I was a teenager, trying to relax, blow off steam. **These days, my idea of relaxing, having a good time is to go fishing or snowboarding, put my feet up with my family, do a little CrossFit, shoot some arrows, throw some knives, maybe fire up the drone or the grill.** And yet I'm still out there at all these clubs and events. I'm not there to party, at least not in the way you might think. I'm there to see what's up, listen to the hottest new music, check out the new styles, tune in to what people are talking about.

Bottom line: this is how I network. It's like speed-dating for business . . . for *my* business. My thinking is, if these people are in the clubs spending money, that means they're out there making money, and it serves me to tap into what they know.

Yeah, I have an incredibly busy schedule. It sometimes feels like I'm on a plane or in a hotel room more than I am at my desk or in my own bed, so if I barely have enough time to sleep, why do I make time to go out to the clubs? Well, best way to answer that is to offer up the same advice I give to business leaders: **know what's up**. When I'm called in to consult with companies—whether they're huge Fortune 500 brands or boutique operations—I'm often giving them strategies for keeping relevant and dialed in. Here I'm reminded of a comment from a good friend of mine, Chris Latimer, the well-known brand builder: "Companies start to fail when the decision-makers at that company make decisions from ivory towers or thirty thousand feet in the air." What he meant by that was that when you stop touching people, you lose touch. When you lift your ear from the ground and your foot from the gas, you lose whatever energy you might have had in the first place. You lose what created you.

At FUBU, we took our marching orders from the streets. That was our energy, our drive. And we weren't just plugged in around our neighborhood in Hollis, Queens—we were all about the emerging hip-hop culture, all across the country. So as we grew, we were getting real-time, street-level feedback directly from the consumer—and finding ways to take that feedback into our designs and products. There was a synergy between the way we lived and the way we worked—it was all tied in, in a totally natural and authentic way.

....

POWER FACT: 54 percent of business professionals see golf as "the sport of business." . . . *My thing is, it doesn't matter if it's the golf club or the nightclub, you need to put yourself where deals happen.*

....

A lot of my consulting clients, they think this kind of feedback is available to them only through expensive market research. Their first impulse is to organize a formal focus group to study a market trend, and a lot of times that's the only kind of research available to them because they're stuck in the office all day, manning the phones, taking meetings, staring at their computer screens. But my thing is to get out there, whenever possible. Nobody says your R&D efforts have to be all buttoned down and boring. And with all the advances in technology, there's no good reason for a CEO or even a division head to be tethered to a desk. In fact, I'm here saying just the opposite, so get out there and make some noise, and know that the noise that comes back to you will inform your business. Does this mean everyone should go out and hit the clubs? Absolutely not, but you do have to go where your market is. This just happens to be where my consumers are at—been that way since we launched FUBU and still remains true today. **Whatever it is I'm doing, whatever it is I'm selling, my time in the clubs gives me a leg up, because that's where my market lives and breathes.** If I want my finger on the pulse, that's where I tend to find it.

But that's just me, right? You need to discover where your own *club* might be. Maybe you're in the movie industry, and your version of the club is traveling the world going to all these film festivals, meeting all the best up-and-coming actors and directors, listening and talking to people talk about what's popular, and learning what the hot new trends in filmmaking are. Or if you're a designer, maybe it's walking the streets of Milan, Amsterdam, and Harlem to see what the kids are wearing, or visiting the factories to find out what kind of material is in fashion, what kind of styles are selling, what kind of technology there is to help you punch up your designs. Or maybe you're in the restaurant industry, and you need to hit the high-end spots to see what people are eating and drinking, what the chefs are making and what the bartenders are pouring—what your competitors are selling, and what people are saying about it. It's like they say in that song from *The Little Mermaid*— you wanna be where the people are. (I have daughters, remember?)

I know some CEOs who go undercover, working minimum wage-type jobs at places like CVS, just to see consumer behavior firsthand. That might seem a little extreme—but you've got to go to the source, and sometimes you just can't trust the assignment to anyone else. Flip on an episode of *Undercover,* a series produced for television markets all over the world, and you'll

see what that's all about. And while you're at it, **take a look at
my own show: go up and down our *Shark Tank* panel and
you'll see my fellow Sharks out there taking the same approach to their own businesses:**

- Robert Herjavec spends a lot of time on the racing
  car circuit, where he's able to mix and mingle with
  executives from these huge global corporations that
  are likely to need his cybersecurity expertise. So that's
  his club.
- Mark Cuban is courtside at every Mavericks game—
  and not *just* because he's a big-time basketball fan.
  Yeah, he loves to root, root, root for his Mavs, but
  being in the arena keeps him connected to his young
  players and fans, and allows him in a full-on way to
  soak in the product he's selling. He gets to cheer his
  lungs out, and at the same time inform his business
  decisions going forward. So that's his club.
- Lori Greiner has got her theories on consumer
  behavior down to a science. You see her doing her
  thing on QVC, where she uses up-to-the-second
  analytics to understand why customers respond in
  certain ways to certain products or on-air pitches. She
  studies that stuff like it's nobody's business, except of
  course it *is* somebody's business—namely, *hers*. She
  gets her feedback on the fly, and puts it right back to
  work, and when she's not in a television studio she
  spends as much time as she can in the retail outlets
  that carry her stuff. She makes a careful and constant
  study of her marketplace. So that's her club.
- Barbara Corcoran flies all over the world to her
  various speaking engagements, and wherever she finds
  herself she finds a way to connect with the people

and the community outside the venue where she's appearing. She came up in the world of real estate, so she's got a kind of sixth sense on housing trends and urban growth and all those little clues that give her the information and insight she needs to assess a deal. She keeps plugged in, in a ground-up sort of way. So that's her club.

- And Kevin O'Leary's club is sipping wine and globetrotting because he deals with the international markets. He made his bones in computer software, but once he had his first couple of successes he was into a little bit of everything. He's a true Renaissance man—he knows *a lot* about *a lot,* and what he doesn't know he makes it a point to learn. The world is his club.

What's yours?

GET YOUR HANDS DIRTY

How many business owners do you know who've slipped up because they got a little too satisfied, a little too comfortable taking the advice of someone who was on the ground level of things, on the streets, in the marketplace, instead of actually getting out there and figuring some of this stuff out for themselves? Maybe one of those business owners is *you*—and now here you are, trying to learn from your mistakes. Well, it's never too late to take in this all-important point: **someone else's impressions and opinions cannot take the place of your own**. So get your hands dirty. Meet your customers where they live. Step outside your comfort zone, break from your routines, and take the temperature of the market you hope to serve. Put yourself out there.

So that's one reason I go to the clubs, why I'll *always* go to the clubs. Another is that it's an insanely efficient use of my time. What do I mean by that? Well, a lot of times when I'm traveling, I can set it up so I meet with a dozen or so different people all in one night. In a city like Miami, all the clubs are within twenty blocks of one another—same in cities like Los Angeles, Atlanta, and even New York. You can get a lot of face time with a lot of people in a casual setting.

Of course, when I was first coming up, it was a very different club scene. Back then, you could hit up a club and it wouldn't much matter if you were in New York or Los Angeles or anywhere in between; they were all dark and cavernous and thumping. These days, "clubbing" now takes place in broad daylight—in the hot, hot light of the sun, even. The big thing lately is daytime pool parties, especially in places like Las Vegas. That's where you find the true trendsetters and tastemakers . . . so that's where you'll find *me,* whenever I'm in town. And I'm not the oldest dude on the pool deck, just so you know. Some of these poolside cabanas are filled with VIPs and high-rollers who have a couple of years on me, but they're out there soaking in the scene, same as me. We're all just looking to plug-in to the mood of the moment, and to keep up with these kids.

Alongside of that, you have clubs where the focus is on a crazy show that's completely unlike anything you've ever seen before. The crowd *really* gets into it. The entire scene is built around this one shared experience and everybody comes away feeling like they're in on this amazing something. When you throw in festivals, especially the big properties like Ultra, Electric Zoo, and Coachella, which bring hundreds of thousands of people to an outdoor venue for a whole weekend, you come to appreciate how endlessly fascinating and shapeshifting the club scene can be.

And yet the more things change, the more they stay the same.

Many of today's top deejays, like Lil' Jon and Steve Aoki, are the new rock stars—and I'm lucky enough to call them my friends. EDM is the new music of the youth, like hip-hop before it, and rock and roll and jazz before that. There's a pulse to it, an energy, and it's seeping into the culture. And just like during the hip-hop era, brands are capitalizing on it—so I absolutely have to tap into it, in whatever ways I can, as often as I can.

....

POWER FACT: The nightlife industry generated more than $25 billion in 2016.... *By some estimates, it provides more than 400,000 jobs, so if EDM is your thing, say, pull a page from my hip-hop playbook and find a way to make a living from your passion.*

....

You have to realize, I have always looked on our popular music scene as a major agent of social change. It's the music of our times that stamps the *look* of our times, the *sensibility* of our times. It tells us what's going on and where we're headed. Just look at the success of Dr. Dre and Jimmy Iovine, who sold their Beats headphone line to Apple for more than $3 billion. That's a lot of paper, especially when you stop to consider that these guys didn't invent anything new. They simply capitalized on a cultural trend they spotted in the clubs and found a way to deliver a smart, stylish product everyone was already familiar with, at a price that made sense. It's no wonder Apple was interested, although the numbers kind of blew me away—that is, until I stopped to remind myself that Steve Jobs himself had built Apple on the back of that very same strategy, perfecting, *not* inventing. Am I right? Those MP3 players had been around for years before Steve Jobs and company got around to perfecting them and started calling them iPods.

So that's my deal: I'm in the clubs because they offer me the best focus group out there. People bring their A-games to the clubs. They want to look their best, be their best, experience the best . . . and I want to be there to see what those *bests* have to show me. I want to see where certain types of clubgoers are going, what they're drinking, what they're wearing. I want to hear what they're listening to, how they talk to one another, what they say with their body language. How do they interact? Are they always on their phones? Or do they set those devices down for a beat and lose themselves in the moment? Either way, what can I learn? Is there some killer new app out there that goes from table to table that allows you to connect with new people as soon as you get into the club? Is there a competing brand coming out onto the scene that I need to be aware of? So I might huddle with the deejay for a while, pressing him or her to share what's new, what's hot, what's not. I look, I talk to people, I listen . . . I take all kinds of notes, to make sure I remember what I've learned. A lot of times I'll wake up the next morning with a whole bunch of questions that I immediately set about answering. I might have come across some band or artist I'd never heard of before, or caught an unfamiliar phrase or expression. Or maybe there was a reference to a new product in some new song and I'll want to know how the folks behind it managed to afford that kind of play.

Or, whatever.

Take the show on the road and spend some time in the *clubs* that matter most to your business. Get out there on the golf course, go to the museum, hit the racetrack, take in an afternoon movie at the multiplex . . . find your market and make yourself a part of it. And if it works out that you have a great time in the bargain—well, then . . . that'll just be our little secret.

Deal?

BE ON TIME

KNOW WHEN THE MOMENT IS RIGHT

JAKE KASSAN AND KRAMER LAPLANTE
Movers, Shakers, Founders of MVMT Watches

SO HERE I am writing about time management and organizational strategies and it just works out that I know a couple of guys in the watch business with some relevant stories and insights to share. How's *that* for synergy? Come on, who better to hear from on the subject of time than two creative, hard-grinding entrepreneurs who've been making a killing designing and selling stylish, affordable timepieces?

I first met Kramer LaPlante and Jake Kassan through the work I do with Shopify's "Build a Business" competition. If you don't know about this event, you should put it on your radar—it attracts all these brand-new start-ups, some of them just a couple of months old, some of them already doing millions in sales. Shopify holds it annually, and it's a chance for aspiring entrepreneurs to meet and compare notes with leading entrepreneurs and to network. I remember being struck by these two young men and their passion for selling and design, so we got to talking. When we first met, the online watch company they started, MVMT, had already raised more than $300,000 in a crowdfunding campaign—and for those of you who don't keep track of such things, that's a lot of coin from a bunch of strangers online. I've never gotten close to that number, so these two were already starting to kick some tail and turn some heads in the watch industry. They had a few prototypes ready to go, a plan for production and distribution already in place. Their concept was built into their name: MVMT, or *movement*. One of their taglines was "More than just a watch, it's a movement, a movement we want you to be a part of."

And their *watches* . . . oh, man, they were sharp! The idea behind them was as important to the brand identity as the watches themselves, because Kramer and Jake were looking to fill a hole in the market, and offer stylish timepieces to young, aspiring, fashion-forward individuals like themselves who maybe couldn't afford a high-end brand.

In this way, and in a whole bunch of others, they reminded me of me and my boys when we were starting out with FUBU, because what they were selling wasn't just the watch itself—they were selling a lifestyle. They were looking to build a community of customers who would come to feel connected to one another and to the brand. Their mandate was simple: to make watches with a minimalist look, suitable for work or play. They would use only the highest-quality materials. And they would look to keep prices down to at least half of what name-brand companies were charging for comparable watches so that people would buy two or three or four watches, and keep coming back to check out the new styles and trends.

EMBRACE THE THRILL OF THE CHALLENGE

Just as we'd done with FUBU, these guys moved to fill a hole in the market, in this case with a line of reasonably priced timepieces that would look great on your wrist at work, or on a night on the town with friends—a watch that could speak to your professional and personal sense of style at the same time. In success, they would be out in front as the face (or the *wrist*) of their brand.

POWER FACT: Start-ups launched by two or more partners have a much greater chance of success than solo efforts. . . . *Working with a partner, you will raise 30 percent more in seed money, and grow your customers three times as fast, so don't think you have to go it alone. Sometimes two heads are better than one.*

When I first met them, they had the concept and prototypes in place but not much else, so I convinced them not to go retail, to sell their merch exclusively online. I *got* these guys—we were cut from the same cloth. Jake, for one, had been hustling since he was a kid. It was in his bones. He grew up all the way on the other side of the country from me, in California, and I think I had about twenty years on him, but he had the same entrepreneurial streak— only he wasn't chasing all these different opportunities to keep out of trouble, but rather just to keep himself amused. He seemed to be wired in a way that left him thinking anything was possible. When he was about thirteen, for example, he built a motorized bicycle— because he was too young to drive, of course, and he needed a better way to get around town than a regular two-wheeler. Guess you could say he was the kind of kid who didn't like to take no for an answer. Every puzzle was a thing to be worked over and solved. In the same way that I used to fix up old bikes using the discarded parts I harvested out on the curb back in Queens, he built this bike with parts and plans that were available to anyone who thought to go looking for them.

POWER FACT: A recent Gallup poll reports that 43 percent of students in grades 5 to 12 want to be entrepreneurs.... *I don't know if that speaks to the popularity of* Shark Tank, *or if there's a new spirit of enterprise in the air and in the water, but I think this is a stat to celebrate—how 'bout you?*

"They used to sell these kits where you could build your own Beach Cruiser for like three hundred bucks," he explains. "Or, you could buy one already built for about eight hundred bucks, so I bought the do-it-yourself model and then I realized, 'Wait, now I can make another one and sell it for eight hundred.' That was probably the first little business I had."

Jake always had a deal going. (Sound like anyone you know?) Once, his father, who ran an indoor soccer center, received a surprise shipment of 1,500 lollipops that some company had sent his way hoping he'd start carrying the lollipops at the concession stand. Jake's dad had no plans to sell the item, so he told Jake he could have them. He said, "Listen if you want to take these to school, do what you want with them," Jake tells me.

So Jake stuffed those suckers into his backpack—removing all the books to make room—and lugged them off to school, thinking he'd sell them for whatever price the market would bear. It ended up, he sold through his entire stash—making about $600. **Wasn't the money that got him going so much as the thrill of it, the challenge. It was a way to judge his effectiveness, his ability to accomplish what he set out to do,** to solve the puzzle of what to do with that windfall of lollipops. Out of that, he started selling T-shirts (*now* does it sound familiar?), and he grew that effort into a rave, lighting, and accessory business and started working the dance festival circuit. Soon he had no time for school—or, at least, not *enough* time for school. First year of college, he was falling behind in his classes—no surprise given that on weekends he was always driving to some event, nursing a retail operation he was trying to get off the ground, and all week long he was promoting and selling and hustling. And with Jake, it wasn't *just* that there was no time for school. It was more like he didn't see the point. His heart wasn't in it. Instead, it was in making money, making deals, making noise, and all that time in the classroom and in the books just kept him away from that.

Meanwhile, his rave business was growing so fast he took space in a local mall and almost immediately logged a $50,000 month in sales—that's how crazy-busy (and how crazy-successful) he was, while still trying to carry a full course load at school.

Not exactly a recipe for success on all fronts—something *had* to give.

Jake's partner, Kramer, also a California kid, was cut the same way. The two didn't know each other growing up, but they met as roommates, around the time Kramer was deciding college wasn't for him, either. The key difference was that Jake was in his first year when he came to this decision, while Kramer was in the last month or two of what was supposed to be his final semester. I thought that was pretty bold, pretty interesting, that you could be so close to a goal and then step away from it, so one of the first things I asked him once we got to know each other was what the hell he was thinking.

"I think I knew in the back of my mind I could always go back to school if I needed to," Kramer says. "Wasn't planning on it, but the option was there. I could always take a year off and pursue whatever I was working on at the time, and after that I could go back and finish my degree."

But that's not exactly what happened. What Kramer had been working on at the time was another crowdfunding campaign— his first, this one for an innovative wallet design. When he found himself sharing an apartment with Jake, the two started comparing notes and they quickly found a lot to like and admire in the other. Jake was blown away by Kramer's success in the crowdfunding space, while Kramer was struck by Jake's familiarity with retail. They kicked around ideas they could maybe pursue together. Underneath all of this, it's important to note that Jake's rave business was now beginning to falter, and the way he remembers it is that he was simply outhustled. "These other guys, they just put me out of business," he admits.

These other guys, it turned out, was a company called EmazingLights, which was started by Brian Lim, who actually turned up on *Shark Tank,* seeking a $650,000 investment in exchange for 5 percent of his company—a deal I almost ended up taking, in partnership with my fellow Shark Mark Cuban, before we all parted ways in the due diligence phase after the show was taped, something that happened every once in a while.

Still, deal or no deal, I was enormously impressed by Brian (that's one of the reasons I'd pursued this partnership), so I understood right away the competition Jake was facing.

"They were doing exactly what we were doing," Jake says, "but better. I'd just renewed my lease in the mall for another year, had just had that big fifty-thousand-dollar month, and within six months I was done. I was out of business. Brian's become a good friend of mine now, and if you go to his facility you understand why he put me out of business. He's an amazing entrepreneur, and I was still doing the college thing, the balancing thing, working eight hours a day and thinking I was putting in the time. Meanwhile, Brian was putting in sixteen, seventeen hours a day, rising and grinding, and making all the right moves. It was a real eye-opener for me."

UNDERSTAND WHERE YOU CAN COMPETE, AND WHERE YOU MIGHT BE BEAT

Guess you could say his ears were now opened as well, and when Kramer started talking about the money he'd raised for his wallet design, Jake was listening carefully. The two roommates tried to come up with a good idea they could work on as a team. With Kramer's experience in crowdfunding and Jake's experience in retail, they thought they could position themselves for a serious run . . . once they came up with the right business or product.

"The great thing about crowdfunding," Kramer shares, "is that your business can almost take off by itself. If you have a good video, if you're telling a good story, you don't have to spend money on advertising and marketing. All you need is a good product that people can believe in."

He's right: on the back of all these great crowdfunding sites, we're seeing the removal of the traditional barriers to entry in most businesses. Along with that, we're also seeing a spike in the number of new products being sold directly to consumers, through innovative platforms like Shopify. And now here you had these two young watch designers who'd been savvy enough to leverage them—and savvy enough to throw in on an enterprise that made full and focused use of their complementary skill sets and an appetite for risk and hard work.

It used to be you had to really pound the pavement, and seed your market, before you sold a single product, but now you've got dynamic young people like Jake and Kramer who are able to push through those development stages on their laptops, and even raise a bunch of capital while they're doing it.

....

POWER FACT: Did you know that despite all the talk about the rise of e-commerce and the decline of traditional brick-and-mortar stores, just 8 percent of total retail sales in the United States are conducted online? . . . *What this means is that there's tons of room for growth, even in an environment where an e-tailing giant like Amazon posts 480 million products for sale.*

....

One of the ideas they kicked around was the concept that grew into MVMT. They were both into fashion, both in agreement that there was a need for a trendy, affordable, high-quality watch line, and both willing to work like mad to see if they could develop one. Trouble was, they didn't know the first thing about watches, beyond what they liked and what they didn't. The good news was they knew how to get things done, and whatever shortcomings they might have had as students, whatever was missing in terms of *grind* in their academic careers, it was a different story when the time they were putting in was to launch a business. Plus, they were quick studies. They learned what it was to design and manufacture a product, how to arrange for shipping fulfillment, which customers to target and where to find them. Trouble was, they didn't have a whole lot of money to do these things, so they harnessed the power of broke and raised it—to the tune of $300,000. The day they completed their crowdfunding campaign, they sold four watches on the MVMT website. It wasn't much, but it was something—and it would grow from there.

All signs indicated they had a good concept, but what they needed now were customers. So they took what they call a growth hacking approach. I'd never heard the term (I'm a little *too* old-school, I guess), but growth hacking is all about experimenting with a series of making-it-up-as-you-go-along marketing efforts across different channels—what we used to call "guerrilla marketing" in my day.

"Basically, we were trying to advertise without spending a dollar," Jake explains, and they did this in a variety of very fluid, very creative ways. One strategy I really admired, as they walked me through it, was the way they looked to tap potential customers through different platforms, liked Reddit, where they'd create a bunch of dummy accounts and change their IP addresses and "upvote" their watches on certain sub-Reddits—earning thousands of clicks.

Here again, they were making things happen the same way we made things happen back in the day with FUBU—reinforcing my belief that there is nothing *new* in how we make and market our products and services, other than the platforms we use to do it. Here it just so happened that the rules of the game had been reinvented, thanks to social media and the rise of online marketing, but these guys were able to assess and address all the ways the playing field had changed. They identified the resources available to them on their nothing budget and took full advantage of them.

At the end of their first year in business, MVMT had $1 million in sales; the following year, they did $7 million; the year after that, $30 million; then, $60 million. As the company grows, they're hoping to expand into new lines and products, such as sunglasses.

In order to keep this growing empire ticking (see what I did there? *ticking?*), Jake and Kramer stick to a fairly set daily schedule. They came into this thing with discipline and focus, and now that they're working together, they've doubled down on those aspects of their character. Each of them drives the other, they say. They're both early risers, both off to the gym first thing, both always trying to cram in as much information as they can on the fly. The idea, to hear them tell it, is to keep sharp in mind and body, to approach each day refreshed and recharged. Jake, for one, likes to listen to an audiobook or a podcast as he commutes—about thirty minutes each day. "At that rate," he says, "I can put down twenty-four books a year, which is just crazy to me, because I can't remember the last time I actually *read* a book."

One of the books that's had the biggest influence? *The Hard Thing About Hard Things* by Ben Horowitz. "It's the best management book I've ever read," Jake says, "with all kinds of insights on hiring and firing and almost going bankrupt. There's also a lot of stuff in there about building a corporate culture, which is one of the things Kramer and I talk about all the time."

Evenings, he'll take some time to decompress with a little meditation, maybe listen to some music, go over what he needs to hit the next day.

Kramer tends to be the gadget guy of the two, so when he's not putting out fires at work or working on that fire in his belly at the gym, he's looking at new apps to help keep him and his MVMT team productive. Lately, he's got his staff of about forty using Evernote to organize and archive notes, and the cloud-based tool Slack to integrate the company's communication devices.

"I don't know where we'd be without the technology," he admits. "We'd have to do twice the work, just keeping track of everything, and in the end it'd be like we put in half the time."

He finds his inspiration in the example of others—like Gary Vaynerchuk, the author, motivational speaker, and serial entrepreneur we met earlier.

"This guy just has so much energy," Kramer says. "I don't know if Gary sleeps at all, with all the things he's got going on, but I look on and see the passion he brings to everything he does and it pushes me to want to do the same thing."

These guys might be college dropouts, but they're bursting

with common sense, and when I hear them talking about all the different ways they've tapped the very latest in technology to help maximize their efforts, I'm reminded yet again what an exciting time it must be to come of age as a young person in business. And what it can do for your *rise and grind* state of being when you're helped along by all those tablets and screens that allow you to get even more done, in less time.

One of the things Kramer worries about now that MVMT has found its footing is keeping his focus, his drive. Right now, the *grind* of building his company doesn't feel to him like a grind at all. He and Jake have created a fun, dynamic workspace, populated with friends and employees of similar ages and interests. But what will happen to his hard-charging work ethic if MVMT continues to grow at its current pace? If his dream of financial freedom is realized when he's still pretty young?

"We talk about that all the time as well," Kramer allows. **"Where are we going to be in twenty years? I don't know. But I have to think we'll find our motivation as we grow. Because, let's face it, there are lots of successful people out there who continue to grind and hustle, long after they've made it."**

There's a lot to like about these guys, a lot to respect. Their story makes me think of that great line from Jim Rohn: "There are two types of pain you will go through in life: the pain of discipline and the pain of regret. Discipline weighs ounces while regret weighs tons."

Discipline . . . Jake and Kramer have got this in full. Regret . . . I don't think that's a weight they carry. Why? Well, they were each smart enough to walk away from a college degree that wouldn't have really served them in the end, and instead went and got educated in the school of real-life business. They saw their time to shine and stepped to it—and I don't see that clock running out on them anytime soon.

Jake and Kramer's Grind Checklist

✓ keep loading up on those podcasts and audiobooks—when I'm not returning phone calls or answering emails as I work out, I should be "reading," and for someone like me who's dyslexic, there's no better, more efficient way to read than to have someone else read *to* me . . .

✓ seek creative partnerships with like-minded people whose interests and energy levels match your own . . .

✓ create a workplace culture that reflects your personality and the spirit of your product or service . . .

✓ put in the time you need when you're just starting out, and pull back once you've found your footing . . .

✓ get your sweat in early—this way, if the day runs away from you, you'll know your workout is in the bag . . .

✓ understand how you plan to scale your business *before* the time comes when you have to do so . . .

✓ be prepared to pivot—the marketplace will tell you if you're headed in the right direction, but you have to listen to it and change things up accordingly . . .

. . . .

For more information on Jake and Kramer and how they use the Rise and Grind mindset, check out
www.DaymondJohn.com/Rise/JakeAndKramer

BE EXCITED

BEAT THE SUN

GRANT CARDONE
Bestselling Author, Motivational Force, Real Estate Investor,
Success Multiplier

FIRST THING THAT strikes me about Grant Cardone, author of megaselling books like *Be Obsessed or Be Average* and *The 10X Rule,* is that he doesn't use a watch. **(Shhh . . . don't tell Jake and Kramer.)** Oh, he wears one—he says he's got about forty!—but he doesn't bother setting them or replacing the batteries when they wind down. He likes how they look, is all.

"I use the sun," he says, when I ask him how he keeps time. "That's my first goal when I start each day, to get up before the sun. **Doesn't matter what time zone I'm in, if I can beat the sun in the morning, I feel like I've had this major victory already.** I try to do it every day."

First thing Grant does each morning when he gets out of bed is "take a piss." He tells me this in such a matter-of-fact way it strikes me as funny, but then it strikes me as kind of telling, that of *all* the people I've interviewed for this book, talking about their daily routines, he's the only one who mentions that he goes to the bathroom as soon as he gets out of bed. "These are the things people don't tell you," he jokes, when I mention that he stands alone in this. "The details behind the greatness."

But that's the thing about Grant Cardone. He tells it like it is, plain talk. I get the sense that he's the kind of guy who's too busy to waste time worrying what people think about him. It's just not a priority. Like how he tells me he's got to eat while we're doing our interview, because it's the only way he can get through everything he needs to do each day. True to his word, someone brings him a plate of food as we're talking, and he pretty much inhales it. Doesn't skip a beat.

"I don't think much of food," he says between bites. "Food, to me, is like gasoline. It keeps me going, but I eat while I'm going because that's how you create time. I don't even think about it. I just throw it in the tank and keep moving."

This kind of plain talk runs all through the morning meeting he holds every day with his entire team, but I'll get to that in a beat, after we plow through the rest of Grant's morning ritual. After he hits the bathroom, he sits down and writes his goals. He does the same thing each night, before he hits the pillow. His goals, he says, are "massive, unachievable targets, probably not attainable in this life."

Such as?

Well, one of his goals during the week I interviewed him for this book was to amass a $10 billion real estate portfolio. Yep, you read that number right—$10 billion! Another is to build an estate that could earn $200 million a year in the year 2065, long after he's dead and gone. Yep, you read that number right, too. Another goal is one that's driven him since he was a kid—to meet 70 million people in his lifetime. Yep, you read that number right again.

"Whatever's on my mind, that's what I put down," Grant says of his approach. "What I'm looking for here, really, is what's repeating itself. I might want to lose some weight, but I might put that down for a couple of days before it drops out. So when I notice that the thing about earning two hundred million dollars a year in 2065 keeps showing up, that's the one that wants to stick."

After writing down his goals, he moves to breakfast—"just a little bit of protein," he says. "Then a quick workout—just twenty minutes or so," he figures. "I'll do some cardio, some weights, some Pilates, possibly a quick swim," he says. **"I'm not looking to build muscle. I'm just trying to get moving, trying to get that sense of being in control of my body.** And the concept here is, if I can't control my body, how am I going to control my business? How am I going to control my money? How am I going to control my customers? How am I going to control the rest of my day if I can't even control 158 pounds?"

It's a fair point and says a lot about a man who lives his life with a military-style discipline and precision. Take that morning meeting I told you about. It happens every day at 9:06 a.m.

Why such a weirdly specific time?

"Because our COO tells me we need to start at a set time," Grant explains. "He wanted to do it at nine o'clock. We've got sixty-five people walking into a meeting, sometimes one hundred, they need to know what time it is. So I said, 'Don't make it nine o'clock. That's lazy.' My point was, nine o'clock is not a decision. **Tell someone you want to be a millionaire, that's a lazy goal. Tell someone you want to be worth $1,184,912, that's a guy who's actually thought through what he wants.** If you set the meeting at nine-oh-six, you've given it some thought. It's specific."

That 9:06 start time reminds me of that super specific goal of mine, to cash a check for $102,345,086.32, where I visualize my fantasy payday all the way down to the penny—because you really do have to put some thought into a thing if you want to make that thing happen. Grant puts a whole lot of thought into these 9:06 morning meetings. He gathers everyone in his company, an industry leader in sales training products, from top to bottom. His finance people, his Internet staff, the folks in shipping. Everyone from C-suite executives to hourly employees is expected to be there, at 9:06 sharp. The focus of the meeting is success, and the only items on the agenda are the winning moments the members of his team think to share—whether or not they are strictly business related. "If there's someone we've helped to lose fifteen pounds, we'll talk about that," he says. "If there's some company that earned an extra fifteen million dollars because of something we did for them, we'll talk about that, too. And it's not like one success story is more valuable than another. They all have great value."

Grant believes those morning meetings are the most important part of his day, and he considers them the one thing he's put in place that really defines his corporate culture. He looks forward to it as he heads into the office, and he looks back on it all day long, as a real highlight. "Look," he says, "I've been in business for thirty-five years. I need to stay excited. I need to keep the people who work with me excited. The salespeople, the accounting people, my executive team. **I know that the plateaus are where the death starts, so I need to keep the focus on possibility and potential.** I've made a lot of money. It would take a lot of work for me to spend all my money, a real effort. So what's going to keep me excited other than money? Potential. The power to help more people realize *their* potential. So what I want to hear in those meetings is, Who are we reaching in the crevices and corners of the world? How are we using technology and change and communication to reach more people? Remember, one of those unattainable goals that keeps sticking for me is to reach seven billion people. I want seven billion people to know my name, in hopes that seventy million of them become friends of mine."

LIVE THE 10X RULE

Grant got his start as a car salesman, and the lessons learned on that job can be found in his books, his keynote speeches, his blogs, and his live-stream posts. He's used the selling technique he picked up in the automobile business to help small companies and Fortune 500 giants of all types discover overlooked markets and opportunities. One of the common threads in the advice he gives to clients and shares with readers is to shake free of the tired constraints of the marketplace, and to shatter the limitations we place on ourselves—and, in the case of companies, on our employees.

His great innovation in this space has been "the 10X rule," which basically tells us to reach for success on a massive scale—the same way Grant pushes himself with some of those crazy, pie-in-the-sky goals he sets for himself each day.

I was pleased and proud to take part in Grant's 10X Growth Con—a three-day conference for entrepreneurs, featuring guest speakers like yours truly—which takes Grant's powerful multiplier concept and encourages people to apply it to *all* aspects of their life. But I couldn't help but wonder where the inspiration for the 10X idea came from in the first place.

"It started out, it was a financial thing," he explains. "I was trying to calculate what it would take, coming out of the financial collapse, to make sure my family was never vulnerable to a market crash or correction. How much money would I need to have? And then, when I was multiplying everything out to get to that number, I started to see that in order to get ten times more money, I'd have to generate ten times more income, get ten times more customers, acquire ten times more real estate. I needed to be ten times bigger, across the board."

CREATE TIME

Grant's *rise-and-grind* mentality came to him as less of a choice, and more of a necessity. He grew up the youngest of five kids—though he has a twin brother, so I guess he technically grew up as one of the two youngest of five kids.

But what stamped his childhood more than the fact that he came from a big family was that his father died at a young age. "He just ran out of time," Grant tells—a sad fact of life that wasn't lost on Grant, who was just ten at the time. "He worked hard his whole life, got his dream house when he was fifty, and he was dead eighteen months later. So that's why you hear me talk a lot about how we're running out of time. The last thing I'm going to waste my time doing is to try to control time. I'm going to try to multiply it instead. I'm going to do two things at once, three things at once. I don't try to manage time, because it's a losing proposition. I don't try to balance life, it's a losing proposition. No one can show me a person who's got that work–life balance thing working and is being super successful, because it just doesn't exist in the same format. It's one of those massive goals, impossible to achieve."

....

POWER FACT: In 2016, there were over 2.3 billion people on social media worldwide, including 207 million in the United States alone.... *Grant's dream of making a meaningful connection to millions of people might be massive, but the reach and power of our information age might put him in the ballpark.*

....

Grant tells me he knew at eight years old that he wanted to be successful. Back then success meant making a lot of money, but once his father died, the definition changed. Now it also had to do with time, and making the most of his time, and finding ways to connect with other people in the time that was available to him. That 70 million number I've mentioned a couple of times already in this chapter? It comes from this time in Grant's life, when he remembers feeling a little angry that his father was taken from him so young, so soon.

"Look," he says. "When my dad died, I knew the guy who was going to teach me about money and success was gone. So I'm like, 'Who's gonna teach me?' My mom was a great mother, but she couldn't teach me about money. She couldn't teach me how to be successful. I got a little pissed off about it, to tell you the truth. And I can remember one day when I was sixteen I told my mom I was going to be super successful. I just announced it. I said, 'I'm going to be super successful and I'm going to help other people.' Because I was just so angry that I'd been so dependent on just one person and that one person wasn't there to help me figure this stuff out. I don't know how many people there were on the planet back then, not seven billion, but that's where I started saying things like I wanted to meet everybody on the planet. I needed to meet everybody, so I wouldn't be dependent on just one person, or just a few people."

An impossible dream? Maybe, but Grant Cardone puts it out there and rises before the sun each day to meet it. He doesn't try to manage time, like he says, but he looks to capture it in what ways he can. That's one of the reasons he bought a jet—not because he wanted to throw his money around, but because he wanted to spend more time with his wife and kids, without taking anything away from his business or his dreams. It's just another way he's trying to create time to do the things he believes he is meant to do—like meet all those people, all around the world.

The truth is, I've never met someone who spends so much

time thinking about time, and so it's probably no surprise that Grant has figured out how to squeeze every last ounce of productivity from his days before he powers down each evening. He's usually in bed by nine o'clock each night, but not before he does a live stream on one of his social media platforms. He's got the themes all worked out ahead of time: on Mondays he does a real estate show; on Tuesdays he shares something he's learned from a power player he's reached out to during the week; on Wednesdays he and his wife, Elena, team up to do a show about business and marriage; on Thursdays there's a sales-focused show for millennials; on Fridays he does a show called *The Cardone Zone*; on Saturdays and Sundays he loosens things up, maybe focuses on relationships or spirituality.

Grant is all about teaching and inspiring others to live their best life, and he's not about to give up on that dream just because he's now a father. "I know that sounds ugly, but that's how I see it," he says. "I think my responsibility to be a father or an uncle or a mentor to many, to seventy million, is as important as me being a good father to two. I've had that dream of helping people since I was ten years old, when there was nobody to help me. And I'm not about to give up on that dream just because I had two kids. It's my purpose, and I'm going to make time for all of it."

Grant's Grind Checklist

✓ be precise—I love the way he starts his morning meeting at 9:06 a.m., how it keeps everyone on their toes . . .

✓ create time by doing several things at once . . . go ahead and walk and chew gum and make things happen . . .

✓ work out to get the juices flowing . . . I tend to think of opportunities to exercise in big, hour-long blocks, but a guy like Grant is able to jump-start his body and get something going with just twenty minutes . . . his workouts are even short enough that he can squeeze in a second one at the end of the day . . .

✓ extend your reach . . . the more people you meet, the more people you're likely to collaborate with, learn from, inspire . . .

✓ keep your short game going, but keep the long game in mind—in other words, do what you have to do, but at the same time do that thing nobody expects . . .

For more information on Grant and how he uses the
Rise and Grind mindset, check out

www.DaymondJohn.com/Rise/Grant

SEVEN

STEP BACK

END OF THE day, it's the *grind* that gets us where we're going, but we need to remember to take a little time for ourselves along the way.

Now, I don't think I meant to offer that kind of message when I started in on these pages—no way! And I don't think it's a message most of you expected to find when you picked up this book. But here it is. Why? Because as I take in the stories of the people who shared their insights and routines with us, and as I look ahead to the few people we're still due to meet in the pages to come, I'm realizing that we all need to take it down a notch from time to time—to hit Pause, or Refresh, or whatever.

'Course, I *know* this, deep down. We all *know* this. And on some level, I guess I've *known* this all along. But we live in a world where hard work is celebrated, expected. Where the space between what we *know* and what we actually *do* can be hard to spot. In this area especially. So let's be honest with one another on this. When it comes to work, we push one another to where it's a point of pride, to be the first one at the office in the morning, the last one to leave at night. It's part of our corporate culture—and now part of our entrepreneurial culture—to put in those long hours. We stick out our chests and crow about it when we have to *grind* all weekend or pull an all-nighter. We post pictures on social media and shout it out to the world when we're off on a never-ending business trip. Hey, I'm as guilty as anyone, the way I amp up the *grind* and encourage the folks who follow me to break a sweat and keep pushing in pursuit of their goals.

But I know better.

Deep down, we all know better.

So let's spend some time on what it is we all *know better*— namely, that **we need to take our foot off the gas every once in a while**. To *step back,* like it says right up top in the title to this chapter.

I was reminded of this in a full-on way by my friend Chris Sacca, the well-known venture capitalist and *Shark Tank* guest panelist, who posted a blog as I was finishing this book. Actually, to call Chris a friend is probably overstating things, because I don't know him all that well, outside of his few appearances as a guest Shark in seasons 7 and 8. Still, I'd come to admire the way he handled himself on the show, and what he was able to accomplish as a first-stage investor in monster companies like Twitter, Instagram, Uber, and Kickstarter, back when they were just scrappy start-ups with a bunch of dollar signs in their eyes. I knew Chris as a guy with a smart mind and a relentless work ethic who was famous for his commitment to his companies and to his partners. There was no letup to this guy—until, at last, there was.

What do I mean by that? Well, in his blog post, he wrote very movingly, very passionately about making the tough decision to step away from the day-to-day of his firm, Lowercase

Capital. He wrote about finally taking the time to slow things down. About holding on to those pieces of himself that maybe get lost sometimes in the hustle and bustle of jump-starting all these different businesses. He wrote about how the *grind* had just about *ground him down.* . . . To get this message from someone like Chris, a hard-driving guy who attacked everything he did at full-throttle, was a real eye-opener.

"Startup investing is one of my things, but it is not my everything," he wrote. "The only way I know to be awesome at startups is to be obsessively focused and pegged to the floor of the deep-end gasping for air. I succeeded at venture capital because, for years, I rarely thought about or spent time on anything else."

Take another look at that last line: *I rarely thought about or spent time on anything else.* . . .

That's not what we're after here, is it? I know that's not what *I'm* after. And yet, too often, we get caught up in the chase. We're chasing paper, chasing prestige, chasing power, chasing our own sense of self-worth . . . and there can be no end to it. **When do we take a step back and start to think about whether we have everything we need? If we're always chasing a number, a dollar amount, a goal, when do we stop to ask ourselves: what are we really chasing, after all?**

When do we let ourselves realize that the life we dreamed about is the life we've already been living?

SMELL THE ROSES

Think back to some of the folks you've met so far in these pages and see how they've been able to recognize this truth. Remember Brian Lee, who had to live, breathe, eat, and sleep Legal-Zoom when he was getting his company started, but once he found—or, I should say, *earned*—success, he was able to pull back a bit, and slow his *grind* down? His was the kind of dedication and killer work ethic many of us can't avoid when we're just starting out, but like Brian Lee we need to keep it in perspective.

Or what about Lola Alvarez, the mom who worked tirelessly, ferociously to help her three boys power past their learning disabilities? When her kids were little she rose before the sun to get them ready and organized for school, and stayed up late, after going over everything their teachers had tried to teach them during the school day. It was a never-ending *grind* for this young mom—but the idea, over time, was to give her sons the tools they needed to get through their schoolwork on their own—and when that day eventually came, Lola was able to go back to work and start taking care of herself a little bit. From Lola, we see that sometimes the *grind* is an investment we make to get us to a place where the *grind* is no longer necessary, where the objectives we seek might become sustainable on their own.

Got time for one more? Kristina Guerrero completed three combat tours before she ever thought about starting a business, so she knew all about squeezing every last drop out of each and every day—but then, after she launched her TurboPUP line of doggie meals and had a child, she found a way to rebalance the work-life scale so that she could squeeze out every last drop of mom time as well. These days, she takes the same tireless work ethic she rode through the Air Force and attaches it to her days as a hardworking mom, making sure to set aside some of that precious quality time for her daughter.

They all chased and chased until they finally caught what they needed, and then they changed up their pace as their lives took on a new shape. We need to pinch a page from their playbook and remind ourselves to push when we must, to pull back when we can, and to find balance somewhere in the middle.

Doesn't matter who you are or what you do, there are

times in your life and career when you have no choice but to go after it, *hard,* and there are also times when you need to put a pin in what you're doing and chill. I don't always recognize this need in myself, and I'm the first to admit I can be a little over-the-top sometimes in the way I work, but it took hearing from Chris Sacca on this to set me straight. Matter of fact, I was so moved by what he wrote, so moved by his honest take on what it is we're all working for, after all, that it brought me to tears. I sent him a text, to let him know the impact he had on me with his post—and I guess what I'm doing here is hitting him back with another text, a *really long* text, to stand as a reminder to all of us to keep our work in perspective—to keep an eye on the long game.

POWER QUOTE: "Everybody is blessed with a certain talent. You have to know what your talent is, maximize it, and push it to the limit. . . ." *That's a line from boxer Floyd Mayweather, and I share it to make the point that we've got to push ourselves to the limit, but we've also got to pull back. Part of fighting the good fight, as Floyd would tell you, is knowing when to power down to make sure you can fight another day.*

Chris's post resonated with me, for sure, though I wouldn't say it got me to change my game. I'm still powering through my days, working double-time to hit my goals. But it did push me to reflect on *why* it is I work so hard, and how long I'll be able to keep at it in this all-consuming way, and when the fire that burns inside me will start to flicker. And it's pushed me to get more organized, more efficient, and more mindful about how I spend my days.

HUSTLE AND FLOW

One of the most famous examples of the balance we should all be seeking in our lives and careers comes from Google. For a while now, the company has been encouraging its employees all over the world to spend 80 percent of their time on their day-to-day assignments and long-term projects, and 20 percent of their time on outside-the-box activities that may or may not have anything to do with Google directly.

That works out to one day each week. On paper, from a management perspective, that seems like a whole lot of time to just give away to the whims of your staff, up and down the line. But Google executives are finding that it's a great investment in their ultimate resource—their *human* resource. Why? Because spending just that one day focused on something totally removed from their regular work allows the company's key people to work harder, smarter, and more creatively on the other four days

They call it the Innovation Time Out policy (ITO), but a lot of folks know it as Google's 80/20 approach, and it's led to the development of such great in-house initiatives as Gmail and Google News. Whatever you call it, the model has been adopted by dozens of leading companies in tech, engineering, and creative industries, and I believe we'll see more and more companies sign on to their own versions of this policy as our business landscape continues to change.

Essentially, the idea is to give ourselves a chance to stretch and grow away from the *grind* of our jobs, and there's a lot of research to support it. A lot of that research has to do with a concept social psychologists call "flow"—basically, those times in our life where we're firing on all cylinders, and so intensely zeroed in on a task that requires our full attention.

Have you ever had the feeling that you've lost track of time?

Been left thinking the clock has stopped while you lost yourself in this or that activity? That's what flow feels like, though for many of us, it doesn't happen all that often—only one in five people say it happens to them several times a day, and 15 percent of people say it never happens to them at all. Me, I find it happens more and more as I make a conscious effort to look beyond my daily goals and my daily *grind* and connect in some new, meaningful way with the people around me, and with my environment away from work.

Everyone finds "flow" in different places, depending on our interests, but we've each got a special groove that's unique to us, and when we're doing our thing in service of that groove, when the rest of the world falls away because we're so passionately and naturally focused, that's when we're at our best.

WHERE DO YOU FIND YOUR FLOW?

For a lot of us, these tasks don't always find us as we work. Oh, we might love what we do, but when our days are packed and crazy, there's no time to *step back* from the work, because there's no end to the work. That's why it's so important to find other ways to tap into flow in our daily lives.

Figure out what moves you, what excites you, what lifts you from the *grind* of your day, and then figure out a way to go there in your mind . . . even if it's just for a little while. According to an article in *Psychology Today,* when your mind is engaged on a specific task, and it's a task that gives you pleasure, it nourishes that part of your brain that keeps you feeling vital. Maybe that comes from playing a musical instrument, or painting a picture, or snowboarding down a difficult trail. Point is that we should all seek out those tasks and create those all-important moments whenever and wherever possible.

....

POWER FACT: 64 percent of people surveyed report feeling "most productive" between the hours of 8 a.m. and noon. . . . *That tells us that we can get the most out of our teams, and the most out of ourselves, when we're feeling fresh and focused, before the grind of the day gets to us.*

....

For me, since my youngest daughter, Minka, was born, that can mean just taking a walk with her, or reading a story together. Or maybe I'll take the time to go fishing when I'm at my place upstate, and lose myself in the sounds of the water and the rhythms of routine.

Some things to keep in mind when you want to get into the *flow*:

- *don't pay attention to the clock* . . . when time starts to fly, that's when you're really getting into the flow . . . try to go with it . . . looking at the time takes you out of the moment . . .
- *keep moving* . . . this isn't a passive deal . . . hey, they don't call it an "activity" for nothing . . . your flow activities should be *active* experiences, which means *you* have to make things happen . . .
- *try not to think of anything other than what you're doing* . . . eliminate distractions, so that nothing else gets in the way of the task right in front of you . . .
- *try not to think of yourself* . . . yeah, you've got to watch what you're doing—like, if you're fishing, you don't want to stab yourself in the fingers as you bait your hook . . . or if your thing is going for an amazing drive on a scenic highway, you've obviously got to pay

> attention to the road . . . but as much as possible, try to separate yourself from what you're doing . . . it's not about you, it's about the zone . . .
>
> • *stick with what works* . . . what I mean by this one is if you find something that brings you pleasure, that takes you outside yourself for a bit, that lets you exercise a part of your mind that doesn't always get tapped in your regular work, then go ahead and make it a habit . . .

So what's in it for us? Why should we buy in to this concept that we need to set aside some time in our busy days and weeks to seek out moments of flow? Well, for one thing, we'll be happier—and not *just* during those moments when we're engaged in our outside activity. Psychologists say there's a carryover effect, and you'll be happier overall if you take the time to lose yourself in the flow in some type of regimented way.

Some of the other benefits: better coping skills, higher self-esteem, and an increase in performance. Matter of fact, there was one Harvard Business School study I came across that found that creative teams in a business or corporate setting tended to have more breakthroughs when they were able to work with a set of clear goals and a great deal of flexibility—a lesson I've tried to take to our Shark Group offices, where I look to set things up so folks can approach straightforward tasks in ways that allow them to get into flow states.

Plus, we usually find flow in activities that tap into our strengths, and according to Dr. Martin Seligman, the father of positive psychology (essentially a field of study aimed at helping people develop their full potential and live happy, meaningful lives), if you're able to recognize your own personal strengths and use them regularly, you'll not only be happier and more fulfilled but healthier as well.

That's the ultimate goal, right? I mean, what's the point of all that *rising and grinding* if it doesn't take us to a place of happiness and fulfillment?

Why run yourself into the ground to make a dollar if that dollar doesn't enrich you in a spiritual way?

THE ENERGY PROJECT

As important as it is to take time out of your daily grind for activities that light up your brain, nourish your soul, and enrich your life, let's not forget the value of powering down entirely. My younger self, when I was getting things going with FUBU, would never take the time to just . . . sit . . . still. The older I get, the more I realize how important it is for me to shut off my brain and power down—even if it's just for a short stretch. These days I find myself looking for these little pockets of calm throughout my day, where I can be alone with my thoughts—even better, where I don't have to think of anything at all. Maybe I'll take a power nap, or head out for a quick walk just to clear my head. Maybe I'll find a quiet room and meditate. It's a rejuvenating thing, to just *be,* and when my day runs away from me and I don't steal a little time in this way, I'm dragging.

And it's not just me—we can find some pretty persuasive arguments for grabbing a little mental downtime right here in this book, through the people you've met in these pages. Take Carlos Santana, with his morning routine of simple prayer and thankful reflection. Catherine Zeta-Jones, lighting all those candles and setting just the right mood to make her feel relaxed and at home. Nely Galán, making sure to get her eight hours of sleep each night—just so she can get up at five o'clock the next morning and meet the day feeling refreshed and recharged. And Tyler, The Creator, climbing a tree in his neighborhood park just to find a little peace and quiet and a perch that lets him look out at the world in an uninterrupted way.

> POWER FACT: The website GoHealthInsurance .com reports a 200 percent bump in productivity in work environments that allow employees unlimited vacation time. . . . *That model might not work for you or your business, but if you try it you'll find that committed workers don't abuse the freedom this kind of vacation schedule allows, and the "returns on investment" can be enormous.*

I found a really great quote in a *Scientific American* article when I was looking for some more information on this subject. It comes from an essay written by a guy named Tim Kreider and published in the *New York Times:* **"Idleness is not just a vacation, an indulgence or a voice; it is as indispensable to the brain as vitamin D is to the body. . . ."**

Here's another way to look at it. Remember how at the start of the book I talked about finding time and making time and using time to full advantage? About how there are only twenty-four hours in a day, which means it's on each of us to *spend* that time wisely? But what happens when it starts to feel like time is running out on us? When our deadlines are approaching and we're not even close to where we need to be? When our goals are looming large and the clock, as it tends to do, keeps ticking? Time is a finite resource. They're not making any more of the stuff, right? **If time is no longer on our side, we've got to find another resource to take its place, and that resource is *energy*.**

Because energy, unlike time, is *not* finite: that's a concept I learned from Tony Schwartz, who runs an organization called the Energy Project, which is devoted to making people and organizations more productive through the practice of positive psychology. You might know Tony as the ghostwriter of Donald Trump's *The Art of the Deal* and other bestselling titles, but he stepped away from journalism to devote himself to promoting the ideal of wellness in the workplace—and he's teamed up with a bunch of Fortune 500 companies like Ford, Genentech, Apple, Facebook, and Coca-Cola to put his ideas into action.

After interviewing more than 150,000 people around the world, Schwartz and his team found that 74 percent of employees are experiencing a "personal energy crisis." What to do about it? Well, he says, "the greatest untapped resource in your organization is what's happening inside your people."

But energy is a renewable resource, right? The Energy Project teaches companies to embrace the concept of "strategic renewal"—meaning to encourage employees to recharge by taking time away from their desks for short afternoon naps and daytime workouts, and to offer longer (and more frequent) vacation time. Studies show that these initiatives boost productivity and job performance, and that people who find ways to renew and restore their energy on the job are generally happier and healthier in their lives and careers.

Let's be clear: you can't *rise and grind* on an empty battery. So what are *you* doing to renew and restore your energy?

While you're thinking about it, let's take some time to meet just a few more people and see how they're finding ways to recharge and refresh.

BE HUNGRY

COME BACK TO WHAT YOU KNOW

AL AND BRITTANI BAKER

Father-Daughter Entrepreneurs, Finger-Lickin' Tastemakers, Partners in Barbecue

"I WILL PERSIST until I succeed."

That's a quote from Og Mandino, once thought by many to be the world's greatest salesman. It's also a line that has motivated my friend Al "Bubba" Baker throughout his career—both as a thirteen-year veteran of the National Football League (and a three-time Pro Bowler!) and now as the owner of the best damn barbecue joint in Ohio (Bubba's-Q World Famous Bar-B-Que) and co-owner of Bubba's-Q Boneless Ribs, the best damn ribs on the planet.

I should know, because Al and his daughter Brittani are two of my favorite *Shark Tank* partners—and their ribs are the best reasons I know for cheating on my diet.

"Hey, I was a pass rusher," Al says, referring to his football days. No lie—*Sports Illustrated* once named him the ninth-best pass rusher in NFL history. "You don't just walk across the line and tackle the quarterback. **The opportunities come when you least expect them, and you have to be moving in**

order to benefit from that opportunity. I had quite a few moves back when I was playing, and I've still got a few moves, and a lot of them came from guile and determination. We live by that in our family. Sometimes you can rise and grind, and rise and grind, and rise and grind, and just grind, grind, grind, and nothing happens. And then you have a breakthrough. But if you don't grind, I can assure you, nothing's going to go your way, because you haven't lined yourself up for it."

Al and Brittani are textbook examples of how I invest in people as much as I invest in products or services. Don't get me wrong, their ribs are out of this world. Their barbecue sauce is to die for. But it's their work ethic that gets me going most of all, and it's out there for the whole country to see—and to enjoy. As I write this, I'm in the middle of a national tour to dozens of Hardee's and Carl's Jr. locations as part of their promotion for Al and Brittani's killer new Baby Back Rib Burger. It uses a patented deboning process that Al and Brittani have developed that lets you bite into these juicy slabs of ribs without having to deal with the mess and bother of a bone.

Al had been noodling with the idea of a boneless rib, had made some real progress on it, but it was his daughter Brittani who gave him the final push to perfect it.

"This was his great project, but he kept getting sidetracked," Brittani says. "He just had so much going on, so he told me it was my job to keep him focused. I stayed on him, kept asking him where we were with the patent attorney, where he was with the process."

One of the ways Brittani kept her father on track was to remind him of the time he wouldn't let her quit the track team when she was in high school. She ran the 100 meters and the 200 meters, and she didn't think she had the time to put in to practice every afternoon, but Al wouldn't let her step away from her commitment. "He never let me quit on anything," Brittani says.

....

POWER FACT: More than 30 percent of family businesses survive into the second generation, but only 12 percent reach all the way to a third generation. . . . *Don't know where to put Al and Brittani in this equation, since they jump-started the business together, but I'm betting they'll be around a good long while.*

....

Now, I'm not about to tell you how Al and Brittani get those bones out of their delicious ribs, because they've sworn me to secrecy. But what I *can* tell is that it's a good thing Brittani kept driving her father on this, because I believe it's one of the greatest inventions in the history of Western civilization. Don't believe me? Well, then . . . I'm guessing you didn't stop in at your local Hardee's or Carl's Jr. and try one of these babies during the limited time offer.

(If you missed out, don't sweat it: there's a good chance we'll bring 'em back!)

DO WHAT YOU LOVE, LOVE WHAT YOU DO

Let me walk you through the story of how Al got his start, because it's a great illustration of how we find ways to stay charged and energized when we're doing something we love. See, he'd come up in the barbecue business. "I had barbecue running through my veins long before football," he likes to say. He grew up in and around his uncle's restaurant, Jenkins Quality Barbecue. His uncle was like a father to him, so Al spent a lot of time helping out, learning the business.

Like a lot of entrepreneurs I've worked with over the years, Al was raised by a single mother, who taught Al and his three older brothers to *rise and grind* by her example. She was up every morning at five o'clock, out the door by six to go to work, and back at it nights and weekends, perfecting her brother's barbecue sauce and finding local merchants willing to sell it. So, barbecue was a family affair, all right, but Al wasn't one of those athletes who look up when their playing days were over and figure they'll just up and start a restaurant. No, sir—not that there's anything wrong with that, but it just wasn't what was going on here.

What was going on was Al had been making barbecue for his teammates since his rookie year with the Detroit Lions. See, on travel days, the team would prepare these terrible box lunches for the players, premade ham sandwiches, maybe a candy bar and an apple. And there'd be Al with his juicy pork chop sandwich, dripping with coleslaw, and you can just imagine how everyone was drooling, watching him eat his homemade lunch while all they had where these nasty slabs of white bread and processed ham.

First person to ask Al for a bite was a defensive back named James Hunter, a former first-round draft choice out of Grambling State who at that point was one of the team leaders. Al was just a rookie, so you'd think he would have offered up that sandwich, no problem. But if that's what you think, you don't know Al.

He said, "Hell no."

Turned out Al had made two sandwiches for himself, and two for his roommate, Dave Pureifory, which he kept in a small cooler at his feet. But he wasn't about to give away something for nothing. James Hunter told Al he'd give him anything for one of those sandwiches, so Al threw out a number. He said, "Give me ten dollars."

Done deal—and Al had his proof of concept right there. And his first repeat customer. Next thing Al knew, he had a business.

The sandwiches cost him less than a dollar apiece to make, including the coleslaw, and they practically sold themselves thanks to James Hunter, who was like a product spokesperson because he kept talking up that delicious pork sandwich. For a couple of weeks, Al took orders, using that same $10 price, but after a while he started to feel guilty about making all that money off his teammates so he dropped the price to $5. For the next five years he fell into this routine of selling sandwiches on every travel day. He had a whole system. He'd do his shopping on his off day, fry the meat, marinate it, prepare and wrap the sandwiches. He was his own little assembly line.

In those days—late '70s, early '80s—unheralded rookies didn't make a whole lot of money in the NFL. Al remembers that his take-home pay was about $1,500 each week during the season, so pretty soon he was making more money from barbecue than he was from football.

In time Al grew the sandwich business to where he started slinging slabs of ribs as well, at $50 a pop. He'd set things up so he could cook eight slabs at a time, and his teammates would come over and pick up their orders—sometimes they'd just set themselves down and eat their fill right there in the backyard, while Al did his cooking.

Meanwhile, Al was running into some trouble with his informal catering business. Truth be told, he didn't really think of it as a business at the time—to him it was more like a sideline deal—but that's really what it was. "I was a professional football player," he says, "but that just set me up to get into the business that was already in me." The trouble was that one of the coaches had complained about the smell of all those sandwiches he'd bring along on the bus or the plane. You see, that small cooler Al used to bring along and keep at his feet when he was just feeding himself and his roomie was now a giant cooler holding thirty, forty, fifty sandwiches, and there was no hiding the delicious aroma that came from inside. He was called into a disciplinary hearing, but by this point Al had so many customers up and down the organization, including some of the other coaches, that the trouble went away.

"What's amazing to me now, looking back, is that none of these guys could cook," Al says.

Not Al. He could cook up a storm. His mother had seen to that. She was gone all day, so she taught Al and his brothers their way around the kitchen—same way my mother taught me to sew, I guess. She taught them how to cut a chicken, how to make the sauce, how to fix up a fine feast. And he took that basic training and kicked it up a couple of notches at his uncle's barbecue joint, so that by the time he started slapping together his own sandwiches and smoking those ribs for his friends and teammates, it was like second nature to him.

LOOK BEFORE YOU LEAP

You'd think, with all that barbecue running through his veins, Al would have started cooking full-time once he left the game, but when he retired from football he and his wife bought a Mail Boxes Etc. franchise in Shaker Heights, Ohio. It wasn't meant to be a permanent thing. The idea was to learn how to run a business within the support structure of a national franchise operation, because Al thought he might need some help figuring out how to handle things like payroll, and taxes, and the general running of a day-to-day business. For all of you would-be entrepreneurs out there, this is a tight strategy—it lets you learn on the job with a kind of corporate safety net underneath you, even though you're still in business for yourself. It was around this time that Al started bottling his signature barbecue sauce—Bubba's-Q All Purpose Sauce—and selling it out of his store, but the Mail Boxes Etc. folks put a quick stop to that because they didn't want their franchisees selling merchandise that wasn't their own.

Brittani was born in 1985, after Al had been traded to the St. Louis Cardinals, but he took his barbecue business with him—and from there, on to Cleveland and Minnesota, where he finished out his career. Brittani remembers growing up around all these big, beefy guys who'd come over to their house with these huge appetites, but even more than that she remembers how much fun her father always seemed to be having, surrounding himself with all this good food, all these good people. In the back of her mind, she set it up so this was something to shoot for.

This goes back to the message of the previous chapter, where I talked about how important it is to fill your days with joy. Hard work is great, but it will run you into the ground unless there's a heaping helping of fulfillment in it, and here Al had himself a big ol' spoonful.

Jump ahead a couple of years, and Al was running his famous Bubba's-Q barbecue joint in Avon, Ohio, but it was a tough slog. They had a whole line of sauces and rubs that seemed to be outperforming the restaurant business itself, so there was talk around the family table of shutting down the restaurant and focusing on their product lines. That's where Brittani's *grind* kicked in. She was a big-time *Shark Tank* fan, and she got it in her head that her family's story would play well on the show, so she went ahead and threw their hat in the ring.

She didn't say anything to her father about it at first, but when her application cleared the first few hurdles and she started hearing back from the producers, she clued him in. He wasn't all that excited. He said, "I have too much stuff to do right now to try to get on some television show."

But Brittani kept after it, and when the producers finally called to invite Al and Brittani to participate in a Skype interview as the final step before coming out to Los Angeles to appear on the show, Al was at the bank trying to arrange a refinancing. Really. How's that for timing? Specifically, he was about to default on a loan—that's how up against it, how broke, he was at the time.

....

POWER FACT: Family businesses generate 62 percent of US job opportunities and create 78 percent of all new jobs. . . . *Take the time to assess the resources around your family dinner table, because you just might find your best prospects sitting there right next to you.*

....

Well, you can pretty much guess the rest of the story. The producers "ate up" what Al and Brittani were selling. (Sorry, folks, but I couldn't resist!) When the day of the taping came around, Al nearly blew his part of the pitch. He and Brittani had gone over it a bunch of times, rehearsed it into the ground, but in their final run-through, just minutes before they were about to step onto the *Shark Tank* set, it felt to Al (and Brittani!) like he was about to blow it.

"This was the biggest stage I'd ever been on," he says now. "Way bigger than any football game."

So what happened? Brittani took her father's hand, looked into his eyes, and said, "It's okay if you ruin our lives, Pops."

"That kind of broke the ice," she remembers. "After that, he was fine."

So fine, in fact, that I was on board almost instantly. And it wasn't just their sauce that won me over. It was their heart, their hustle. And their sense of humor. If there's a secret ingredient in what these good people bring to the table, other than the finest herbs and spices and the best cuts of meat, it's their sense of humor. They find something to laugh about all day long, and when I'm with them the time just flies. Doesn't mean we don't get down and get to work, but they also know how to kick back and relax. In fact, a lot of times it feels to me as if that's their default mode, so they've got the happiness part of Tony Schwartz's Energy Project on lockdown. Whether they're grinding or chilling, there's a joyousness to their pursuit that I've come to love and admire.

I believe their sense of humor is a big part of what keeps them energized, what keeps the battery charged. The other is daily prayer—nowadays Brittani gathers her family each morning to give thanks for where they are and to seek strength for where they're going. I've come to love and admire that, too.

"Even though we've been on *Shark Tank*," Brittani says, "we're still *grinding*. Every day, we *grind*. We have to get up, and get our minds right, and face the challenges we're going to face on this journey as we look to share this boneless rib with America and show them why we believe in this product."

Al echoes the same point: "We have not arrived," he says. "We're on the journey. Every single day, we remind ourselves of this. We tell ourselves that the only way to win is to get up earlier than the competition, and to go to bed later than the competition. And in between those proverbial football lines, if you will, something good will always happen, if you put yourself in a position to play. That is the only guarantee."

Al and Brittani's Grind Checklist

✓ if at first you don't succeed, come at it another way . . . it's an old lesson, but it's tried and true, and here if Al had stopped selling his barbecue sauce from his Mail Boxes Etc. location, I wouldn't be carrying all this extra weight around my middle from these boneless ribs!

✓ carve out your areas of strength when you're working with a partner . . . Al knows ribs and barbecue . . . Brittani knows sales and marketing . . . they know to leave it to each other to do their separate thing . . .

✓ take the time to pray and give thanks . . . I'm repeating myself, I know, but if there's an important lesson in these pages it's this right here . . .

✓ don't quit . . . Brittani took in that message loud and clear when she was in high school, and she was quick to put it back on her father when he needed to hear it . . .

✓ turn your accidents into opportunities . . . Al tells a story of how he forgot to defrost the turkey one Thanksgiving, so in desperation he put it on the grill while it was still frozen . . . it turned out superduper juicy, and that's how his smoked turkeys were born—one of his most popular items!

✓ baby-stepping is better than overstepping . . . when Al and his wife started that Mail Boxes Etc. franchise, their idea was to learn on someone else's dime . . . yeah, they were running their own business, but they had this big corporation behind them, so they could figure things out with a kind of cushion . . .

✓ just when other folks start to think you've "made it," that's when you need to double down and really get to work . . . it's one thing to make it onto the big stage, but it's another thing to stay there . . .

✓ it's always darkest before the dawn . . . keep the lights on as long as you can, so opportunity knows where to find you . . .

....

For more information on Al and Brittani and how they use the Rise and Grind mindset, check out

www.DaymondJohn.com/Rise/AlAndBrittani

BE QUIET

HARNESS YOUR EMOTIONAL ENERGY

JOEL OSTEEN
Televangelist, Author, Spirit Guide

ONE OF THE great side benefits to being on television is the chance it gives you to connect with so many amazing people. Back when I was all about FUBU, I met my share of movers and shakers, but it always felt to me like I was the one chasing down a meeting, like they were doing me some kind of favor by giving of their time. And they were—better believe it, they were! Nowadays, though, the connections run two ways. It's flipped. I'm always hearing from people I admire, telling me they're fans of the show and thanking me for putting out a positive message and creating opportunities for aspiring entrepreneurs. At the same time I'm reaching out to folks who've touched my heart or sparked my creativity in some way.

Whoever it is, I'm usually able to get a dialogue going.

Got to say, it's a great good thing. A blessing. And I take time to appreciate it, every single day. So when I heard that Joel Osteen, the senior pastor at Lakewood Church, in Houston, and whose televised sermons are seen by millions each week, was a

Shark Tank fan, I was all over it. Even better, he was eager to visit with me and talk about the ways we might work together and maybe motivate readers to harness their *grind* to help them live a more meaningful, more purposeful life. I was stoked. I mean, this guy's sermons are seen in more than one hundred countries. He's got a gig on Sirius satellite radio, and one of his books *Your Best Life Now* was on the *New York Times* bestseller list for almost four years! Four years! That's *sick,* right? Really, the way this man is able to lift people up, to change lives, with the strength of his words . . . it got me wondering how you carry the weight of that kind of responsibility, how you rise to meet this type of calling. How you manage to sustain the emotional energy needed to do that type of heady work. And how you make it look so easy.

The short answer: you don't. Meaning, you don't think of the weight. You don't think of what you're doing as any kind of burden. You don't *rise* to meet anything. You just get up and get out there and do your thing, and after you do it long enough it starts to seem effortless—even though it isn't.

As for emotional energy, Joel recharges by making time for *quiet,* time to get in touch with himself—whether through reading, writing, or prayer. Here's what I mean: Joel starts his days with a moment of prayerful reflection. I'd kind of figured Joel got to his prayers straightaway, but what struck me was *how* he prayed, and *when,* and *where,* and *what* he hoped to get out of the transaction.

"The first thirty minutes or so, I use that time to get quiet," he says. "I take that time to pray, to be thankful. To me, it's how I start each day with balance, and I really focus on what's going on with me. I search my heart. I ask myself, 'What am I doing today?' I try to search my motives. I ask, 'God, is this the right thing? Is this the path I'm supposed to be going down?' I view that time as a chance to be honest with myself and to prioritize the day."

> POWER FACT: According to *U.S. News & World Report*, 41 percent of people who pray believe their prayers are frequently answered.... *Why is that, do you think? Personally, I think it's because once you put an idea or a goal or a wish out into the world, you're more inclined to dig deep and find a way to make it happen.*

Joel sits by himself and reflects. And he tries not to ask for things when he prays. He uses the time to express his gratitude, and to think about the things he wants to accomplish in the day ahead. Sometimes he'll read his Bible, or revisit a favorite psalm. And when he does find himself asking for something specific in prayer, it's never for him—he asks on behalf of a friend or family member, or a parishioner, or a complete stranger whose story has touched him in some way. He asks on behalf of the planet, or of all mankind.

Also, Joel is patient with himself when he prays. **He's careful not to start his day off in a hurry, doesn't want to rush out of the house, or cut any corners on expressing his gratitude for the new day. The way he sees it, how he starts his day determines the kind of day it's going to be.** "If you start it off negative," he explains, "and you focus on, 'Oh man, it's raining,' or, 'Oh man, I don't want to go to work,' I just believe you're drawing in negativity. I think it's important to get up and say, 'Lord, thank you for another day.' Find something to be grateful for. So I thank Him for my health. I thank Him for my children. I thank Him for the opportunities He has given me."

Joel's office is like his sanctuary. It's where he feels most connected to his faith, and to his mission. But it's also where he feels most in tune, where the writing that makes up the bulk of his work these days seems to come most easily. Basically, it's where he finds the peace and quiet he needs to explore the big themes he talks about in his sermons each week. His office is filled with all these little touchstones from his life and his ministry, and it looks out on his property down in Texas. He spends most of his reflective time there, soaking in the wonders of his world. He keeps a ton of photos and mementoes, reminding him of where he's been and where he's going. **On one of his shelves is a pair of his father's shoes**—as many of you might know, he took over his father's ministry when he was just thirty-five years old, after his father died of a heart attack, so those shoes are a very literal reminder to Joel that he's walking in his father's footsteps. And he draws energy from the quiet of this sacred space, where he gives thanks for his legacy, for the people in his life who inspire him, for the people he gets to inspire in return.

Joel's weekend sermon might only run thirty minutes, but the writing of it dominates most of his workweek. Everything else falls from this right here, and Joel's staff knows not to bother him once he slips into writing mode. The day-to-day *grind* of running the church, his business dealings, his broadcasting responsibilities . . . that stuff is for Mondays and Tuesdays. On Wednesdays he immerses himself in the news of the day. He reads, he studies, he goes over his notes, looking for ideas, sorting through trends and themes and finding something that speaks to him—something that will hopefully speak to his millions of followers as well.

Thursdays and Fridays, he's in his office by seven o'clock in the morning, writing.

"I feel like I'm the most creative at that time of the day," he says, "so that's the most important part of my day."

When he's deep into writing or researching mode, Joel makes

sure to put a pin in what he's doing and get in some exercise. At these times he'll start to feel like this physical release for his emotional energy is essential. He'll do this at a couple of points throughout the day. When the weather is cooperating, that can mean a one-hour walk, usually at a brisk pace, and usually with an inspirational CD to keep him company. Or maybe he'll be so lost in what he's listening to, he'll walk for a couple of hours. For a lot of people, listening to music or a podcast or a sermon is a way to pass the time as they exercise, or a way to catch up or multitask. But for Joel, these long contemplative walks are really just extensions of the work he's doing when he's at his desk, and he listens to draw inspiration from what other people have had to say on whatever it is he's writing about.

Now, I don't mean to compare the books I write to the sermons Joel gives each week, but I understand the pressure he's under—only with me and my books, I get to finish the assignment and set the writing aside for a year or two before I start thinking about the next one. With Joel, he has to come up with something eye-opening, something stirring, something uplifting *every week*. With no letup! I never went to college, but I imagine it's like the pressure of having a term paper or a thesis hanging over your head, constantly. That's got to be pretty intimidating (and probably exhausting!), but Joel has found a way to isolate that pressure and keep it as just a part of his workweek. He doesn't let it overwhelm him. Once the research is done, he's able to pull back, wait for the words to come. He's learned to trust that if he carves out his week in this way, if he's diligent in pursuit of each new sermon, the words will find him.

And they do. Maybe not at first, but they get there eventually.

His exercise routine is key, he says, because he's not just moving his muscles and working up a sweat—he's freeing himself to find inspiration away from his desk. Three or four days each week, he'll set aside time to lift weights, and in the *grind* of that kind of exertion, his mind is free to wander. He can tune in to parts of his body and leave the sermon to percolate in his brain. Most afternoons, he'll head out with his wife, Victoria, for a bike ride, and here too he makes room in his thinking for inspiration to strike.

"I'm a big believer in being active," he says. "Your readers probably know this, but there needs to be a balance. Physically, spiritually, and emotionally. We need to exercise in all three areas, and when I work out, I work out in all three areas. I feel like I'm more creative when I can get out and walk and see creation. So **while I'm putting out that effort, I want to make sure I'm also putting something in**. And then, at the end of the day, I'll sometimes go for a walk in the evening with Victoria. Even if it's nine o'clock at night, it helps to take that time together at the end of the day. It helps to rediscover the quiet I had at the beginning of the day. Just to get back and feel centered again."

On some nights, when he doesn't take the time to walk, Joel might step outside for five or ten minutes and stand in his backyard and look up at the sky—just to grab another few moments to thank the Lord for another good day.

And, always, he's thinking, thinking, thinking about what he'll say on Sunday.

ACCENTUATE THE POSITIVE

One of the most important lessons I took in from my talk with Joel was on **the power of positive thinking**. That's a concept that's been around a long time—in fact, that was the title of a megaselling motivational book by Norman Vincent Peale originally published back in the 1950s, another book I took the time to read as a young man. I also listened to some of Joel's sermons before we talked, and this positivity really came through. What I also kept hearing was the idea that we're all out here doing the best we can with what we're given. He empowers people, and basically tells them, "Hey, what's in you is greater than what's coming against you."

During our visit, Joel shares one specific strategy he has for staying positive—to banish the negative. He illustrates this through a simple story about the lady who used to cut his hair.

Check it out:

"For ten years, I got my hair cut by this person," he tells. "I liked her very much. She was a very nice lady. But every time I went in, she told me her problems. She talked about her marriage. She was having a pride problem, and I tried to help her with it, but I always left feeling drained. Finally, after all that time, I thought, You know what? I dread going to get my haircut. I really did. As much as I wanted to help this person, I just couldn't face the idea of seeing her like this, every time. So I made that change. All of that negativity, it can pull you down, so I try not to be around negative people so consistently. Time is too short, and it can get to be a real drain."

Oh, he continued to care for this woman, checked in on her periodically, but it was no longer attached to the routine of getting a haircut.

One of Joel's most positive qualities is his humility. I remember, as a kid, the way some ministers would talk down to you all the time. The televangelists I'd sometimes catch when I was channel-flipping would do the same thing. Religion, to these guys, was all about the don'ts. They'd put it out there that they were perfect, without faults, and then they'd start to scold you for screwing up—which, of course, is inevitable, right? We all screw up, from time to time.

Joel Osteen recognizes this and works against it in his sermons. **His message, almost always, is to admit that we're all works in progress.** "That's all we can do," he says. "I tell people we can all rise a little higher. We're all overcoming things. We're not here because we're perfect. I think it's good to be open with people and let them know that everybody's dealing with something. We're all on a journey."

Joel looks back at the journey his father started, and he marvels at how their church has grown. There were just ninety people in the congregation when his father started out, and it was pretty much a one-man operation. His father swept the floors, turned out the lights at night, went to visit members if they were sick, and performed all the weddings. He went to the office every day, and made himself available at all hours. There was no end to the *grind,* and Joel can't imagine running the church the same way. For one thing, it's gotten way too big. But for another, it's not his personality. Joel sees himself as more of a big-picture guy. He likes to pull back and empower the people who work with him to run their end of the operation, leaving him to do his thing.

"I'm more of a hands-off leader," he says. "I'm a big believer in getting people in who know more than me in their area. I don't want to be pulling everyone along. And when they succeed, I'm grateful to be a part of their journey."

Joel Osteen's sermons succeed because he makes them a priority. Oh, he's got other things going on that pull him away from his desk, away from his thoughts, away from his routines. He might be called on to deal with a problem at the children's church, or maybe he'll have to council someone who's lost a loved one. There are all these tasks, big and small, lining up for his attention, but then when Wednesday rolls around, he tries to hit the brakes on the daily business of leading his church and focus in on his writing.

....

POWER FACT: In a *Newsweek* survey titled "Is God Listening?" it was reported that 54 percent of people prayed on a daily basis and that half of those people prayed at least two times a day.... *I guess the lesson here is that if you believe in something so deeply that you put it out there and ask for divine assistance, might as well double down and ask again.*

....

"I'll sit down to write," he says, "and some weeks I'll just have no emotional energy for it. I'll just have to step back and regroup. And then I'll get back to it and find a way to make it work, because that sermon, those thirty minutes, that's what everything is built around. I've got thirty minutes to speak to all these people, and I had better do a good job of it, because the next thing I know it'll be Wednesday and I'll have to start in on the process all over again."

Joel's Grind Checklist

✓ don't be afraid to grow a business or a project beyond its original size and scope, just because your parent or your partner who started it is no longer around to shape his or her vision . . .

✓ seek out a quiet place that's just for you where you can recharge—whether by meditation or prayer or silent reflection—on the goals in front of you . . .

✓ it's not enough to simply chase the negative thoughts from your head—sometimes you have to chase the negative people from your life as well . . .

✓ acknowledge your flaws and your failings and try to learn from them . . .

✓ focus on the one true thing you do that's yours and yours alone—in Joel's case, that's writing and delivering his sermon each week, and he's learned to line up his time so that all his energies are directed in this way . . .

....

For more information on Joel and how he uses the
Rise and Grind mindset, check out

www.DaymondJohn.com/Rise/Joel

EIGHT

THE POWER OF GRIND

THE BEST WAY to put an exclamation point on the stories and strategies I'm sharing from these amazing, accomplished people is to help you find patterns in their wildly different approaches to grow your own game.

The best way to do *that* is to share some of my thoughts on the common threads I see running through all these lives and careers. The tips offered in this book may seem like they're a little all over the place, but that just reminds us that there's no one recipe for success. **We each throw our own stuff into the soup, based on whatever ingredients we've got in the kitchen.** We get it done in our own way, in our own time. Look closely at the stories in this book and you'll see that these tips range from general and all-about-the-attitude to specific and all-about-the-action. Some of them might not even come across as tips at all—just a pattern or collection of behaviors that helped to place this or that person on a positive path.

I realize that not every strategy will work for every reader. In fact, some of the strategies are in conflict with one another. For example, some people like to "think big" and chase lofty goals and others try to hit simple, achievable targets. But there are a few basic principles that seem to run through *all* of these stories, and if we look at them like a common current we can light up the way we think.

With that in mind, I've identified three basic principles at play in *all* of the individuals profiled here:

1) They believe that what they do matters.

2) They risk only as much as they can afford to lose.

3) They focus on what they have, not what they don't have.

Let's accept that in order to be successful, you need to be dead certain that you have control over what you do and that you can influence outcomes. **Success is not a destination to be found, it is an outcome to be made.** You have to believe that everything you have, and everything you *are,* is an asset. Doesn't matter what your background is or what resources are available to you. Doesn't even matter what your circumstances are when you're starting out. Me, of all people . . . I *get* it. It only matters that you tap the will to learn and grow and move ever forward—consistently, persistently—until you get where you're meant to go.

Also, on the risk-reward front, the idea is to *get* in the game and then to *stay* in the game. (Gotta be in it to win it, baby!) Remember, this is all about the *grind*. Remember, too, that we're talking about a long-term play. Think about how successful **entrepreneurs increase their longevity and pump up the odds in their favor by making small bets on ideas along the way**. At each step, they buy themselves time and opportunity to take it to the next level. Once an idea starts to gain traction, they might make more substantial investments, and take slightly bigger steps—and so on, and so on. It's an incremental deal. The same applies to a traditional career in a corporate or office setting. We start at the bottom and climb our way to the top of the ladder one rung at a time. If we look to bypass a couple of rungs along the way, we might stumble and fall.

And finally, **successful people can't help but keep the accent on the positive**. If you're an entrepreneur, you're wired to see everything and everyone around you as a potential asset. This is a good and necessary trait, and if you don't recognize it in yourself, you should take a fresh look at what you've already got going for you. A hidden life "asset" can be a tangible item, like a vehicle or a piece of hardware you might need to advance your idea. Or it can be an intangible item, like extra space in your home or access to individuals in a position to open a couple of doors for you. Even items others might see as "junk" can be converted into an asset, in certain situations.

All it takes is thinking along these lines to start seeing the world around you in a more positive way, which is something the successful individuals you've met in this book have all been able to do—in one way or another, at one time or another.

SEE ME, FEEL ME

Turns out, I can see these principles at play in myself. I might not have recognized them as such when I was just starting out, but here they are—and there they were, back in the day. I'm betting, hoping you can see bits and pieces of yourself in these pages, too. I mean, there was a reason you reached for this book in the first place, right? Must be you've got a hunger to learn about what *already* motivates you, as much as you want to learn from the good habits of others. So keep in mind, **these behaviors aren't simply good workplace strategies. They're strategies for living, too.** They're life skills. Taking these approaches and attaching them to your own will advance your goals and your creative capacity, no matter what field you're in. They'll help you to power through your days *and* to build meaningful, sustainable relationships. And if it works out that you've been doing some of these things all along, without recognizing them or giving them a name, then you're off to a winning start.

There's something in these pages for everybody, people. Corporate managers use the skills on display in these pages to bring about innovation in the workplace. Creatives use them to experiment and push the envelope. Advocates for social change use them to build coalitions and create movements. Entrepreneurs use them to turn ideas into viable businesses. And *you* can use them, too, to create the success and happiness you desire.

Think back to those **GRIND** Points I shared with you at the beginning of the book—the easy-to-remember G-R-I-N-D acronym I came up with to highlight our themes. Let's spend just a little more time on these before I sign off, but here I want to focus on *your* **GRIND** Points. I already gave you mine: **G**et *on it* . . . **R**epeat . . . **I**nsist . . . **N**avigate . . . **D**esire, **D**rive, **D**etermination . . .

Go ahead and come up with a set of your own, so we can frame this discussion about good habits and motivation techniques in a way that reminds us that *everything* is on the table when it comes to powering through your days in a meaningful way. Remember, **there is no *one* way to grind**—I said it earlier, but might as well drive the point home.

Hit me up on social media—on Instagram (@TheShark Daymond) or Twitter (also, @TheSharkDaymond)—and let me know what you've got. Spell it out for me: **G-R-I-N-D**. I'll be sure to repost and retweet so we can keep the conversation going.

Tell me, *what you got?*

As you close the pages in this book, let's look ahead to the ways we can *rise and grind* together. Let's recognize that we've tapped into the innermost thoughts and faced down the deepest doubts of a group of people who've accomplished incredible things, like climbing Mount Kilimanjaro on their stomach, or becoming an Oscar-winning actress, or creating a $60 million men's watch empire in just a few short years. And let's also recognize that through the examples of these game-changers you now have the power to tap into some of those same thoughts of your own, to face down doubts of your own, and find a way to come out on top.

I hope this book has inspired you to harness your passions, your talents, and your drive in such a way that you power past any obstacle in your path.

RISE AND TAKE CARE

MARK TWAIN WROTE that the two most important days in your life are the day you are born and the day you find out why.

I was born on February 23, 1969.

I found out why on April 14, 2017.

That's the date I learned I had stage II thyroid cancer. Amazingly, I heard this as good news instead of devastating news, and before you set this book down I want to spend some time explaining why. Short answer: because it all ties in. Longer answer: because it took this giant wake-up call for me to realize that the reason I was put on this earth was to make life better for the people around me—not *just* the people I love and keep close, but the people *all* around me, which these days runs into the multi-multi-digits, thanks to the reach of *Shark Tank* and the power of social media.

Here, let me explain:

I'd always taken good care of myself, got a physical every year, went through all the usual tests, exercised regularly. Sometimes

I'd party a little too much, or eat a little too much, but I'd always be aware of these slipups in a back-of-my-mind sort of way, and balance those periods of excess with long stretches of dieting and moderation. Basically, I was like most everyone else. I was doing the best I could with the information I had, with the willpower I could get together, with the resources available to me—probably like *you're* doing, right now, in your own lives. I was taking care—I just wasn't making it my number one priority.

But as I got to talking with all the people you've just met in these pages, I started to realize that every single one of them *does* make their health a priority. It's first and foremost. It's how they start their days, most of them, working out and making sure to eat right. They all take care to surround themselves with healthy, holistic influences, and they all have practices—whether it's meditation or prayer or reading or time with family—to nourish body and soul, heart and mind. So I started to think I should be living some of the principles and practices on display in this book in a more full-on way. Whatever it is we're doing, we can always do *more,* right?

We can always do *better.*

And then, in the middle of all that, I got to talking to a friend—Bernie Yuman, one of my great mentors. I'd just had my annual physical, and we were comparing notes, and Bernie told me that if I really wanted to take care of myself I should sign up for an "executive physical." I'd never heard of an executive physical, so he filled me in. It's a complete, super-thorough workup, usually conducted at a cutting-edge medical facility like the Mayo Clinic, usually over a two- or three-day period. It's also way, way expensive, and of course it's not covered by insurance, so I'm afraid it's only available to the very fortunate. It's called an executive physical, I learned, because it's typically paid for by major corporations who want to make sure their CEOs and top executives stay in the game—they look at it as a small investment in the health and well-being of their companies. Top actors, athletes, heads of state . . . basically anyone charged with running a huge business or enterprise, or anyone who almost single-handedly supports a big organization or controls a family fortune, has access to one of these physicals, because so many people rely on them to keep running things. Is this fair? No way. Do I wish everyone could have access to the best medical care money can buy? Absolutely. But wishing these things doesn't make them so, and we've got no choice but to live inside our own reality.

The more I looked into it, the more I learned about it, the more I started to think I should do whatever it takes to get one of these babies. I started thinking about my three beautiful daughters (including the most gorgeous toddler on the planet!), and how I want to make sure I'm around for them for a long, long time—for them and for all the people I cherish in my life. I've got all these people depending on me, not just my family and loved ones, but my employees at the Shark Group and my other partners who rely on that steady paycheck to provide for the people they cherish in their own lives. So I decided to put my money where my mouth is. In a lot of ways, I saw it as an investment. Only instead of investing in a bright young entrepreneur bursting with potential, or a promising start-up with a winning concept, I was going to invest in . . . *me*—specifically, in my health and well-being.

So I did, and as I made all the arrangements and found a two-day hole in my schedule—which wasn't easy, by the way—it never occurred to me that these super-thorough doctors would ever, ever, ever turn up something in their exam. I was just being thorough. It was a precaution. I was expecting to be sent home with a monster bill, but a clean bill of health and blessed peace of mind.

That's not what happened.

Sure enough, one of the doctors found a small growth in my

neck that had him "a little concerned." Like I said, I'd *just* had a physical with my regular doctor, and he had checked my throat the way he's done every year for the past twenty years. But now here was this executive-physical doctor telling me there was this growth, about the size of a marble, I should think about having removed. Probably wasn't anything, but might as well, right?

What's interesting is that nobody came right out and said this growth could be cancer. It's like they were afraid to even mention the c-word, so we were all talking around it. But I knew the deal. Wasn't anything *just yet,* wasn't anything to worry about *just yet* . . . but still, it was something.

Obviously, I decided to have the surgery. That was the whole point, making sure all my bases were covered, making health a priority. This one was a no-brainer. When an examination shows a potential problem, you remove the problem—boom, end of story. And so we scheduled the surgery for a Friday morning, and I fully expected to relax at home for four days.

During the preop, the surgeon drew four little dots across the word GOD I have tattooed at my throat, right over the word BLESS. It's a collar tat I proudly wear but that most people don't see, unless I'm at the beach or sitting by a pool. It reads: "Who God bless no man can curse."

I see those words in the mirror every morning (backward!), and I'm inspired to fill each day with purpose.

The plan was for the operation to take about ninety minutes, and there was no reason to expect anything other than a routine outcome. My loved ones had gathered at the hospital, and the mood of the room was like it was all no big deal. They'd take out the marble in my neck—half my thyroid!—and I'd be sent home to rest and recuperate for the next four days.

At least, that was the idea.

As I went under, the anesthesiologist told me to think happy thoughts. He said that if my head was filled with negative thoughts, I'd wake up with a bad headache, so as I drifted off I thought of everything I was grateful for in this life. I know it might seem a little cliché or melodramatic, but I took the doc at his word, and I really did watch all the good things in my life flash through my mind, all the things I was grateful for. . . . My mother, working her butt off to keep me grounded and fed and out of trouble. How she'd encouraged me to "think big," instilled the belief that I could do anything, be anything, despite the fact that "keeping out of trouble," in my neighborhood, meant steering clear of the drugs and gang violence that had taken the lives of too many of my friends, who ended up dead or in jail. I thought about how grateful I was that despite my pretty humble beginnings, I managed to find a band of like-minded souls to partner with, and together we built a brand out of an idea, a passion, we all shared, because we refused to be counted out by a fashion industry that didn't seem to want our business. How I'd somehow grown that business to the point where we made enough money, and enough noise, to eventually be offered a spot on a prime-time reality show on network television, alongside people I deeply respected and admired. How my experience on that show helped to transform my personal brand from urban fashion designer to television personality and change agent and serial entrepreneur, and how I'd transformed my business to support start-ups in a dozen different industries, and speaking engagements all over the world. How I'd found the time to start a family of my own, and then to start another one, and how despite all the money I'd made and the people I'd employed and the shirts and jackets and widgets I'd sold, it was the love of the people around me that was my greatest achievement, my greatest legacy.

The last thing I remember from before I went under was a picture I held in my mind of my three daughters, and the thought that came with it: This is what success looks like. I closed my eyes and thought, This is why I *rise and grind* . . . all day, every day.

Next thing I knew, I was coming out of surgery. My family was worried, because the operation dragged on an hour longer than expected—a long time for the people who love you to be sitting out in the waiting room twiddling their thumbs, when they were told the procedure would take an hour and a half, tops.

The kicker to the story was this: when they ran the tests on the marble-size nodule they took out of my neck, it came back as stage II cancer. If it had gone undetected for another couple of years, it would have been a massive problem—maybe even killed me. But because I was lucky enough, blessed enough, to undergo all this preventive care, we were able to find it and remove it and, thankfully, move on from it.

Big sigh of relief, right?

A lot of folks might have just counted their blessings and left it right there, but that's not how I played it. For one thing, it wasn't lost on me that this particular Friday, April 14, was also Good Friday. I'd known that going in, of course, but now, with this report from the doctor, I took special notice. As you've read, I'm a pretty spiritual person. I pray. I believe. I thought it had to be some kind of sign, me having this operation and dodging this kind of bullet on Good Friday, of all days. Already it was a day of great meaning for me, because it was on Good Friday in 1989 that I first stood outside the Colosseum Mall in Queens selling tie-top hats from a duffel bag—a decision that would change my life. And now here I was, all these years later, on Good Friday in 2017, making a decision that would *save* my life.

See what I mean, how it all ties in?

And it ties in to the themes of this book, the ways we *rise* to the challenges and responsibilities in front of us, and *grind* to meet them. One of the ways I rise to the primary responsibility in my life—taking care of the people around me—is by taking care of myself. That was my key takeaway from this cancer scare. And, I'm hoping, it's the one that has resonated with you.

WHO GOD BLESS NO MAN CAN CURSE

I wear those words around my neck, across my chest . . . and, now, from this Good Friday forward, I carry them in my heart as well.

Let us never forget that we *grind* to get and keep ahead, but that we also *grind* to make our world a better place for the people we love. For some of us, that might mean our world close to home. For others, we might keep a bigger picture in mind. For me, it means I am now meant to shine a light on the all-important message of awareness and early detection. That's why, right after my surgery, I started giving all these interviews, talking about my cancer scare, and it's why I'm closing out this book with the same message. After all, my goal has been to inspire people to *rise and grind* and set about their days with power and purpose. A lot of times, that power and purpose has nothing to do with making money—it's about how we touch the lives of the people around us, and I don't know about you, but I hope to be around for those people for a good long time.

Look, I know most people don't have the means to do this kind of comprehensive, state-of-the-science medical exam. But while we've still got access to health care in this country, we should be out there taking every early-detection measure within reach. **We should *all* be taking full advantage of every resource we have in order to keep ourselves healthy and whole.**

Whatever it is you're already doing, whatever it is you can afford, you can afford to do just a little bit more. To take even better care. Colonoscopies, mammograms, pap smears, endoscopies . . . we've got to get out in front of whatever forces are out there threatening to set us off our path, so that we can keep on keeping on.

That's what this book is about, in the end—putting ourselves in position to thrive!—so here on the last page I just wanted to throw this out there, to get us all thinking about what's at stake as we move about our days.

Take good care . . . and do what you have to do to keep *rising and grinding.*

ACKNOWLEDGMENTS

One of the things I love about this book-writing business is the chance it gives me to work with so many smart, creative, insightful people. Just like my *Shark Tank* gig opened up a whole new world to me, my book projects put me in the room with so many people I wouldn't get a chance to work with in my day job, so I consider myself blessed to be able to learn and grow on the backs of these good people.

First, I want to thank everyone who took the time to sit down with me and share their thoughts and motivation strategies. As you can tell from reading their profiles, these are busy, busy people, but they took a little time away from their own rise and grind to help me shine a light on what it takes to live a fuller, richer life, and to succeed at the very highest level. Without them, there's no book.

I also want to thank my friend and cowriter, Dan Paisner, for helping me to organize everyone's thoughts (and mine!) in a way that really captures my voice and the spirit of what I do. This is our fourth book together, and I'm looking forward to working with him on a whole bunch more. Without him, there's no book.

Thanks also to my literary agent, Kirsten Neuhaus of Foundry Media, for finding a home for us at the Crown Publishing Group, where we're in the good hands of our editor, Talia Krohn; publisher, Tina Constable; associate publisher, Campbell Wharton; publicity director, Megan Perritt; publicist, Owen Haney; marketing director, Ayelet Gruenspect; art director, Tal Goretsky; and editorial assistant, Erin Little. I couldn't ask for a better team of publishing professionals—without them, there's no book.

Thanks also go to my dedicated team in the offices of the Shark Group, led by Ted Kingsbery, who as president of my company helps to run all my projects, and Champ Nichols, the head of our speaking division, who always has my back and helps to polish my keynote speeches and keeps me focused on all the new thoughts and theories on entrepreneurship. Really, I'm grateful to the whole team at work, for pushing me to be the best I can be and for sharing their knowledge and passion every day. Got to say it . . . without them, there's no book.

My management team rates a shout-out here, including Eric Ortner of Ortner Management Group, Zach Rosenfield of Stan Rosenfield & Associates, my entire team at William Morris Endeavor, and the members of my FUBU family—Carl, Keith, and J, my brothers for life, and my partners Norman and Bruce. Without them, I wouldn't be in the position I am today.

Same goes for my *Shark Tank* family, starting with Mark Burnett and the crew at Mark Burnett Productions, especially Holly, Jamie, Yun, and Clay, and the executives at ABC and Sony. And, my fellow sharks—Mark, Kevin, Robert, Lori, and Barbara—for their friendship, and for bringing out the best in me, on and off the set. I also want to thank CNBC for being such a strong syndication partner. Without all of these folks, there might be a book, but there wouldn't be a whole lot of people lining up to read it.

Of course, I've got to thank our *Shark Tank* fans, who keep me humble, and my *Shark Tank* partners, who are always teaching me something new. Without all of you, I wouldn't have so many great reasons to get out of bed each morning and start grinding.

Last, I want to send a special nod to everyone out there who's chasing a dream . . . hitting a goal . . . reaching for a bigger, better, more purposeful life. This book is for you, after all.

INDEX

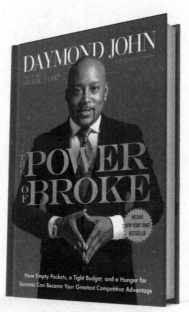